A Little Love in Big Manhattan

A Little Love
in Big Manhattan

Ruth R. Wisse

Harvard University Press
Cambridge, Massachusetts
London, England   1988

This book is printed on acid-free paper, and its binding materials
have been chosen for strength and durability.

The bird ornament for chapters is reproduced
from a Halpern manuscript.

Library of Congress Cataloging-in-Publication Data

Wisse, Ruth R.
   A little love in big Manhattan / Ruth R. Wisse.
      p.   cm.
   Bibliography: p.
   Includes index.
   ISBN 0-674-53659-2 (alk. paper)
   1. Leib, Mani, 1883–1953. 2. Halpern, Moshe Leib,
1886–1932. 3. Yiddish poetry—New York (N.Y.)—History
and criticism. 4. Poets, Yiddish—20th century—Biography.
5. Poets, Yiddish—United States—Biography. 6. Poets,
American—20th century—Biography. 7. Jews—New York
(N.Y.)—Intellectual life. 8. Manhattan (New York,
N.Y.)—Intellectual life—20th century. 9. New York
(N.Y.)—Intellectual life—20th century. I. Title.
PJ5129.B7Z9 1988   87-29036
839'.0913'09—dc19   CIP

For Len and our children,
Billy, Jacob, and Abby

Preface

This book is about two Yiddish poets in New York. Mani Leib (who dropped his patronym Brahinsky when he began to publish) and his contemporary Moishe Leib Halpern may not be familiar to most readers today, but they were known in their lifetime to hundreds of thousands of Yiddish readers in the United States and over the world. Two outstanding figures in a constellation of writers, they came to New York City as young men in 1906–07, to try their literary fortunes. Their poems, which appeared almost from the moment of their arrival in little magazines, journals, newspapers, and miscellanies, gave voice to a new cultural experience of the modern Jew in America.

Yiddish was the spoken language of most Jewish immigrants from Eastern and Central Europe, and it initially served the Jews in America just as it had in the lands of their birth. The product and expression of a distinctive way of life that had developed in Europe over some thousand years, Yiddish was spoken by Jews as naturally as Italian was by Italians and Polish by Poles, but with this difference: whereas Italian and Polish newcomers often thought themselves only temporarily separated from their homelands and continued to identify the old country with their national culture, the Jewish immigrants knew themselves to be permanently uprooted.

The finality of their resettlement and the size of the Jewish immigration stimulated a uniquely independent Yiddish culture in America. Unlike those newcomers who remained yoked to their native lands, the young Jews who came to settle in New York knew that they were opening a new chapter of Jewish history. Of course they would write it in Yiddish, their language and the language of the Jewish immigrant mass that grew denser with each arriving shipload.

Never before had so many speakers of a Jewish language come to-
gether in one place, and never was there better opportunity for a
cultural renaissance.

By the end of the nineteenth century, many Jews hoped that Yid-
dish could help sustain a community rapidly losing its earlier
sources of cohesion in religion and lacking the compensating factor
of a national soil. The Yiddish language was so integrally identified
with Jewishness that some speakers considered it a vehicle of Jewish-
ness, a repository of Jewish ethics and values that could continue to
unite secular Jews worldwide. This sense of a culture contained in
language was essential to the poets who are the subject of this book
and to the readers who looked to them for new inspiration. (In the
Rare Books Collection of McGill University is the library of Joe
Fishstein, a sewing-machine operator of the International Ladies
Garment Workers Union, who lived in the Bronx and assembled a
remarkable collection of Yiddish poetry. On Saturdays he made
protective dust jackets and decorative bindings and copied his fa-
vorite poems into a special notebook. His family observed that he
had transferred the more traditional values of the Jewish way of life
to a passion for Yiddish poetry.)

But the transposition of religious observance into secular form
had other, unexpected consequences. For two millennia Jewish law
and custom had sustained the Jews in all the lands of the diaspora.
When they moved from one country to another, Jews studied the
Talmud and codes and rabbinic responsa in the various languages of
their dispersion, maintaining their unique way of life in Aramaic or
Ladino, Arabic or Yiddish. Their religious civilization, based on
continuing reinterpretations of biblical teachings, was never depen-
dent on language alone.

Secular literary culture, on the other hand, is limited by definition
to the language in which it is created. And the same factors that
stimulated the great flowering of Yiddish culture in America also
precipitated a linguistic decline. Whereas Italians and Poles often
maintained their mother tongue as an essential bond with the
homeland, the permanently relocated Jews in America took up the
local language as part of their new way of life.

In his fictional autobiography *Family Chronicle*, presented as a
series of narratives by his mother, his father, and himself, the Amer-

ican poet Charles Reznikoff gives a vivid account of this process of acculturation. His mother, a recent immigrant from Russia, describes how impatient she grew with her husband for his lack of initiative:

> He was still reading a Yiddish newspaper. "You will never learn English if you do that," I said. But he kept on. At last I said, "If you bring a Yiddish newspaper home again, I'll tear it up." Next night he brought his newspaper with him and after supper settled down to read. I snatched it out of his hands and tore it to bits. He was furious, of course. "I'll do it again," I said. But I did not have to. The very next night he had an English newspaper, and soon knew more English than I.

For Reznikoff's mother, America demanded a changeover from Yiddish to English because without it one could not take proper advantage of the land's abundant opportunity.

This scene dramatizes why, by the time he became a poet himself, Charles Reznikoff had lost contact with the poets of his parents' generation who would have been his natural predecessors, if the lines of cultural transmission had not been so rudely snapped. Mani Leib and Moishe Leib Halpern, and scores of other American Yiddish writers and poets, published much of their work in the very newspapers that Reznikoff's father was discouraged from reading. This book is a modest attempt to return to modern Jews part of their lost inheritance and, more important, to locate for American Yiddish poets their rightful place in the American canon.

Mani Leib and Moishe Leib Halpern were so thoroughly different in temperament, background, and style that it is hard to imagine them as part of the same literary group. Indeed, after the first few years their coterie began to lose what cohesion it had at the start, and the two poets rarely met except on the pages of newspapers and magazines, at an occasional literary gathering, or at one of the cafés they frequented. Nevertheless, they were aware of themselves as opposites in the same artistic movement, as rivals or contraries in a group that aspired to change the very nature of Yiddish writing. The play of their names—Mani Leib/Moishe Leib, *leib* meaning *lion*—seems further to have sharpened their consciousness of one another, whether in envy or admiration.

Mani Leib and Halpern impressed others almost from the beginning with their originality and that intangible quality known as genius. The tension between them appealed to me as a dramatic framework for a book about American Yiddish poetry. For the modern reader, Halpern is the more interesting of the two, and more accessible in translation. But I do not intend to use one poet as a foil against the other, and if I did not like them equally I would not have undertaken to write about them together. Discussing them in tandem affords many advantages:

—Their contrasting poetry suggests the depth and range of a creative movement that could produce at the same time two such different voices. Rather than summarize the literary achievement of an entire circle of writers, a few pages or a short chapter devoted to each in turn, this concentrated study lets us appreciate at least two of the poets in something like their full stature while providing a glimpse of the dozens of writers around them.

—The presentation of Yiddish poetry in translation deprives the critic of many tools of analysis that would be available in the original. Contrast is a partial compensation for this handicap. Even untrained readers of poetry will recognize the distinctive characteristics of one kind of poetry when it is presented alongside another that is quite different.

—This book covers a period of approximately fifty eventful years. During that time the two poets were affected in contrasting ways by changes in American life and in Jewish society. Mani Leib's temporary decline as a poet coincided with Halpern's most creative years. Halpern died before Mani Leib did his best work. Looking at their poetry as the product of the same environment, we can better understand how each of them was affected by its pressures and responded to its challenges.

It was the peculiar fate of these poets to foresee the waning of a tradition of poetry that they had but recently initiated. By the end of their lives they were burdened by the knowledge that they would have no literary heirs. One of their finest critics, Abraham Tabachnik, was nevertheless right to exhort them in their period of late reckoning not to forget what *shkotsim* they once were—with what irreverence they had come on the scene. His reminder serves equally for us.

Contents

Illustrations follow page 104

Then from the tight cell of my narrow grief
The voice of all who suffer rising strong
Will cry to me like kin to kindred crying,
Will ring out cleansed, transmuted in my song.
(Mani Leib, "Ode to Simplicity")

There in the shadowy, dank hall
Right alongside the ground-floor stair—
A weeping girl, attended by
A grimy hand in the mussed-up hair.
—A little love in big Manhattan. . . .

It isn't that he's ill, the sad one
Who contemplates these things at night;
But sick of his own sadness only
He lies and broods, his pipe alight.
—A little love in big Manhattan.
(Moishe Leib Halpern, "Song: Weekend's Over")

A Home for Art

Among the estimated two million Jews who arrived in the United States in the first decades of this century were dozens of young poets, writers, and intellectuals, some of exceptional ability. They had been raised, most of them traditionally, in small disciplined Jewish communities between Kalish, on the German border in the west, and Niezhin, in the easternmost section of the Pale of Settlement. Driven to seek a new home by the same conditions of poverty and oppression that routed almost all immigrants, they arrived in the new land with heady expectations and great energy. The gathering of so much creative potential in one place stimulated a flowering of literary activity.

At first sight, no setting could seem less conducive to the pursuit of poetry. Bursting with newcomers, the Lower East Side must have struck the young immigrant who had just passed through the sobering initiation rites of Ellis Island more like Babel than Parnassus. Adjoining the Jewish neighborhoods were pockets of Poles, Rumanians, Ukrainians, and Germans, all speaking their own languages.[1] Although Yiddish was the common language of most Jewish immigrants, each Jew spoke his own regional dialect and often had difficulty understanding another's speech. The demands of English were also unsettling, even for those who did not aspire to master its strange labials, diphthongs, and the impossible *th*. When the poet Mani Leib, shortly after his arrival in New York, tried to send his lyrics to the editor of a new Yiddish newspaper in Philadelphia, the manuscripts were repeatedly lost in the mail because he could not address them properly.[2]

Most of the young people who became part of the new literary movement arrived in America without professional training and only a religious Jewish education. To support themselves they had to compete for available unskilled jobs—as tailors in small factories and sweatshops, as apprentice housepainters, paperhangers, and carpenters, or, more menially still, as window washers and waiters. The writer Meir Blinken worked first as a carpenter, then as a masseur. Joseph Rolnik sold newspapers. They were subject to seasonal layoffs, and dissatisfaction drove them from one job to another. Whatever time they could give to writing had to be wrested from a worker's hard routine.

The first encounter with America was often unpleasant in unexpected ways. The small towns and villages of their youth, however poor, could not prepare the newcomers for the squalor of Jewish New York. "I can't forget the disgusting impression that my first American 'toilet' made on me," recalled Isaac Raboy in his autobiography. "Had I but had the money, I would have sailed right back home . . . I couldn't understand how people could live without falling sick in such unsanitary conditions."[3] There were no trees, not even in the so-called parks. The noise was thunderous and unabating. The constant press of people only increased the sense of isolation of those who had come without any welcoming family.

Yet along with the hardships came a freedom that the writers had not known before. Though the Lower East Side was not the hospitable place they had expected, it was improving. They still found traces of the "Jewtown" described by Jacob Riis in 1890, where "penury and poverty are wedded everywhere to dirt and disease."[4] But like Hutchins Hapgood, who celebrated the spirit of the voluntary Jewish ghetto in 1902, they also recognized its better prospect.[5]

By the first decade of this century, New York was the most populous and lively Jewish center in the world. The partisan Yiddish press, still young, had become a strong source of authority, almost a new cultural establishment. Without the censorship that hobbled the Yiddish press in Europe, Jewish writers and editors of every ideological stripe vied for public support. From a single Yiddish newspaper with a circulation of 3,750 in 1887, the Yiddish press of New York City alone rose to five dailies with an approximate circulation of 190,000 in 1905 and of 525,690 in 1915.[6]

Spurred by the entrepreneurial possibilities of an expanding audience of immigrant readers, Abraham Cahan, who dominated Yiddish journalism for over half a century, shaped the socialist *Forverts* (Jewish Daily Forward) into the largest foreign-language daily newspaper in America, and other editors who did not quite achieve his personal prestige also wielded considerable influence. The market for magazines was expanding as well. *Di tsukunft* (The Future), originally launched in 1892 as a dogmatic socialist journal, lapsed between 1897 and 1901, but when it was reconstituted as a monthly for "science, literature, and socialism," it became a prestigious forum for new writing, offering its contributors small but significant honoraria and a circulation that eventually reached 20,000. Other magazines, such as *Der yidisher arbeter* (The Jewish Worker) and *Der yidisher kemfer* (The Jewish Fighter), tried to gain a foothold in the fluid immigrant market with emphasis on good literature.[7] In the absence of any overarching communal structures, the press acquired something like the power of a Jewish government; with the decline of religious authority, its writers were accorded the status that had once belonged to rabbis.

The Yiddish theater was another vital new arena. Liberated like the press by America's guarantees of free expression, the theater prospered here as it never could in Europe. It offered immigrants "a glimpse of something that might transcend the wretchedness of the week: a . . . touch of the Sabbath, even if a debased or vulgarized Sabbath."[8] To provide a few hours of glamor and excitement, it used flamboyant staging, music, slapstick comedy, and shameless sentimentality. The theater was a transmutation, sometimes a parody, of the synagogue, with rival loyalties to directors and stars replacing loyalties to the renowned Hasidic rabbis of yore and with orchestrated emotions taking the place of the rhythms of Jewish ritual and prayer. The institutions that could not survive the transition to America left a need in the immigrant community for new forms of association and inspiration. Fraternal orders and *landsmanshaften* of newcomers from the same town or region were established to provide social regroupings.[9] Socialist parties, to which many of the young writers had belonged before coming to America, created branches in New York, where the familiar debates continued.

Most important for the new literature, the Lower East Side had developed its own version of the literary cafés that dotted the major European cities. In small cafeterias clustered around Rutgers Square, writers, editors, and educated readers gathered after a day's work to argue the merits of a recently published story, essay, poem, or editorial. These cafeteria debates had the flavor of the yeshivas and houses of study where some of the participants had spent their youth. Talmudic habits of interpretation and close textual analysis were here transposed into secular form as young men argued over political nuances or an unfelicitous phrase of a work in progress. The competitive male camaraderie of traditional Jewish society stimulated a new kind of culture, at once freed of religious restraints and yet reminiscent of them. The critic Shmuel Niger said, "these are writers who cannot stand and pray, that is, create, in the middle of the street, but who must have for their literary minyan a special corner, a literary shul, an artistic *mokem koydesh* [holy place]."[10] Such use of traditional vocabulary to describe their modern situation, intended by the writers to place ironic distance between themselves and their past, reveals how much of the past still clung to them.

In some respects, the writers who came to America resembled their idealistic counterparts of the Second Aliyah, young Jews who left their native communities in the same decade between 1903 and 1914 to settle in Palestine. Products of a religious education and traditional upbringing, they had already rebelled against orthodoxy; they read secular books, attended classes at the university, usually as day students, and joined political movements that were twice forbidden, by their parents and the tsar. They imagined a Jewish existence unrestricted by either religious coercion or antisemitic oppression. But while the young immigrants to Palestine and the United States left their homes for similar reasons—to avoid military service, to escape trial and imprisonment for revolutionary activity, or to resist the humiliation and restrictions of Jewish life in the Pale—the two groups developed differently in their very different surroundings. To overcome the physical hardships of life in Palestine and to hasten the ideal of national sovereignty, the Second

Aliyah pioneered collective structures. Its members wanted to forge a new Jewish community based on socially functional rather than religious considerations.

A similar transference of religious impulses to social action was widespread among young Jews who remained in Europe and who, through such political organizations as the Jewish Socialist Bund, tried to ameliorate the condition of their people. Formed in 1897 to promote united action among the Jewish workers of Lithuania, Poland, and Russia, but restricted after 1905 in its political aims by the repressive measures of the tsarist police, the Bund channeled much of its energy into cultural work and stimulated the development of Yiddish literature and language as part of its proletarian program.

But the young Jews who came to America could also pursue their individual aims in a country that made a virtue of free enterprise and provided generous possibilities for its realization. The freedom from persecution in America and its abundant natural resources also permitted its immigrants to feel less urgent concern for national survival. Even poets and writers who continued to sympathize with the revolutionary cause to which they had once been fully committed, felt justified, upon arrival in America, in leaving the collective struggle for the nuanced, private life of the individual.

For the writers especially, the experience of separation was crucial. The Jewish boy from a yeshiva or the ranks of a socialist organization, the girl from a small Jewish town, felt a shock of dislocation during the long, unaccompanied voyage across the Atlantic and the bewildering arrival in New York. Both frightening and liberating, the lonely ocean passage loosened the bonds of immigrants to their past and launched them *in der fremd,* on alien ground. Moishe Leib Halpern's first long work was a poem by that title, describing the stages of the Atlantic crossing as both a final leave-taking and an omen of permanent displacement.[11]

It was this ambiguous process of self-discovery that the American Yiddish writers charted in their early works. Their discovery of the self had in it something of the excitement of Renaissance artists who explored human anatomy with a passion that had once been reserved for intimations of God. Each poet examined his moods as if he were the first ever to find himself unique. In a culture that insisted on fraternal interdependence and was treated by the surrounding world as an indissoluble collectivity, this emphasis on the first-person singular felt renegade and therefore rich in creative potential.

In the winter of 1907–08 the term *Yunge* became associated with a number of American Yiddish writers who were said to be taking literature in a new and dangerous direction. The immediate source of the name was a little magazine called *Di yugnt* (Youth), a slight affair of twenty-four pages, which declared that it would publish only the works of young writers. By the second issue it was already taken over by "younger" writers dissatisfied with the conservatism of the founders. With the third issue the magazine folded, but "the Yunge," at first used pejoratively by the critics, was worn proudly by the aspiring writers and the term stuck.[12]

Many magazines of the period emphasized novelty. There was *Dos naye lebn* (The New Life), a prestigious political and literary monthly edited by the outstanding Yiddish intellectual, Chaim Zhitlowsky; *Di naye velt* (The New World), launched in 1909 by Jacob Milch for the study of American life and institutions; *Dos naye land* (The New Land), a short-lived illustrated weekly dedicated to literature, criticism, and the arts. These and many similar publications were dedicated to new ideological positions and visionary ideals of society and culture.[13] Zhitlowsky's progressive Jewish nationalism was particularly influential in converting many estranged Jewish radicals to nationalism and in raising the prestige of Yiddish as the language of Jewish discourse.

Di yugnt was novel in a more radical sense. It did not oppose one or another part of the Jewish ideological spectrum, but set itself apart from all national and social concerns. With a program that could best be described as aestheticism, the magazine declared that the goal of the artist was not to transform society but to transcend it through the creation of lasting works of beauty. The new Yiddish writers said they had an artistic obligation to explore their own feelings, not the problems of "the people."

By any standard save that of contemporary expectations, *Di yugnt* was a mild offering. Each issue contained about ten poems and stories with titles like "My Goddess," "Regret," "Love," "Night," "Clouds," "Storm," "Two Angels," "Two Friends." The single most provocative item was a story by Isaac Raboy in which a young man, taking his girlfriend on a sleighride, tells her a story that reaches the following climax:

> I arrived at a spot where no foot had ever trodden. The snow was unblemished, chastely protected by the splendid blue sky, as if a pure and innocent maiden were covering her head with a blue silk kerchief, lest a single strand of hair escape to tempt a stranger's eye to lust.
>
> I caught sight of a red snowflower growing low and piously near the snow, and I desired that flower. Approaching softly, I stooped to pluck it with burning fingers.[14]

Everything here conspires against material reality: the symbolic suggestiveness of the prose, the eroticism of the images, the haziness of time and place. Indeed, among all the snowy and cloudy landscapes in the three issues of this magazine there was, with the exception of one reference to Rivington Street, no specific designation of any locale in either the new country or the old. Raboy's story was characteristic of the magazine's contents not only in its first-person narrator and individuated theme (few subjects are as intimate as seduction), but in the opaque language and obscure intention.

The story was also characteristic in its remoteness from the author's actual way of life. At the time he wrote it, in a tiny bedroom so cold that the ink often froze in the inkwell, Raboy was working long days with five of his eight brothers in the basement shop of his father's house in New Lots, Brooklyn, sorting and sewing fur pelts. From the basement window in winter, he did look out on a snowy field, but it was not the pure landscape of his fiction. Further, without the prodding of others, Raboy admitted, he probably would have lacked the stamina to sit down to write after his day's work. Borukh Senter, Yoel Entin, Moishe Shmuelzon, M. J. Haimovitch, Yedidye Margolis, and a group of recent newcomers to America were generating so much excitement over *Di yugnt* that they infected even the shy and withdrawn Raboy with their enthusiasm.[15]

The magazine was certainly far more haphazard than its editors' ambitions. The spelling is reminiscent of early Elizabethan publications, where the same word appears on the same page in two or three different versions. Sometimes the Yiddish adheres to German orthography, which was still the common practice in Yiddish publishing, and elsewhere words are spelled phonetically, according to the more modern custom of imitating actual pronunciation.[16] The same pattern of inconsistency prevails elsewhere. There are startling stylistic shifts, sometimes within a single short item. Some poems and stories are written in an oral folk style, as if modeled on the works of Sholem Aleichem. Others avoid the Yiddish idiom and, in trying to achieve elegant diction, read like stiff translations from a foreign tongue.

But though too slight to bear the full weight of its cultural mission, the little magazine was determined to create for Yiddish belles-lettres a "separate independent home":

> Yiddish literature here in America has been boarding out with the Yiddish press that treats it as a stranger, a stepchild. The purpose of the press is either to turn a profit or to spread certain social or nationalistic ideals. It has never had any pure and authentic interest in literature . . .
>
> As professionals, the young Yiddish writers in America are in love with literature, and it hurts us to see Yiddish belles-lettres in exile here, being treated with cynical abandon. We have united in *Di yugnt* to create for Yiddish literature its own home to free it from its bruising battering exile.[17]

It is not difficult to see in the image of the humiliated boarder the writers themselves, many of whom lived in the rented backrooms of overcrowded apartments or with relatives. Nor can one miss their high-minded idealism, as if a new sect of priests had arisen to purify the masses.

Despite its obvious shortcomings, *Di yugnt* did throw a gauntlet at the powerful Yiddish press. And while the press did not quite shudder to a halt, it did reward the young upstarts with a show of pique. Critics objected to the obscurity and incomprehensibility of the new writing and to its disturbing eroticism. Abraham Cahan summed up the objections with his customary acerbity by likening the Yunge to Turkish women who always wear a veil so that no one can tell whether they are beautiful or ugly.[18] Above all, the critics protested the social irrelevance of this kind of art. The retreat of the writer from public concerns seemed an act of betrayal among immigrant Jews who had so recently been torn from their established way of life. Instead of assuming the leadership and moral instruction of an uprooted people, the Yiddish writers "had followed the Russian

Symbolists into the clouds."[19] Claiming that "whatever the Russian authors chew, the Yiddish writers spew," critics accused the literati of blind imitation and willful irresponsibility.[20] Thus the battle was engaged: the earth-bound press against the heaven-bound literary sect.

Yet in what sense was the Yiddish press an enemy of the Yiddish writer? In Europe modern Yiddish literature had been a by-product of the Yiddish press from the 1860s onward. It was in the first Yiddish supplement of a Hebrew weekly that Sholem Yankev Abramovitch introduced his brilliant creation, Mendele Mocher Sforim, Mendele the Book Peddler, the ubiquitous pseudonymous narrator who would travel around the Pale for fifty years, picking up stories and unpublished manuscripts that he would then bring to the attention of his newspaper readers. It was the Yiddish press as well that welcomed the stand-in of Sholem Rabinovitch, Sholem Aleichem or "Mr. How-Do-You-Do," and featured him in its pages until the moment of his creator's death. The rise of I. L. Peretz to the third hallowed place in Yiddish literature began when the press was curtailed by censorship, but from about the turn of the century he too appeared regularly in its pages.

The Yiddish press that greeted the young immigrants in America was more varied and influential than the dailies that squeaked by tsarist censors in Russia. The first Yiddish daily in America preceded the first Yiddish daily in Russia by eighteen years, and its spread was correspondingly quicker and greater. *Dos yidishe vort* (the Yiddish word), a link with the world left behind, was for millions of immigrants also the best guide to the society they entered, a source of news and information, healer of bruised spirits. When Cahan, protean editor of *Forverts*, initiated the popular question-and-answer *bintel briv*, the paternal advice he offered in its columns was really an extension of the rest of the newspaper, which tried to orient its immigrant audience to unfamiliar surroundings.[21] And why would Sholem Aleichem (his pseudonym having taken over his identity), when he visited America in 1906 and then came permanently in 1914, gravitate to the newspapers like a religious Jew to the synagogue, while the fledgling writers who arrived within that same period recoiled from its embrace?

The immediate answer came from the Yunge themselves. The

press was utilitarian, providing enlightenment or public entertainment or occasionally, as when it published the Yiddish writers, both at once. Whether a newspaper had as its particular goal the consolidation of the working class, loyalty to Jewish tradition, the development of Jewish nationhood, or any other combination of ideals, it regarded literature as subordinate to its larger purpose. The earlier Yiddish writers were untroubled by this functional view of their craft. Just as Addison and Steele felt themselves at one with their audience when *The Spectator* began to appear in eighteenth-century London, so the pioneering Yiddish writers a century later shared with their readers a common culture that the newspaper acknowledged and intended to reinforce. Each of the three "classic masters" of modern Yiddish writing began with the question, "For whom am I working?" and remained committed to improving the lot of all Jews. Sholem Aleichem's choice for a pen name of the common words of greeting reveals his desire to be accessible, and every word he published, including his autobiography, invited readers to recognize that they still shared the same community.

The American Yiddish poets who preceded the Yunge sought a somewhat different but no less passionate involvement with their readership. Known collectively as the "labor" or "sweatshop" poets, Morris Winchevsky, Joseph Bovshover, David Edelshtat, and Morris Rosenfeld came to London and then to New York after 1881, part of the first great wave of emigration from Eastern Europe. Their identification was no longer with the Jewish community as such, spread throughout the great cities of England and America, but with the working classes, which now included the poor and oppressed Jewish mass. The verses of these worker-poets became a staple of the Yiddish press, expressing more poignantly than any editorial could do the hardships of daily life and the immigrant's cry for help. When it was translated into English as *Songs from the Ghetto*, the poetry of Morris Rosenfeld was described by William Dean Howells, then at the height of his influence as a writer and editor, as "the 'Song of the Shirt' by the man who had sewn the shirt," a judgment that confirmed the poet's own premise that the sweat of labor authenticates the poetry it generates.[22]

The sweatshop poets fully shared the misery of the early immigrants. Edelshtat died of tuberculosis at the age of twenty-six.

Rosenfeld buried several children, and his most popular song, the lullaby of a father who can see his son only when the child is asleep at night, arose as naturally from his own experience as it did from the harassed lives of thousands of other tailor-fathers. But it was also a convention of their poetry to demand a public and folklike posture for private themes. The poets subscribed so faithfully to the idea of solidarity with their people and class that they resisted the alienating idea of special talent. Edelshtat wrote:

> I never learned how rhymes may be polished
> How prettily thoughts can be dressed.
> The bloody dramas of the age
> Were staged within my breast . . .
>
> Stop knocking, Muse, at the door of my heart!
> No hope illumines my room
> Which is crowded with tears and terribly dark—
> Go to the poets in bloom!
>
> To those familiar with golden salons
> Who have reached the rapturous isle;
> As for me, crippled by fetters and wounds—
> Leave me alone for a while![23]

Similarly, Rosenfeld instructed his muse to seek him not where myrtles bloomed and fountains sprayed, but where the blood of the workers flowed thick.[24] Self-isolation and artistic refinement were the prerogatives of the rich and of those prepared to betray the collective struggle for a better life. The familiar rhymes, *noyt, broyt, royt, toyt*—need, bread, red, dead—united workers and poets in awareness of their common plight.

Although most of the Yunge were unskilled laborers who shared the socialist ideology of the sweatshop poets and had typically belonged to a revolutionary group before coming to America, they distinguished art from politics, identifying the writer with all that was inward and particularistic. The deepening emphasis in western culture after the Renaissance on the emancipation of the individual had taken a long time to penetrate the consciousness of East European Jews, and when it did they often exchanged one collective identity for another, the religious community for a social movement. Only gradually, with the failure of the Russian revolution of 1905 and the massive exodus to America, did some Jews begin to feel the problem of personal identity or accept its challenge as a goal in itself.

The young American Yiddish writers questioned and occasionally resented the compulsory brotherliness that traditional Jews accepted as central. In America the poet Menakhem Boreisho observed that the ghetto "forced us to breathe one air and we became the most socialized creatures on earth. If we wish to free ourselves now, we must free ourselves first of all from these collective social instincts and return to the stychic freedom of the individual."[25] If they continued to live crowded together in ghettos and to breathe the common air of factory and shop, at least their art could be refined and singular, beyond public rhetoric and journalism. The Yiddish press thus served as the most obvious, or perhaps merely the most convenient, antagonist of their resolve. The daily newspaper or the political magazine addressed a mass audience, adjusting style, language, format, and content to the perceived level of its readers. Adapting from other literatures the idea of art as an end in itself, the new writers announced their intention of trying to satisfy only their own standards of good writing. Reuben Iceland, the man who did most to interpret the philosophy of the Yunge, complained that "the older Yiddish poet did not recognize any mood. He therefore never encountered his own individuality. Even when he did . . . he had a ready-made general concept for everything."[26] The true writer had an obligation that could only be met if he discovered the personal language, style, form, and content that revealed his experience.

One might as well note at the outset that this argument had ramifications even beyond the grave. Implicit in the discussion over the proper function of literature was the very fate of the Jews, whose survival seemed threatened by the simultaneous breakup of religious authority and cohesive community. Shelley's idea of poets as the unacknowledged legislators of the world assumed greater urgency among the immigrant Jews in New York than it could have in England, which at least continued to enjoy its acknowledged legislators. Among Jews, who had in any case learned to function without a legislative body, writers could logically be expected to stand in for rabbinic authority since they alone worked in the same medium of words. Thus aestheticism, the acceptance of artistic truth and beauty as a fundamental self-referring standard independent of social, ethical, or national value, was a challenge not only to traditional Judaism, which generally opposed secular art, but to the expectations of newly emancipated Jews who turned to literature for an elucidation of ethical and social problems. It is no wonder that the Yunge were accused of subverting the national interest.

In practice, though, the lines between the Yunge and the press soon grew blurred, and a policy of reengagement arose from within the group itself. The cover of *Di yugnt*, designed by the artist most closely connected with the Yunge, Zuni Maud, already alerts us to the group's ambivalence. The list of contents is framed by two lions in a design normally reserved for the ten commandments. Overhead is an arch bearing the title of the magazine, and above it, in a star-and-cloud studded sky, two muscular angels with outsized wings play the violin. These unlikely angels, fiddling in an artificial sky above the Lions of Judah, draw attention to the incongruities of the new aesthetic. The desire to escape into ethereal realms in pursuit of an ideal—in this case, an ideal of higher art—was subject to singular suspicion in Yiddish culture, even among some of those involved in its promotion.

Artistic movements, much like their political counterparts, require the guiding hand of a leader, and David Ignatoff was the Yunge's organizing force. It was he who wrote the "position paper" of the group in the second issue of the magazine and who later edited their best publications. Earnest, impetuous, fiercely loyal to his friends, Ignatoff was the most jealous promoter of the new movement. Once when the printer refused to release copies of the magazine without cash on the table, Ignatoff argued so eloquently that the man extended him credit and even lent him a wheelbarrow to carry the magazine down Canal Street to the public hall where a celebration was under way.[27]

Ignatoff was born in 1885 in the Ukrainian town of Brusilov and educated until the age of thirteen in the local cheder. The region of the Ukraine in which Brusilov is located had been the cradle of the

Hasidic movement a century earlier, and its Jewish communities were still enthusiastically pious, resonant with the teachings of the Baal Shem Tov and the stories of his many disciples. (Ignatoff later wrote Yiddish versions of some of these wonder tales.) But by the time Ignatoff was in his teens, the spirit of the Jewish enlightenment had begun to penetrate even the outlying Hasidic strongholds of the Ukraine. Along with thousands of other young Jews, he taught himself Russian and mathematics with the hope of entering the university to study a profession. In 1903 he moved to Kiev, audited university classes, and prepared to take the entrance examinations. This was the period when the revolutionary drive for the liberalization of Russia was reaching its peak, especially among disaffected and unemployed young intellectuals like himself. He joined the Iskra faction of the Social Democratic Party and quickly developed a reputation as an effective political organizer.

The unsuccessful revolution of 1905 brought in its wake the seemingly inevitable by-product of any Russian civil upheaval: pogroms against the Jews. Ignatoff joined the swelling exodus of disillusioned Jews and left for America, where his brother had already settled. He arrived in 1906, at the peak of Jewish immigration, and took his first job as a window washer. Hoping for better employment, he set out for Chicago and then St. Louis, but soon returned to the "whirlpool," as he was to call New York. For a time he worked as a maker of hat frames in a millinery factory, where he also got jobs for his fellow writers, Reuben Iceland and Isaac Raboy, and applied his reformist zeal to union organization. As his writing began to take up more time, he turned this same organizing skill to literary projects.

It was during these years that he befriended Mani Leib, Zishe Landau, and Iceland, who with him were to constitute the core of the Yunge, and many others who were associated with it at the beginning—I. J. Schwartz, Joseph Rolnik, Moishe Leib Halpern, M. J. Haimovitch, Raboy, Joseph Opatoshu. Every shipload brought new writers. Ignatoff enjoyed making introductions, taking the newcomers to the homes of friends, and drawing them into literary discussions. His effectiveness as an editor began with his prodding of friends after a long day of work to sit over a poem or story until its completion. Dubbed "the thinker" for his intellectual seriousness, he persuaded these immigrant writers that together they constituted a new cultural force.[28]

The different backgrounds of the young writers lent a certain piquancy to their meetings and exchanges. Mani Leib, like Ignatoff, was from the Ukraine, but from its Russian-speaking northeastern region, from a poorer family, and with no formal education after childhood. Zishe Landau, who became one of Mani Leib's intimates, was the grandson and great-grandson of noted Polish rabbis. He had been tutored privately in Hebrew, Polish, and secular subjects, and though he was forced to leave home at an early age because of the family's impoverishment, his relatives expected him to remain worthy of his aristocratic descent. As the young writers met, they took wary measure of one another. There was, for example, the prickly first meeting between Iceland and Landau not long after the latter's arrival in 1905. Iceland had come to America two years earlier from Radomishli in western Galicia, where he had studied in a cheder and taught himself Hebrew and German. His first poems had just appeared in local magazines, and the chance meeting with a fellow poet was an occasion to show off his familiarity with the local artistic scene.

"So you're Zishe Landau," he said to the Polish newcomer, "and where are your whiskers?" This was a jibe at a poem of Landau's recently published in a New York magazine, which included a forced rhyme between a man's whiskers, *vontsn*, and his dancing, *tantsn*. Since the more natural rhyme for *tantsn* would have been *vantsn*, bedbugs, the poem had aroused its share of merriment in the literary cafés. Landau, not easily cowed, shot back, "My whiskers are with your evening gold!" He hit the mark. Iceland, perhaps in an attempt to prettify the drab circumstances in which he lived, made excessive use of gilded phrases like "flaming gold," "evening gold," "golden dreams." That night he reportedly wept with shame at the insult. The bantering tone of these young poets was like the first bout between up-and-coming boxers or like the first encounter of two yeshiva students each with a reputation for genius.[29]

The male competitiveness of this intellectual environment may help to explain why some talented women, also experimenting with new kinds of writing, found it hard to gain a foothold in the movement. Yente Serdatski wrote a spirited defense of the Yunge, but though her themes of disappointed hope and unrequited love well suited theirs, she did not become a member of the inner circle.[30] This may have been due in part to her age: at twenty-eight she was older than most of the Yunge and already a mother when she arrived in America in 1907. The same cannot be said, however, of Fradl Shtok, a young and prolific poet who was highly praised from the moment of her debut in the American Yiddish periodical press in 1910. Her work was featured in many publications of the Yunge, as were her theoretical discussions of art. Nevertheless, respectfully as her contributions were received, she is not mentioned socially as one of the group, which may be part of the reason she later turned from Yiddish to English.[31] Although the Yunge did not seem to have been aware of their maleness as a stimulus to cohesion, their many references to themselves as a new kind of minyan evokes a vigorous masculine world.

Both at the time and later, everyone insisted that the Yunge represented no specific literary tendency, "no synagogue in the ideological sense," "no consistent literary school."[32] All the same, the gathering of so many eager young writers in Sholem's Café and in the pages of periodicals gave the impression of an active movement, the sort of "youth" movement that had already surfaced in the literary life of England, Poland, and Germany but that was the first of its kind in Yiddish literature.

Certainly this was the impression of many writers who arrived in New York in these years. Aaron Leyeles, having acquired some English in London during a stayover of several years, went to his first meeting of the young writers, and it was not what he had expected:

> I saw and heard before me a bustling country fair . . . I don't remember who was in the chair, but I do recall that the novelist David Ignatoff was the main speaker, the director, although he had a hard time getting a bit of order in all the noise. The talk was of practical matters, something about uniting two separate groups of young writers. Expressions like "it was decided by *bolshinstvo* [Russian for majority]" offended me as sins against the purity of the language. I was eager to hear something having to do with literature itself . . .
>
> Ignatoff demonstrated a clear organizational talent. With reference to the plan for unification he kept complaining that nothing had been

heard from the other side, and "How can we know if the deaf man understands French?" Then there stood up a tall, thin, somewhat slouching and handsome young man whose comments were laced with the words "quiet, quiet," though no one was actually interfering with his talk. But what he wanted I found impossible to understand. I recall him arguing that the problem was not one of getting published because "most of us are already getting published." This last phrase, as I clearly observed, provoked no little surprise on the part of most of the audience. Apparently, the said declaration was for most of those present far from consonant with the facts. The speaker was Mani Leib, already one of the "acknowledged" young poets, at least in some sectors of the literary public.

I also heard some sharp words directed against the press and editors who don't give you the time of day. The sharpest of these comments came from a man with thick red hands, a fairly coarse face, and aggressive manners. He was excitable, passionate, hurling accusations in language far from select. He had to be called to order, and after getting angry a few times he left the hall in protest. A little later he returned . . . and soon began to rant again—this time not only against the editors of the newspapers and journals, but against those running the meeting and the whole organization. All of this extravagant behavior went along with a certain elegance—at least by the standard of most of the others—in dress, the crease of his pants, the boldness of the tie. I was intrigued, and when I asked who this was I was told: Moishe Leib Halpern.[33]

Although this literary reminiscence might inspire more trust if it did not echo in so many phrases and images the published memoirs of other veterans of the movement, it conveys no less than the others the mood of an emerging new culture. Whatever the continuing argument over the composition of the group and the nature of its writing, the Yunge had about them the aura of an artistic coterie strengthened by a common sense of injury.

When the contributors to Di yugnt declared their independence from the press, they were prepared for criticism from professional journalists but not from some of the established Yiddish writers. David Pinski, a well-known playwright and novelist who the Yunge regarded as a potential sponsor, published a slighting review of their efforts in Der yidisher arbeter. A reviewer in the leading Yiddish monthly Di tsukunft, which they had also expected to support their work, mocked the ideal of beautiful literature, the sloppiness of self-publishing, the ignorance and inexperience of the young writers. Stung by criticism that seemed to be leveled against them as a cohort, even those who did not fully subscribe to the aesthetic idealism of Ignatoff and Mani Leib felt implicated in the attacks and rallied to the defense of their colleagues.[34]

To retaliate and to demonstrate the strength of the new movement, and to have some literary fun, a second group of young writers launched a new publication, very different from *Di yugnt* in style, format, and substance. *Der kibitser*, a satiric review as light-hearted as *Di yugnt* was earnest, first appeared on April 15, 1908, and proved so immediately popular that it changed within the year from a monthly to a semimonthly and then to a weekly. Its success prompted the creation of a rival publication, *Der groyser kundes* (The Big Stick), which drew on many of the same contributors and attacked the same sacred cows.[35]

Der kibitser took up the cause of its friends by mocking the mockers, serving notice that anyone who attacked the new direction in Yiddish poetry and prose would also be subjected to ridicule. At the same time, the Yunge themselves were too good a target to ignore, and no one understood their weaknesses better than those who shared or half-shared their artistic dreams. The very nature of the medium demanded that the satiric reviews lampoon their own contributors as well as the daily press and the "Jewish street," the public at large:

> Call us Yunge
> Call us goyim
> As you will.
> Write reviews, write criticism
> To your fill.
> No! We'll not perform
> Tradition's dance.
> Our two-step is the modern
> Decadence!
> From the void
> From aery nothing
> From the abyss

> Lacking form, without much grace
> Or artifice,
> Our verse, too proud perhaps,
> And happenstance
> Will tunefully accompany our
> Decadence![36]

Such parodies punctured the inflated rhetoric and pretentiousness of some of the new writing. The same week that a poem or story appeared in one of the literary magazines, its comic counterpart was already circulating in the pages of *Der kibitser:* "On Rutgers Street, in a tiny room, on the third floor, there we secretly gathered . . . It was evening, when God's creation is restless . . . We, lovers of the goddess Youth, came from behind the shops of this purple and gold striped globe of ours, where eternity hovers eternally in violet dreams."[37] The sharpest sting was a cartoon in one of the early issues showing a New York graveyard with the stones of all the little magazines standing neatly in a row. The recently deceased *Di yugnt* is the last in line, with a fresh gravestone beside it engraved with a question mark.[38] The mortality of highbrow culture stood in ironic contrast to the enormous popularity of the "low" magazines that had come to its defense.

Recurring references to the young Yiddish writers in the pages of these satiric magazines brought them to the attention of audiences that would otherwise have remained ignorant of their existence. But this raised uncomfortable questions. How could this playfulness coexist with the ambitions of writers who did take themselves very seriously and for whom the gatherings in a third-floor walkup on Rutgers street were not comic? As long as the humorists were content to recognize themselves as illegitimate offspring of the literati, they could be accorded a useful secondary role, like that of the fool in Shakespearean tragedy. But the aesthetes were certainly not prepared to grant lampoons the status of serious literature, and when Moishe Nadir, one of the main contributors to the humor weeklies, was appointed editor of a literary magazine, Ignatoff fought his election bitterly.[39]

The simultaneous rise of serious literature in Yiddish and the instrument to undercut it suggests why the artistic movement known as the Yunge could not long survive its beginnings. The aestheticist idea was much too foreign to Jewish culture to enjoy the sustained support of writers who were in any case part of the working mass of East Side Jews. Even those writers who talked most passionately about "pure literature" published regularly in labor, Zionist, socialist, and anarchist publications.

Once the first thrill of publication had worn off, writers began to recognize that they did not have as much in common as they thought, that they represented opposing tendencies in art. Programmatic distinctions such as the Yunge tried to establish between individual sensibility and collective identity are useful in the rallying days of a movement, but they seldom survive its beginnings. Friendships snapped, rival publications sprang up, former colleagues became public antagonists. With the passage of years, the writers looked back in wonder to their springtime on the Lower East Side, when their youth, talent, and artistic ambition had briefly united them.

Joseph Among His Brothers

I n an autobiographical poem written twenty-seven years later (of which a paraphrase follows), Mani Leib describes the day he arrived in New York in 1906.[1]

The young man spewed out by the sea onto Ellis Island—the Isle of Tears, as it was known among the immigrants—carries a small leather pouch containing his first poems, written in *zhargon*, in Yiddish, during a rapturous free hour. His crooked index finger and characteristic manner of spitting mark him as a sewing-machine operator, a skilled craftsman who used to specialize in leather boots. The shirt he wears, black with a high collar and green and red checks, is the mark of the revolutionary; it had been embroidered by the same white hands that sewed the red flag for the central committee of their revolutionary group back home in the Ukraine. He is still young, a mere twenty: that's why the immigration official just pretends to take his pulse, marks his sleeve with white chalk to show that he has been examined, and points the way out.

Waiting for him behind the gates is Uncle Zhiame, the hero of his youth. How many stories his mother had told him about this brother's daring! There was the winter night when, at the distant juncture of the Likomir Highway, Zhiame broke into a church and screwed out the diamonds, big as nuts, from the eyes of the Virgin Mary. Then he poisoned the dogs of the priest, stole two of his horses, and flew like the wild wind to his beloved's house in Niezhin to claim Aunt Temme. His pounding woke the household. "I want your youngest daughter!" he shouted, tossing his cap across the floor. "I'll take her with me to America and watch over her every step." He was not about to let himself rot in Russian prisons! Snatching up his cap and his bride, he bade her kiss her mother goodbye and drove off with her through the snowfall that would cover all their traces by dawn. And now here is Uncle Zhiame in America to greet him. He recognizes his green-gray eyes that could go suddenly hard or soft. Zhiame's gruff welcome brings them both to the point of tears, but they soon shake off their mood and stride off together over the New York cobblestones that sweep his young heart up forever into their alien dirt . . .

Thus far the published section of the poem. A further section, which did not appear during the poet's lifetime, describes the visit to Zhiame's house later in the day.[2] The newcomer begins to get an inkling of his host's attitude when his uncle points out the city skyscrapers (cloud-towers or sky-climbers, some Yiddish poets called them), among them the Singer Building, one of the tallest. Zhiame boasts that one hundred of its sewing machines were currently building his own American fortune and offers avuncular advice: "Here you have to know how to make the dollar, not be the fool." Before taking his nephew home with him to Brooklyn, Zhiame outfits him in a light checked suit, hard straw hat, stiff shirt, silk tie with pink and blue blossoms, and tan shoes with shining copper buckles. Thus presentable, he is ready for the reunion with his Aunt Temme and with a dimly remembered Uncle Ben and his wife, who had left home many years earlier. There is also a female cousin with dazzling white skin, who plays the piano.

In the warmth of the family gathering, the newcomer begins to tell of home, of far-off Niezhin, with its muddy roads that stretch out of town to the graveyard. Father, like all the Jews, is on the road from market fair to market fair, from Sabbath to Sabbath. Sometimes he brings home the ring of the bagel and other times only the hole. Mother bears and nurses the children and sells geese to the rich. Though the children sleep on straw on a damp earthen floor, they are jolly, running around barefoot and naked in summer, and "skating" across the ice in winter, as he himself used to do, without skates. The house is always full of music, like a synagogue, and when mother is in form, all the neighbors gather outside the windows to listen to her.

At this evocation of their past, the aunts start to sob, and Uncle Zhiame leaps up with the promise that he will bring the family over from Europe—each and every last one! This pledge apparently opens an old wound between the two brothers-in-law. Uncle Ben, who had been sitting silently until then, croaks, "Yes, Zhiame, but will you really keep your word?" The tension grows dangerously between the vigorous wealthy uncle and the cynical poor one, but rather than try to make peace, their newcomer nephew picks up the poorer uncle's cue: Ah, but you wouldn't recognize our city nowadays; Niezhin is transformed! The young Jews of the town have become so militant that the very earth burns beneath their feet. On Sabbath, arms linked in a chain, they march to Gogol's monument in the square. With their red flags on the First of May, they gather to demand of the local bourgeoisie their bread and their freedom.

The goad is successful. Uncle Zhiame turns on his nephew in anger—"You too, greenhorn? You too?"—then stomps from the room. The poet feels a burning sensation on his tongue and shouts after his uncle: "Bourgeois! I hate you and your house!" Taking hold of the lapels of his new jacket, he rips it clear through to the lining and flees, with the girl at the piano as his final memory of that day.

It is not surprising that Mani Leib should have written a fictional account of his arrival in America. Several of his contemporaries composed prose memoirs of this kind; among immigrants the world over, the point of starting fresh, with the body of an adult but the vulnerability of a child, remains fixed with exceptional clarity. But the circumstances of its composition reflect the nature of the memory. Mani Leib wrote this long work in the winter of 1933, while he was convalescing from tuberculosis at Deborah Sanatorium in Browns Hills, New Jersey.[3] Feeble and frightened, with neither home nor job in the city, he seemed at this time of life to embody the failure of America's depression years, and some of it finds retroactive expression in the bitter outburst of the poor young immigrant in his wealthy uncle's home. The young woman in white who plays the piano was also more than an actual memory. She was, as we shall see, Mani Leib's recurring image of American refinement, and the blurred glimpse of her here is a poetic reminder that beyond the material allure of America there was the further temptation of high culture, even more provocative and elusive than all his uncle's wealth.

Yet Deborah Sanatorium gave Mani Leib an unprecedented opportunity. Lying there he had, for the first time since his arrival in America, endless hours to think and, when strength permitted, to write. Letters poured from his pen. He wrote a number of lyrics and even finished, in the course of three weeks, a five-act play that he hoped to sell to Maurice Schwartz for production on the Yiddish stage. His autobiographical poem "On New York Stones" was thus the product of an unusually fertile period. Though Mani Leib thought that he had found, in the natural rhythm of iambic quatrains, an ideal vehicle for his entire autobiography, he did not write it beyond the rupture with Uncle Zhiame, who figures as a kind of Jewish Robin Hood as long as he is in the old country but is portrayed after his success in America as a crude and greedy capitalist. Like several prominent Yiddish writers—Sholem Aleichem, Mendele Mocher Sforim, I. L. Peretz—Mani Leib interrupts his autobiography at the point of adolescent rebellion and decisive separation from what could be called "home."

When it comes to his recollections of childhood, however, Mani Leib weaves a tale soothing enough to lull even the most fitful of children to sleep.[4] Niezhin, the poet's birthplace, was a city of 35,000 Ukrainians and 4,000 Jews living in complementary harmony. With a statue in the square of its most famous native son, Nikolai Gogol, Mani Leib's Niezhin is renowned for its mud, willow trees, wealthy tobacco merchants, horse traders, and horse thieves; also for the tombs of its holy Jews, its shoemakers and drunks, the great white lycée where Gogol had studied, and above all for its pickles. He found the city very beautiful, "with its pre-Passover and post-Days of Awe muds that reach above the waist, and its winter snows that rise above the straw rooftops to the height of the chimneys."[5]

The family of Mani Leib was poor, gentle, and honest. His father, "the tallest Jewish pauper in Niezhin," would buy animal hides from gentiles at the outlying fairs and sell them to local dealers. A fairly well-educated man, he also wrote letters for those who could not. His mother, a native of Vilna who loved to sing and to talk in epigrams and rhymes, raised poultry and during the winters sustained them by selling potatoes and frozen apples. The eight children—six sons, of whom the poet was the eldest, and two daughters—slept on straw mats. A single blanket covered all the boys, and occasionally the two eldest, who slept at either end, had a tug of war.

During the day the older children looked after the younger ones. At the close of Sabbath, his father's friends and neighbors, butchers, teamsters, horse dealers, and wandering beggars, would sit around the boiling samovar, drinking tea and trading stories about bandits, wolves, witches and warlocks, corpses and orphan girls. When the Ukrainian peasants sang at the outskirts of town and the Jews raised the rooftops with their folksongs and cantorials, the two sets of melodies would intermingle in lovely new harmonies.

The poverty of the household dictated the pace and direction of the boy's development. At the age of eleven Mani Leib had to leave the cheder because there were too many to feed at home. This was the end of his formal education. He was apprenticed by his father to a bootmaker, and if he learned more at first about rocking a cradle and other household chores than he did about sewing leather, this was all part of a normal apprenticeship. Eventually he did learn from his master, in addition to the craft of bootmaking, the arts of playing cards and talking in rhyme, an earthier kind of rhyme than he had learned at home from his mother. He also read his master's books in Yiddish and Russian. Since his mother was a singer, and his grandmother Etl was a gifted storyteller, it was only natural that he too should begin to compose songs and stories in verse. The first poem he ever saw, in Shomer's novel *American Fortunes,* set out in even lines on the page, made him marvel at the visual effect. Encouraged by his master's son, a student at the local high school, he wrote many poems, until one of his satires on a local wedding got him into trouble with those it described. Only later, once he had left his native city, did he begin to publish his work.

When he was fifteen Mani Leib woke one day to find that his master and mistress had run off to America with a good deal of their customers' money, leaving the machinery and shop unclaimed. At his father's insistence, he took over the shop and the younger apprentices. He might have prospered, were it not that another bootmaker came into town from the neighboring city of Homel to organize the first local strike in the industry. He discovered that it was an ugly thing to be a boss, profiting from the sweat of others, and that he would rather be a strike leader, running about all day with students, agitating, and composing rousing rhymes. He worked so effectively to overthrow the tsar that he was soon imprisoned, which was a great honor and, since it gave him some free time, also an occasion for writing.

But the next time he was arrested, he decided to run off to America, where he sat down at the same kind of sewing machine he had used in Neizhin and again began stitching leather. With the money he earned, he brought over his father and mother, married, fathered children, and, whenever he had the time, composed rhyming lines that he then set out in poems.

To these colorful memoirs Mani Leib never added very much. He liked to tell stories about his uncles, the notorious horse thieves.[6] He once told an interviewer about his maternal grandmother, who brought her daughter to Niezhin from Vilna when she was widowed and who fasted every Monday and Thursday all her life to atone for having accidentally smothered her only male child at the breast. He told of the first time he brought home his apprentice earnings: in the house there was only one fork, which belonged to his father. The rest of the family ate with their hands from the common bowl. On this occasion his father insisted that the new breadwinner take the fork in his stead.[7]

All his reminiscences of home are bathed in soft light. Defending himself against charges of sentimentalizing the past, Mani Leib claimed it wasn't his fault that he had grown up in so peaceful a family and region. Yet autobiographies of poor boys who are apprenticed at a tender age to less than scrupulous masters are rarely so carefree; nor are the memoirs of revolutionaries in tsarist prisons. Descriptions of Ukrainian-Jewish relations, particularly when written, as these were, after the Ukrainian slaughter of some 100,000 Jews in the pogroms of 1919–20, are seldom so cheerful. Mani Leib was clearly shaping the old country into an almost magically wholesome place, a rustic paradise that stood in contrast to the harsh conditions of America. From his own background and from Jewish history he erased the most humiliating memories so that the Old World Jews should be revealed in health and hope, with himself as their artless folksinger. His decision to drop his patronym, Brahinsky, when he began to publish emphasizes this folk image.

Mani Leib's recreation of a golden past was not simply an expression of nostalgia for the old country, but the reaching of an uprooted artist for a firm myth of origins. Much as Sholem Aleichem used his autobiography to tell the story of the birth of a folk writer, so too Mani Leib dramatizes choice moments of his childhood to show the Yiddish poet emerging from his native culture like a sapling in rich soil. The details of his mother's singing, his master's rhyming, the inheritance of narrative skills from his father and his grandmother, the merging Jewish and Ukrainian melodies on a Saturday night—all of these stress the child's membership in an integrated family and community and the emergence of his music from theirs. It is a story of the fatherland of Yiddish which nurtured the poet until he had to go into exile.

Mani Leib's actual passage to America followed the typical route of young Russian-Jewish intellectuals. The trip across Europe was interrupted several times because of difficulties crossing borders and a lack of money. He spent the better part of a year in London, 1904–05, probably because he did not have the funds for the trans-Atlantic crossing and had to wait for additional help from his uncle or earn the money himself. In London he took his first poems around to various local Yiddish newspapers and periodicals hoping for publication.[8]

Through the intervention of a friend, Mani Leib was introduced to Joseph Chaim Brenner, one of the most original writers of modern Hebrew prose. Brenner was then working as a typesetter and proofreader at the Naroditski Publishing Company on Mile End Road. His work was complicated by the fact that some of the editors of the local Yiddish anarchist and socialist publications for which he was responsible were not Jews and had an imperfect command of the language. Brenner's influence thus extended beyond his given assignments, and he had a say in the content of the publications as well as their format. Mani Leib showed Brenner his Yiddish translation of the Russian revolutionary song "Vikhri razdrazhennie viutsia nad nami" (Angry Stormwinds Swirl About Us), and years later he still recalled with pleasure Brenner's praise of it. This does not appear to have been enough, however, to ensure its publication.

The extraordinary variability of Jewish literary life during this first decade of the century is manifest in the situation of writers who found themselves in the halfway house of London for weeks or months or years. Brenner, for example, was in London from 1904, when he escaped from tsarist army service, until 1908, when he went to Lvov, Galicia, and from there to Palestine. He was a leading figure in the renaissance of Hebrew literature. His bleak descriptions of the unmoored Jewish youths of his time made his readers believe that the classical language could express their turmoil and ironically, by extension, encouraged them to substitute a Hebrew secular culture for their traditional religious upbringing. Yet Brenner himself voiced misgivings about the future of Hebrew and looked upon himself and his few fellow Hebraists as the last heirs of a dying art. "We are going under, but we shall die in our shoes and on our feet." He called his press Masada, after the stronghold of zealots who committed mass suicide rather than be taken by Rome into captivity.[9]

The Yiddish writers surrounding Brenner felt that their language was the natural choice for modern Jewish literature. Brenner admitted to them that Hebrew did not come easily to him, though he had before him such models as the Bible, the Mishna, the Midrashim, and especially Mendele Mocher Sforim, the crusty old man who was still exerting critical influence over both Yiddish and Hebrew writing from his home in Odessa. Brenner would first think everything through in Yiddish and only then translate his thoughts into Hebrew. He considered it pointless to speak Hebrew to his fellow Jews, since it was so much easier to talk in the vernacular. Nonetheless, neither his employment in the Jewish press nor his proven ability to write Yiddish attracted him permanently to the language.

For their part, the Yiddish writers accepted the logic of Yiddish, despite their own occasional misgivings about its inferior literary status. The Yiddish writer Lamed Shapiro, who befriended Brenner during his own passage through London in 1906, was convinced that it was a waste of historical energy to attempt a revival of Hebrew because it would not succeed and because Yiddish, "that wonderful instrument" developed by Ashkenazic Jewry over the centuries, would make it unnecessary. Another of Brenner's close friends of this period, the journalist Kalman Marmor, who also had a command of both languages, was invited along with Brenner to leave for Philadelphia in 1906 to edit the Yiddish weekly *Yidisher kemfer*, the same paper to which Mani Leib had such trouble sending his poems. Brenner flirted briefly with the idea but finally refused, though he did send some articles to Marmor the next year.[10]

Products of the yeshivas, with a classical education in Hebrew, young men like Brenner, Shapiro, and Marmor had to make the difficult choice between two possible Jewish languages—although, to be sure, the choice was often dictated by their assessment of immediate opportunities. Mani Leib, a boy with only a rudimentary cheder education, had no such option. As his manuscripts and letters show, he could not even spell many common Hebrew words let alone comfortably use the language. He always remained somewhat in awe of colleagues with Hebrew literacy. Perhaps because he knew that Yiddish was his only authentic tongue, Mani Leib imagined it as the unclaimed treasure of its people and himself as the simple native son who would become a princely artist in the act of uncovering its splendor. They were both of equally humble origin, he and the language, but like the peasant of the fairy tale who wins the hand of the princess, they would eventually prove their superiority.

Mani Leib's arrival in New York coincided with the peak of Jewish immigration. From an economic standpoint, he was among the most fortunate of the 150,000 newcomers of 1905, since he found lodging with an uncle and work as a bootmaker at four dollars a week. Among the Yunge he was sometimes envied because none of the others had developed so marketable a skill. Though his work in shoe factories over the next few decades entailed long hours of work, he could at least always have it when he wished. Reuben Iceland remembers Mani Leib in the months after his arrival as a tall, thin young man dressed in a long black coat and a black woolen shirt without a tie. The absence of a tie did not strike Iceland as unusual because in the radical clubs of socialists and anarchists of the time this antibourgeois outfit was de rigeur. Yet there was some-thing exceptional about the length of the coat and the blackness of the shirt. In his dress and bearing Mani Leib was decidedly a poet, issuing forceful pronouncements on what he liked and disliked in art even as he was publishing his own first poems in *Forverts* and in the anarchist daily *Fraye arbeter shtime* (Free Workers' Voice), whose editor, Shaul-Joseph Yanofsky, was hospitable to unpublished writers.[11]

Though Mani Leib might have enjoyed a bohemian existence as a bachelor at least for a while, he acted swiftly and impulsively to secure a family. Unsure of himself, he was homesick and, like most of his fellow immigrants, sought out his local landsmanshaft of Priluke-Niezhin, where he could get the latest news from home and help in arranging the passage of his family to America. Soon after his arrival, he also brought over his childhood sweetheart, Chasia.[12] Marrying the girl next door probably seemed a good way of easing an uncomfortable entry into the lonely new land. The couple had five children over the next ten years, a matter of puzzlement to the poet's friends, who sensed their incompatability. Chasia was a homebody, a silent woman who wanted a solid family life and clung jealously to her husband as the only link to the unfamiliar world around her. Pretty in her youth, she neglected her appearance after the birth of her children. But Mani Leib soon became the most romantic figure of the new Yiddish writers. His handsome, some-what haughty appearance, and the suffering role in which he cast himself in his poems, made him attractive to women and involved him in many romantic affairs. If he had intended to import comfort from the old country, he found that his wife could not supply what he now sought. Or perhaps, once the home was securely estab-lished, he grew restive and hungry for adventure outside it.

The routine of factory worker, husband, and father soon proved to be irreconcilable with the aspirations of a poet. Mani Leib did not spend much time in the small apartment in Williamsburg with its squall of children. Rather than invite friends in, he went to the cafés where he played cards till late in the night or argued literature. Sometimes he would spend the whole night in absorbed conversa-tion with friends, walking through the sleeping city.

He was attracted to the home of David Ignatoff and fell a little in love with Ignatoff's wife, Minna, a woman who played the piano well and created around her the atmosphere of a cultivated salon. Minna's American upbringing and the decorum of her home contrasted sharply with the stolidity of his own wife, who grew more sullen, some said dangerously ill, as he retreated from her. He wrote a poem about the lily fingers of a woman playing the piano that lured him away from his children in their white nightshirts, and then summon up, through the music they play, the image of those white-clad children weeping in the night.[13] His poems of this period express the distaste he was beginning to feel for his wife, complicated by remorse, and the guilt he experienced as he stole pleasure from another man's house. Of Mani Leib's poems during the first decade of his writing, Iceland notes that the words *kind* and *zind*, child and sin, form an essential and not merely recurring rhyme.[14]

When the poet Itsik Manger in later years called Mani Leib "a Joseph among his brothers," he may have been referring to the special role that he began to occupy among the Yunge as the most attractive member of the group, the one generally singled out for attention and praise.[15] Or Manger may have had in mind Mani Leib's dreaminess, the way he set the substance of his verse in opposition to his daily life. Both qualities brought him to the forefront of the movement in 1910. The Farein, a loose association of writers that attracted as many as seventy members to its meetings, decided that year to put out its own literary monthly. The editing entrusted to its three senior members—Yoel Entin, Yoel Slonim, and M. J. Haimovitch—the first issue of *Literatur* was a handsome volume of 144 pages, a significant advance in quality and bulk over other little magazines of the time.[16]

Arguments for a new literature in this first issue outweighed examples of it by a ratio of three to one. Entin defended symbolism over the exhausted western heritage of realism. Philosophically anti-materialist, symbolism, with its faith in the creative spirit, could transform man's vision of himself and thereby improve society. It was really the source of an optimistic new psychology that could free mankind from "earth-bound" social truths and inspire confidence in a visionary future. This neoromantic outlook was buttressed by two other essays, one by Moishe Katz on I. L. Peretz and one by Yoel Slonim on Oscar Wilde.[17] Peretz was praised for moving away from realistic fiction to the mysterious and stirring folktale tradition, and for reinvigorating the ancient Jewish religion with a renewed sense of personal quest. Slonim commended Oscar Wilde for the magical quality of his prose poems, his aestheticism, and his thematic emphasis on the self. Unfortunately, compared with these fervent arguments for a new sensibility, the poems and stories in the miscellany were disappointingly tame.

As in the case of *Di yugnt* two years earlier, some of the younger members of the Farein objected to the conservatism of the editors and took control of the magazine, keeping its aesthetic orientation but inverting the proportion of literature to criticism. To dramatize their innovativeness, they opened the second issue not with an essay or statement of purpose but with a series of lyrics by Mani Leib which had been turned down by the first editorial group. The leading poem, rendered here in my bald translation, became the focus of vigorous debate:

> Dovestill blue evening hours!
> Spread soft evening's dream outspread before me—
> Now my red roses burn redder,
> Fiercer burn my wounds—
>
> Now as noises die in city streets
> Footsteps echo softer, words are stiller.
> Eyes that seek out other eyes burn paler,
> Hands pressed into other hands speak milder.
>
> Now my longing bursts aflame in gold,
> Hotter burns my blood, my eye splays wider.
> Now, my red roses burn redder,
> My red roses—my wounds.[18]

> toybnshtile, bloye ovnt-shtundn!
> shpreyt far mir mayn ovnt-troym tseshpreyter!
> itster . . . itster brenen reyter, reyter
> mayne shtile royzn—mayne vundn.
>
> itster shtarbt in gasn der gepilder;
> trit un verter hilkhn shtiler, veykher,

eygn, benkendik nokh eygn, kukn bleykher,
hent in hent gedrikte redn epes milder.

itster vert mayn benkshaft gold getsundn.
heyser vert mayn blut, mayn eyg vert breyter!
itster . . . itster brenen reyter, reyter
mayne reyte royzn—mayne vundn!

Missing in English are the swishing sounds in Yiddish of falling stillness as against the rough rasp of opening wounds, the musical patterns of the poem that are its most striking feature. This musicality excited the poets. They felt that the Yiddish word had liberated itself from the burden of meaning that, like an overloaded camel, it had been forced to bear.[19] Here, finally, was Yiddish symbolism not in theory but in poetic practice. The critics protested that the neologism "dovestill" was self-contradictory because doves were noisiest toward evening; that the metaphoric connection between a symbol of beauty, the rose, and a symbol of ugliness, the wound, was aesthetically inappropriate; and that the imperative "spread" in the second line did not require the redundant adjective "outspread" to enforce its meaning. The poets, however, admired the emotional intensity generated by just these "senseless" features of synesthesia, soundplay, repetition, and verbal daring.[20] In Jassy, Rumania, the young Itsik Manger, excited by the "halftones and three-quarter tones" of this poem, recited it to the students and workers of the Morris Rosenfeld Reading Circle as a model of the new American Yiddish literature.[21]

The plain sense of the words did violence to the cultural expectations of Yiddish readers. But for the Yunge the poem was proof that Yiddish no longer need be inhibited by its national or social context from expressing private subtleties. At the end of a working day, as others on the crowded streets pair off in shared affection, the isolated man in the poem feels the pain of his yearning, realized in the speaker's independence of his surroundings and in the poem's independence of denotative speech. As many of the British Romantics discovered their humanity in the majesty of European mountains and British lakes, Mani Leib and his colleagues probed their solitude among the tall buildings and rumbling elevated trains of the metropolis. With Mani Leib's poems and other works in the same vein, the editors of *Literatur* felt they had given "the better sort of reader" a new kind of art whose value stood above the literary marketplace. They hoped that the expression of subjectivity would free writer and reader from the clutch of collective identity and the burden of historical destiny.

But lacking the great sweep of natural landscape that had inspired the Romantic poets a century earlier, the experience of self in much of this urban verse seemed exhausted before it had begun to realize its potential. In Mani Leib's poem, the adjectives—paler, milder, redder, softer—are comparative only in relation to their own intensity. The enmeshment of senses and the speaker's indulgence of his pain point up his overwrought state of mind. The musicality of the language requires a considerable sacrifice of natural diction, and the experience of solitude easily slips into sickliness.

In sum, the precocity of this new poetry drew so much attention to itself that, instead of transcending its environment, it unwittingly demonstrated its artificiality. Moishe Leib Halpern, who had been attempting to write the same kind of lyrics (and is represented in the second issue of *Literatur* with a poem of similarly heightened emotionalism), used the pages of *Der kibitser* to parody Mani Leib's "Dovestill blue evening hours" for exactly what characterized his own poetry as well:

A shadow hurries through a street. Another follows. Zounds!
The lampposts when I look at them appear to me as wounds . . .

Wounds! Why yes—not long ago I read that wounds are roses.
Wounds—roses? Woe is me! Then these holes in my trousers
Must be red roses . . . and my heart a blossoming rosegarden.
And the peddler of toothpicks in the cafeteria—
Isn't he an errant red rose domain? . . .
    If wounds are truly roses
By God, I'd swear black chimney smoke must be white underwear
And the soles of cossack boots are matso pancakes![22]

Using the denotative standard of the literalist against the imaginative language of the lyricist, Halpern beats the bushes of poetry to shake out its excesses as if he had never before seen a metaphor. His deflating barbs, no doubt sharpened by competitive high spirits, show his impatience with the unreality of the new art, which seemed likely to explode from its own ballooning pretentions. His satire struck deeper than the critics had by seeming to ask Mani Leib —and himself—whether their myth of The Poet and his inner life was not comically disproven by the contradictory evidence of their immigrant poverty.

It was a question over which the Yunge were soon to be divided. But at least for the young Mani Leib there was no question of reconciling his two lives: in the manner of much of the culture he had left behind him, he used poetry as a means of denying the limits of material realities. The Russian symbolists and decadents of the turn of the century, whose publications circulated among the émigrés, offered the enviable model of an artistic coterie that united creative individualists in a common cause. Reacting against the dominant populist influence of the late nineteenth century that had sought to harness literature as a force in progressive politics, the Russian symbolists developed a competing philosophic justification for lyricism, for the exploration of purely personal feelings and perceptions. Since the poets deemed it necessary to penetrate the ultimate reality beyond this world of shadowed imperfection, they welcomed every passion and stimulated intense emotion. Their swooning love affairs, the self-advertised experiments with mysticism, the eccentric way they dressed and behaved, drew attention to the antibourgeois, antidemocratic nature of the movement. The New York Yiddish poets who followed their pronouncements and read their poetry from afar were inspired by this possibility of self-liberation from the constraints of public taste and the daily affairs of men.

Of course, the economic and social conditions within the Yiddish-speaking immigrant community ensured that the Yiddish poet could never shed quite so much of the material world as those admired Russian poets. The pressures of the immigrant environment continued to anchor the Jewish writers in reality even when they were no longer observing the disciplining rituals of traditional Jewish society. Zishe Landau published a translation of Fyodor

Sologub's mystical *The Magic of Sorrow*, which exalts unfulfilled yearning and intuition over all that is present, logical, and known. Despite the skillful rendition, the work sits oddly in Yiddish, and Landau had to create or import from German all the key concepts of *nitdoikayt* (negative reality, or unexistence) that give the book its flavor. In his own poetry, the references to unexistence and unexistent words are the domesticated yearnings of an ordinary man and poet for something beyond his ordinary experience.[23]

It is easy to see how Mani Leib was attracted by these qualities of romanticism and symbolism in his own poetic theory and practice. Here he was, a Ukrainian Jew, far from the beloved landscape that had nurtured his art and imagination. He was separated from the intertwined cultures of Ukrainians, Russians, and Jews in which he had been raised, and his lifelong attachment to that complex knot of language and influence grew stronger the more it receded from him in time. Mani Leib's whole idea of inwardness and personalism derives from the images and sounds of his distant, enticing birthplace, which he carried within him through the busy New York streets.

His sign of antipathy to the street was his cultivation of the word "stillness," the dimming of sound and the cessation of movement. The speaker in the early lyrics sits, typically, not at his workbench or at the supper table but alone behind his closed door, trying to ignore the ringing phone and buzzing voices in the room beyond and the bustle in the street outside. Sometimes he walks along the paths of the silent park, and the word for those paths, *aleyen*, reinforces the sense of his solitude: he is alone, *aleyn*. The poems create through sound the immigrant's suspension from the crush around him, his desire for inner serenity. Dreams of snowy Russia, with its fading echoes of sleighbells in distant valleys, haunt his memory —and also quicken his guilt, for he knows that he should be responsive to his actual surroundings.

A common prop of the early lyrics is the window that separates the inner from the outer world, creating either a shelter or a cell. Behind the drawn curtains of his tiny room, the speaker almost goes mad in his self-imposed solitude, and even when he opens the curtains, he feels himself separated from the hectic activity outside. Alternately, the poet walking in the street is beckoned by the light of windows overhead, realizing that he will never penetrate their mysteries or their warmth.[24] Set apart from others, the poet is able to see through to the heart of the world he inhabits. He is particularly observant at night, when misery is more keenly revealed:

> Night and rain,
> night and wind.
> In the night and the rain
> in the night and the wind
> people walk the streets
> dog-tired, hungry, wet,
> tempest-tossed and lost.
>
> And where do the people go?
> Ask the night and the wind.
> They never weep, they never cry,
> in the night and the wind,
> in rows walking by,
> dog-tired, hungry, wet,
> driven out and lost.[25]

Rather than invoke the outcast as occasion for a plea or threat or demand, Mani Leib soothes the weary with a song of their weariness, extending the unspoken tenderness of music, like a crooning parent.

This yearning for *nitdoikayt* and the ideal of quietude also had sources in experiences of political hope and despair. Mani Leib had cut his teeth on the strike movement that involved over two million Russians in 1903, and the dedication to reform that brought him one prison sentence would have cost him another had he not decided to leave Russia. The discouragement that overtook young Russian intellectuals when their uprising was crushed in 1905 accompanied its supporters overseas, dulling some of their faith in political activism. Mani Leib frequented anarchist and Russian socialist clubs only for a short time after his arrival in New York. To the writing of poetry he transferred the idealism he had shown earlier as a strike organizer; the servant of poetry could also be the servant of his people.

God raised me from the dust
Set me above other men
To have me sing your worth
To have me praise your honor
That when I am returned to earth
My name remain among you. Amen.[26]

From symbolism Mani Leib adapted the idea of the poet as an
alchemist who distills ordinariness into its purer essence; from hu-
manism and Jewish teaching he took the ideal of the individual
whose striving for moral perfection hastens the redemption of the
world. He did not feel that he was abandoning the poor, but ad-
dressing their deeper deprivation. The labor poets who had limited
their observation to the surfaces of things may have helped to bring
about better working conditions and higher wages. But the aesthetic
poets offered the disadvantaged what the Sabbath held out to its
observers: an interval of perfection in a world where chaos reigns.

A turning point came for Mani Leib when he realized how deeply
his feelings were rooted in the redemptive longing of Jewish tradi-
tion. "I am not a mystic, and I don't believe in miracles . . . but one
Sunday while walking through a lovely section of Brooklyn—trees,
flowers, it was autumn, Rosh Hashonah—I heard the chanting of a
cantor. I couldn't tear myself away from his prayer. Somehow I felt
that a whole new source of images and language had opened for
me."[27] This should not be misread as a traditional religious experi-
ence, for the poet was not inspired to enter the synagogue but to
appropriate its music for his verse. The result of this epiphany was a
poetry of greater resonance and heft:

Hush and hush—no sound be heard.
Bow in grief but say no word.
Black as pain and white as death,
Hush and hush and hold your breath.

Heard by none and seen by none
Out of the dark night will he,
Riding on a snow-white steed,
To our house come quietly.

From the radiance of his face,
From his dress of shining white
Joy will shimmer and enfold;
Over us will fall his light.

Quieter—no sound be heard!
Bow in grief but say no word.
Black as pain and white as death,
Hush and hush and hold your breath.

If we have been mocked by them,
If we have been fooled again
And the long and weary night
We have waited all in vain,

We will bend down very low
To the hard floor, and then will
Stand more quiet than before
Stiller, stiller and more still.[28]

It is strange to think of this poem of 1914 as a product of the political Lower East Side. At the time, streetcorner ideologues and spokesmen for every cause were trying to exhort the immigrant masses to angry protest. Among great orators recently come to the United States were the Zionist Nahum Syrkin, the fiery socialist and diaspora nationalist Chaim Zhitlowsky, and the great theoretician of Labor-Zionism, Ber Borochov. At large public rallies, and by the power of their pens, they were able to sway huge segments of the Jewish community to their views. Labor organization was at its height, and strikes were often made or broken by the rhetorical impact of their leaders. The speaker in Mani Leib's poem, who is also addressing a mass of Jews, inverts all the usual terms of the day. He points his listeners to the past, not the future. He exhorts them to be silent rather than beat a drum and raise a fist. From the secular language of the modern sociopolitical movements, he turns back to religious symbols of Jewish tradition, to the ancient dream of the Messiah that had sustained the Jews for thousands of years.

The excitement over this lyric on the part of the Yunge attests to its perceived cultural importance. It was granted the opening place

of honor in the third volume of *Shriftn*—the most mature publica-
tion of the Yunge to date—and was accompanied by two drawings
by Zuni Maud, one of them representing a prophetic figure and the
other a white-bearded Jew, the symbol of traditional wisdom and
piety. In Yiddish the term for such a man is *sheyner yid* (beautiful
Jew), since the aesthetic ideal of the community derived from just
these qualities of mind and spirit. The illustrations drew attention
to the way the poem united its own aesthetic credo with the age-old
Jewish ideals of beauty and faith.

The first American Yiddish work to introduce the messianic
motif, this lyric was, according to Reuben Iceland, also the first
successful expression of their moral view. The gravest obstacle fac-
ing the group, as he saw it, was the danger of overreaching them-
selves. The ambition to create all at once and in an underdeveloped
language a great literature could easily result in bathos, false infla-
tion, and fatal errors of aesthetic judgment. True excellence of art
and character required self-restraint and creative discipline, espe-
cially amid the inflated expectations that America inspired. By rais-
ing resignation to heroic pitch, Mani Leib had set the standard for
their art, which must know how to resist the urge for illusory prog-
ress in its striving for timeless perfection.[29]

In a small way Mani Leib's modest invocation is reminiscent of
Keats's magnificent "Ode on a Grecian Urn." The splendid pursuit
of lovers around the ancient Greek urn, figures that will never
achieve their goal and on that very account will never age or die,
become for the poet the essence of artistic immutability. Mani Leib
similarly turns to the past, to the generations of Jews who stand in
poised expectancy of the messianic coming as his own culture's ideal
of immutability. He admits the irony of the pose, because the
redeemer's delay is as stubborn as Jewish longing, and the hostility
of the nations who mock and fool the Jews is as passionate as their
trust. Yet the faith of the modern artist must be similarly stubborn.
In the traditional Jew's attendance upon the Messiah, the modern
poet and perhaps the Yiddish poet in particular can find an emblem
for their own impractical quest.

It was in the shorter forms of poetry and fiction that the Yunge
began to excel, and Mani Leib's lyrics were the first to pass beyond
precocity to ripeness. Like a boy whose vocal register changes with

age, Mani Leib's poetic voice took on a deeper resonance about the time he heard the cantor's chanting in Brooklyn, around 1913. Departing from the radical innovation exemplified in "Dovestill blue evening hours," he used the models of folksongs and ballads to achieve natural Yiddish rhythms and diction. Rather than submit the language to his own imported or invented patterns of sound and sense, he tried to elicit music from the spoken language:

> I have my mother's black hair and green eyes,
> my father's delicate thin hands
> and blood that sings and flares,
> blood of grandfathers—Jews along the Dnieper;
> on my head, the many nights with friends
> spent longing for fine and tender lust,
> and sharp teeth indentations on my chest
> of a dependent, apprehensive woman.[30]

This self-portrait, drawn in a tight space between the woman who bore him and the one who now possesses him, has nothing at all of the haziness of Mani Leib's earlier studies of himself. The man in the poem is made of conflicting inheritances that join in uneasy coalition. He is the passive battleground of vital forces that claim him— forces male and female, biological and cultural, past and present. One can recognize here the moody subject of the earlier poems, still at odds with his surroundings. The real change is in the confidence with which the poet now explores the subject.

The ferment in Mani Leib's literary development during the two years prior to World War I reflected the maturing of the group as a whole. David Ignatoff began to edit *Shriftn*, which in its modest editions of between 500 and 1,000 served an elite readership that sought the same standards in an indigenous Jewish culture as did the writers themselves. Because self-publishing was fairly cheap, miscellanies could be funded by whoever happened to have the money on hand and were distributed through the local Yiddish bookstores. One volume of *Shriftn* was put out on the strength of a $75 contribution from Joseph Opatoshu and a gold chain pawned by Mani Leib.[31] Ignatoff intended to send 200 of 500 copies overseas, to Poland. A local bookseller bought up the whole edition for $140, leaving the contributors with a debt of about the same amount they still owed the printer.[32]

The ideal of a high culture was developed in other languages by aristocrats and bohemians, those born or attached to the two extremes of society equally distant from the majority. The aristocrats by virtue of their position and the bohemians because they renounced position were free to espouse independent ideals of perfection because they were not involved in ordinary activities. But the American Yiddish writers were fully part of the common life. Mani Leib was so skilled as a bootmaker that he was sometimes able to complete a day's work in a few hours and take the afternoon off for himself. Nonetheless, the work tired him, and the rest of his colleagues were far less dexterous.

From a later perspective, the incongruous pairing of aestheticism with menial occupations had its charm. "Imagine," writes Irving Howe, "in any other literature the turn to impressionism or symbolism being undertaken by a shoemaker and a housepainter, and the dismissal of the social muse by men laboring in factories! Proletarian aesthetes, Parnassians of the sweatshop—this was the paradox and the glory of the Yunge."[33] The writers themselves struck this note in their memoirs. A favorite story describes H. Leivick checking his bucket and brush with his coat when he attended the premiere performance of his play *The Golem*. Reuben Iceland recalls how desperately he longed to close the butcher shop he was running for his brother-in-law whenever his friends dropped by with a new poem.[34] One young writer who opened a cleaning store in the Bronx was thrilled when it became a gathering place for the writers of the Yunge who were then moving into the neighborhood. Opatoshu came in to discuss his stories, and Moishe Leib Halpern slept there for several weeks. Eventually the business began to suffer: "There were fewer and fewer customers. I was forced to decide whether to take down the classic Yiddish writers from the wall, toss out their grandsons, the Bronx chapter of the Yunge, and turn my 'Literary Hostel' into a real business establishment, or let things go, whatever the consequences . . . I didn't hesitate for a minute and chose the latter."[35]

What may seem piquant in retrospect, however, was often discouraging at the time. Apart from the sheer physical strain of writing after a full day's work, these double lives required enormous mental agility, the ability to switch from the routine of the workplace to the discipline of literary craft and back again, day after day. Though the Yunge always aspired to great works of art, by which they meant works of quantitative as well as qualitative weight, few of them ever found enough uninterrupted time for the epics they dreamed of. (Once, when Ignatoff asked him for a long poem, Moishe Leib Halpern gave him translated sections of Hugo von Hofmannstahl sandwiched between two parts of his own work.)[36] For the first decade, the group miscellany and the little magazine were the group's only vehicles of publication, the short story and the short lyric their characteristic genres. The only poet among the Yunge eventually to write masterly works of epic proportion was I. J. Schwartz who, after leaving New York for Lexington, Kentucky, to help run a clothing store, apparently found the time to compose with sustained concentration. His book-length poem *Kentucky*, the epic tale of a Jewish peddler who settles in the South and becomes part of its history, was one of the few works ever to satisfy the group's early expectations that their work could expand to fit America's limitless breadth.[37]

Yet the myth of their incomparable New York youth grew with the passage of time:

> A literary evening. Morris Rosenfeld recites his poem, "The Candle-Seller," and his betrayed young heroine implores, "Do you remember the night when you swore to be true?" The hall is packed. The audience is young and enthusiastic. On the way out someone is heard sneering at the rhetorical bombast of this verse, someone already familiar with Paul Verlaine's dictum that "in poetry there must be music before all else . . ." Another, secretly envious of the great poet, is thinking, just wait, I'll show the world that I'm as good as Rosenfeld . . . What unites us all is the feeling that we are lost forever to this magical East Broadway that contains in itself all the enchantments of the world.[38]

For Mani Leib poetry was the enchantment he had found and created on East Broadway. Schwartz harbored fond memories of their elders—the old bard Eliokhum Zunzer, who had made his poetic reputation as a performer at Jewish weddings and later opened a small printing shop on the Lower East Side; Yehoash, the great biblical translator and Jewish scholar who befriended the younger poets; Morris Rosenfeld, embittered by life and resentful of those taking his place; Abraham Liessin, powerful man of struggle and song and even more powerful editor of *Di tsukunft*. But for Schwartz as for Mani Leib the magic began with the arrival of *their* ships, "bringing rich tribute to Yiddish poetry." They were:

> a great chorus,
> a band of the young . . .
> the poem burning on their lips,
> flaming in their eyes and hearts.
> And each of them in his own form,
> with his own voice. A young generation,
> new growth in an old field.[39]

Voices of the Chorus

On April 22, 1912, a twenty-five-year-old night watchman, Moishe Varshe, jumped to his death from the top of the building he had been guarding. As his friends accompanied his body to burial, they realized that he was the first but probably not the last victim of poverty.[1] Among the Yunge, Varshe was recognized as a talented translator of Oscar Wilde, Anton Chekhov, and Leonid Andreyev, and as a poet who had not yet begun to show his work. Not long before his death, he and the poet Ber Lapin had published a translation of Andreyev's play *The Life of Man*, in which Fate, in the form of a gray background presence with a shortening candle in his hand, stalks the poor hero who is trying to live a happy life. Varshe, chronically depressed, seemed like this fate-ridden character, except that he gave up sooner.[2]

When Varshe died, his close friends Zishe Landau and Kolye Teper honored Varshe's literary ambitions by posthumously publishing his diary, a series of anguished notes about himself and things he had read, interspersed with several short lyrics. Instead of hidden talent, the diary revealed a pathological self-loathing reminiscent of the Viennese Jew he admired, Otto Weininger. "I am a putrid carcass, crumbling and rotting, that deceives the world with what appears to be life, and itself, with longing." Rather than describe the attic room where he had lived and the poverty in which these miseries had been registered, in their preface Landau and

Teper called their friend an ascetic and wondered whether through the accident of death his soul might not have found its true reality.[3]

Kolye Teper himself was a much more complex person than Varshe, and his failure was correspondingly more spectacular. By the time he appeared among the Yunge in America in 1907, Teper was already something of a legend, having begun his intellectual career as a Zionist orator and then switching so decisively to the side of the socialist Bund that he became one of its great polemicists against the Zionists. When he was arrested after the revolution of 1905, a group of workers engineered his escape from prison. He left Russia for Berlin, then New York, and abandoned socialism for a combination of anarchism and individualism that kept changing over the years. The poet Melekh Ravitch described Teper as victim of a kind of spiritual elephantiasis.[4]

His proficiency in several languages and wide erudition won Teper enormous influence among the Yunge, who looked to him for the theoretical and literary underpinnings of ideas they had adopted instinctively. He held forth on Kant and Lev Shestok, on literature and history, in German, Russian, Hebrew, English, and Yiddish. Among the works he translated into Yiddish were studies of Ibsen and Nietzsche by the critic Georg Brandes, Margaret Sanger's "What Every Girl Should Know," and (together with Varshe) Chekhov's *Uncle Vanya*, *The Seagull*, and *The Cherry Orchard*. At least two of the Yunge, Moishe Nadir and Zishe Landau, always paid homage to Teper as their teacher: Nadir cited his irreverence, Landau his appreciation of literature.

For a short period during World War I, Teper found his own voice. Under the pseudonym Count D'Abruzzi, he published a column called "Zigzags" in the anarchist daily, *Fraye arbeter shtime*, which presented his impressions and judgments in a careening, frenetic manner. Writing, for example, on the subject of "our great age," he begins by quoting the optimistic Labor-Zionist, Ber Borochov; then wonders why Mani Leib spends this great age in mooning about the silent *aleyen*; accuses the head of the local War Relief Committee of publicizing his private charities; asks the Jewish "caretakers" to stop arguing among themselves during a national crisis; and finally challenges Jewish revolutionaries to grant the status of national hero to Rabbi Eliezer Leib Treistman of Lodz, whose intervention with the Germans had saved several comrades from the gallows.[5]

Obviously Teper did not intend to promote rabbis over revolutionaries, but his reduction of so many topics to the same level of importance recalls the etymological source of the word "futility" in loquaciousness, a penchant for talk that exhausts the will to act. As much as he loved literature and tried to promote his friends among the Yunge by mentioning them in his column, he could not help diminishing their seriousness through his technique of frivolous cross-cutting. The world-weariness he manifested and promoted, however, did not prevent Teper from setting out for Russia immediately after the revolution of February 1917, to be there at the dawn of its "great age." He was disappointed almost at once but, for want of a visa, could not get back to America. The rest of his life was spent in geographic zigzagging across the Soviet Union, trying to escape the regime's collectivist passion. His former colleagues heard of him only sporadically: at one point he was living in a remote Siberian village; in the late 1920s the Leningrad library was said to be his place of refuge.[6]

This is how he was remembered in later years by the poet Aaron Leyeles:

> He stood at the head of the young writerdom
> slapping arrogant conventions on the back,
> trying to surprise, urging the youngsters to pounce
> with blaspheming clatter.
>
> He marveled at every chiseled line
> of the new poets. Looked for his own igniting spark.
>
> Found but
> ashes, coals, singed bits and scraps
> of world doom.[7]

Leyeles associated Teper's philosophic pessimism with his failure as a writer. Sympathetic critics interpreted his meagre literary output as the smaller part of his achievement: "Count D'Abruzzi was one of those whose fate it is to enrich others and remain poor himself."[8] The unsympathetic critics of the Yunge thought he had corrupted the group. Everyone agreed that his own literary promise had been wasted.

The case of Zishe Landau, good friend of both Varshe and Teper, was quite different. Landau, who shared with Teper a love of language and a suspicion of social activism, was capable of expressing both casts of mind in verse. Landau believed in the aestheticist ideal and, like Mani Leib, looked for it in a spare poetry of understatement, stillness, natural diction. A poem, he said, required no justification beyond itself. "We would consider a man to be a fool if he said he was getting married not because he wanted to but to swell the ranks of the Jews. The more seriously he affirmed this, the more comical he would seem. Well, marriage is its own aim, and poems certainly."[9] But Landau also knew that a man was a fool if he married blindly for love. Whereas Mani Leib spoke of refining reality, Landau showed some of Teper's self-consciousness about art, an awareness that poetry was "unnatural" in its very essence. He held his own faith in beauty no less suspect than any other belief in the possibility of perfection.[10]

Outsiders who skimmed the journals of the Yunge without paying close attention to every line were not aware of how much tension had developed within the movement by the time David Ignatoff put out the first issue of *Shriftn* in 1912. In fact *Shriftn* left readers with quite the opposite impression. "An edition of this quality cannot be assembled for all the money in the world," read an advertisement in the magazine *Di literarishe velt* (The Literary World), which was offering a copy to every new subscriber, appealing to cultural snobbery by formulating literature in the categories of social advancement: "We know our reader—he has intelligent taste, and no matter how he relates to the ideas of the Yunge, he will appreciate their very honest achievement."[11] *Shriftn* represented the movement so attractively that even writers who did not really share the ideas of the Yunge, and slipped away from the group soon after this, could never topple the impression that had been created of a united, dynamic literary coterie, nor easily pry their own names loose from its roster.

Yet even at this early stage, the ideas of the Yunge were by no means those of a cohesive group. An argument arose, for example, at the core of the group about the function of material reality in lyrical poetry. When Iceland modestly tried to formulate the program of the Yunge at a talk given in 1912 at the Moses Hess Club in Chicago, he was quite sure he spoke for Mani Leib, Landau, Ignatoff, and a few others as well as himself. He said that they were interested in the everyday life of individuals, with all their sufferings and pleasures. His first successful poem several years later, as if in demonstration of this theory, described the life of a factory worker using details of sound, like the shuffle of his wife's slippers on the kitchen floor or a seamstress cracking an eggshell at her lunchtime break, to render the quality of "everyday" (which was the poem's title). Iceland said that poetry was resigned to the reality it evokes.[12] But when it came to publishing the talk, Mani Leib insisted that the word "everyday" be dropped from Iceland's statement of their common purpose. He was not prepared to admit drabness into art except as the raw material that the poem would elevate. Poetry might make a virtue of human resignation, but if it ever accommodated itself to the commonplace, it would simply not be poetry.

Thus, when Mani Leib wrote about the factory, he tried to evoke beauty and mystery in the scene. Though he shows the pricked fingers of seamstresses and the monotony of the work, he concentrates on the multicolored silks rustling through young hands in the ebbing hours of a summer's day. The sensuous descriptions of fabrics and the echoed phrases of fairy tales in the description of their labor bring to mind enchanted princesses of old, who are trapped in high-walled towers, waiting for a bell to free them from the spell of their toil. as they might once have awaited their prince. By linking the harsh conditions of an overcrowded sweatshop with the eternal theme of beauty in plight, the poet can redeem the ugliness he observes.[13]

To this debate on aesthetic principles, Landau contributed his own views. He agreed with Iceland that the mundane joys and minor irritations of daily life were indeed the proper subject of verse, but as long as one was whittling sentences there could be no artlessness. Poets had to acknowledge artifice even when artlessness was their goal. Instead of the Sabbath, the traditional theme of Jewish romanticism, Landau wrote about "Tuesday," when he has

> two glasses of hot tea with milk to drink
> three or four zwieback to eat

> then sits for a long time at the table
> smoking and staring at a nail on the wall,
> translates four poems from German,
> lies down exhausted on the sofa
> folding his hands beneath his head
> and spits up three times at the ceiling.[14]

This was not a representation of ordinariness, but a fetish of ordinariness that denied poetry any special place.

Like Kolye Teper, Landau impudently undercut visible ideals: the striving of the ambitious middle class, the reformist zeal of the press, and above all the faith of the artist in his redemptive mission. By declaring himself a foremost deceiver, the poet invited from everyone else an admission of hypocrisy. Because poetry is involved in deception—Oscar Wilde, to whom Landau was often compared, had written of the importance of lying—the poet is professionally qualified to expose the undeclared deceptions of romance and ideology. Mani Leib tried to reveal beauty where none was immediately apparent. Landau, some said in order to distinguish himself from Mani Leib, exposed the preoccupation with beauty as just another strategy of self-deception.[15]

In the early days of the Yunge, Landau relished his role as aesthetic dandy:

> Because the papers meanly ignore me—
> they think my luncheon menus not fit to print—
> small wonder girls don't give me a tumble
> and day by day my stock goes down.[16]

Tongue in cheek, he dismissed any claims for poetry as a noble pursuit, or the poet as anything but a hustler in a hustling society. But Landau's refinement was never so noticeable as when he was pretending that it did not matter. His pedigree as the grandson and great-grandson of learned rabbis was purer than that of all the other writers among the Yunge, and his reaction against the high expectations of poetry may have been an extension of his own rebellion against the burden of personal lineage. (In later years Joseph Opatoshu wrote a story about a bittersweet meeting in New York between Zishe Landau and one of his pious kinsmen, Rabbi Menahem-Mendl, recently arrived from Poland. The poet recovers from the rabbi a Sabbath melody "that had been in his bones since childhood."[17])

Landau playfully, Mani Leib with romantic intensity, tried to create a body of poetry that was at once rebellious and affirmative. Their rebellion, explicit in Landau, usually unspoken in Mani Leib, was against true believers, old and new, who thought they knew how the world was run or how it should be run. They often applied to themselves the term "resignation" to signify their acceptance of an unredeemed world. In his poem "Shtiler, shtiler," Mani Leib does not seek to hasten the Messiah's coming but to nurture the human capacity of expectation. Landau would have agreed with him that the poet's task was to expand this spiritual capacity, by illuminating the extraordinary spark in ordinary experience or by exposing the falseness of fraudulent messianic claims.

Not surprisingly, the ideological modesty of this position soon began to irritate some of the Yunge. The prose writers especially, and a few of the poets, felt stifled by an idea of writing that engaged the world so little. It was to some extent a matter of temperament. Some young writers were simply not prepared to consign themselves to the kind of "irrelevance" the Yunge cultivated, to boast, as Iceland did, of their handful of readers. Now that the American Yiddish immigrant group had proved itself capable of sustaining a major literary publication, they wanted to make a bid for a larger audience and a more important role in the life of the community.

The leader of the breakaway group was the short-story writer and novelist Joseph Opatoshu (Opatovsky), an odd-looking man with a short neck, darting eyes, and a nose so prominent that Landau's daughters used to wonder when he drank his tea whether he could keep it from dropping into the glass.[18] Opatoshu, vigorous and prolific, liked to be at the center of things. He knew that as long as Ignatoff controlled *Shriftn*, it would remain a coterie publication. At first some of Opatoshu's writing suited the neoromantic outlook of *Shriftn*. The novella "Romance of a Horse Thief," for example, which appeared in the 1912 volume, describes the adventures of a young horse smuggler in a Polish border town. Into the fairly conventional love story of a suitor of low family and the only daughter of the town's wealthiest Jew, Opatoshu introduces a frankly lustful hero and a richer treatment of erotic desire than was customary in Yiddish prose. Yet despite its brothels, brawls, and coarse horse thieves, this romance between an amiable outcast and his beloved was essentially as benign as Mani Leib's Old World tales, revealing the latent tenderness of the thief who does not threaten society nearly as much as it threatens him.[19]

But Opatoshu's contribution to the 1913 volume had a much harsher bite. He wrote about the New York underworld, applying the style of Jack London to characters demoralized by the sudden disintegration of Old World constraints. "Morris and His Son Philip" is about a seedy vaudeville performer who abandons his eleven-year-old son and runs away with his landlady after persuading her to rob her blind husband of his savings. As a final touch the father steals the pillow from under the head of his sleeping son. Opatoshu wrote not as a realist exposing the social roots of private distress but as a naturalist presenting the human animal in his physical habitat.[20] In a sense, his chilling study was as new to the Jewish sensibility as Mani Leib's musical application of words. The two kinds of innovation, however, could not happily coexist.

The rift when it came was painful. Opatoshu organized a meeting at the home of I. J. Schwartz to initiate a rival publication, *Di naye heym* (The New Home).[21] Mani Leib and Ignatoff persuaded Isaac Raboy to join them in trying to head off the defectors. They arrived as a delegation at the Schwartz apartment to argue that the strength of the new literature lay in its unity and that any attempt to splinter the group would damage the growth of American Yiddish letters. But the differences were too substantive to yield to diplomatic overtures, and Opatoshu's ambition too strong to be contained within Ignatoff's publication. In the years that followed, friendships between the two groups waxed and waned, but their essential argument over literature was never resolved. The critic Borukh Rivkin called the split between *Shriftn* and *Di naye heym* a division between the drunk and the sober, indicating his own preference for a literature of greater engagement.[22] Most of the critics were to share this judgment.

Isaac Raboy, torn between friendship for Mani Leib and Ignatoff on the one hand and his own artistic instincts on the other, provided perhaps the most persuasive reason for trying to keep the movement together. His shyness kept him away from the cafés, and his personal preference for a quiet way of life attracted him to the less involved writers. Yet after several years of experimenting with symbolism, his writing had moved in a new direction, one more in keeping with the aims of Opatoshu's publication. Of all the writers of the Yunge, Raboy had most thoroughly explored their new home in America and made it the subject of his work.

Raboy's first stories were written as dreamy escapes from the factory at which he was employed. Then, with the intention of becoming a farmer, he attended the Baron de Hirsch Agricultural School in Woodbine, New Jersey, and proved unexpectedly adept at horse training. After graduation he spent some time on a ranch in the Midwest and later on a farm in New England, which he hoped he could run profitably for his family. The most lasting results of these efforts were the stories and novels that he later wrote about a Jewish boy who tries to find a place for himself among American farmers and ranchers. His novel *Her Goldenbarg*, the adventures of a young Jew who works as a ranchhand, linked the redemptive healthfulness of life on the land with the Labor-Zionist idea of salvation in a national soil.[23]

At first Raboy's American fiction was also colored by neoromantic influences. His descriptions of the lonely Jewish boy in a gentile country are overburdened by imagery, making it hard to get a firm grasp of plot and character. With the passage of time, though, Raboy became one of the leading realists among American Yiddish writers, abandoning his earlier prose experiments for exposures of social injustice. In the late 1920s he joined the Communists and polemicized hard on their behalf. However much he may have wanted to maintain the comradeship of the writers' movement, the direction of his prose took him ever farther away from the Ignatoff group.

I. J. Schwartz, the host but not the initiator of the attempt to create a rival to *Shriftn*, was the most learned Jew among the Yunge. He translated from medieval and modern Hebrew poetry, in which he felt perfectly at home, and taught as did Opatoshu in the Hebrew afternoon schools, an occupation Opatoshu describes in his novel *Hebrew* as having brought them little more profit than they were able to bring their students.[24] At the same time, Schwartz was also the Yunge's most avid English reader. It was he who translated "Salut au Monde" from *Leaves of Grass* for the second issue of *Shriftn*, inserting additional references to America wherever he thought they belonged in Whitman's text. Through Walt Whitman, Schwartz adopted a long free-verse line and a rich-bodied cosmopolitan American voice, which it would take him a number of years to fashion in Yiddish as his own.[25]

The ranks of the "sober" were decisively strengthened by the arrival of H. Leivick, the last of those associated with the Yunge to reach America and the one who achieved the greatest fame during his lifetime. Several of the Yunge had served short prison terms for antitsarist agitation or fled to America because they were being sought by the police, but Leivick was a full-fledged revolutionary at sixteen, smuggling arms for the self-defense units of the Jewish Socialist Bund. Arrested repeatedly, the first time when he was too young to stand trial, he was finally sentenced to lifetime exile in Siberia and spent months under the worst conditions before he managed a daring solitary escape. Lean and ascetic, Leivick exerted a kind of moral authority that derived from his harsh experiences.[26]

Leivick found it hard to gain a foothold in America. After searching vainly for a job in New York, he went to Philadelphia for a few years, where he trained as a cutter in a garment shop. Returning to the center of Yiddish literary life, he made a living as a paperhanger, work that taxed his strength and brought on the first of many bouts of tuberculosis. When his first poems were published, under his real name, Leivick Halpern, he was mistaken for Moishe Leib Halpern, an indignity that prompted him to reverse his names thereafter on everything but his passport.

Leivick's voice was too distinctive to escape notice for long. The mournful evocations of buried life—"Somewhere far, far away, / Lies a land that's forbidden us"—revealed great personal suffering and unlaid charges of injustice.[27] At first he was delighted with the discovery in America of the Yunge, who seemed to him not merely a literary group but a sect with a deep religious spirit. "We separate ourselves from everyone," he wrote approvingly, "not just from other writers but from everyone. We want to be by ourselves, our ears cannot tolerate the false sounds, the cheapened literature." He was prepared to justify the retreat of the Yunge from national and social engagement because their zealous faith in the Yiddish word was itself a bulwark against Jewish decline.[28]

Within a few years, however, Leivick turned against the Yunge to become one of the fiercest critics of their "slippered smugness, their dustiness, their spitting into the alien cold." He denounced their separation from the people as fatal cynicism that emptied their work of all value.[29] Opatoshu, less harsh in his public pronouncements (though not in his private correspondence), shared this contempt, which grew stronger during the politicization of Jewish life in the 1920s and 1930s. Thus the split in the ranks of the young American Yiddish writers was not accidental, not just the reshuffling of editorial power, but the expression of genuine aesthetic and philosophic differences that could no longer be reconciled. Opatoshu and Leivick were naturally much more popular with the press because their avowed social concerns signified a return to public art.

There was also a third faction among the Yunge. Humor magazines like *Der kibitser* and *Der kundes* became the special province of Moishe Leib Halpern and Moishe Nadir, contemporaries from the neighboring towns of Nareyev and Zlochev in Galicia. They were raised with German rather than Russian or Ukrainian as the coterritorial language, and were exposed to the poetry of Heine and Peter Altenberg rather than Lermontov and Blok. The Viennese-Jewish fashion of irony and the medium of the humor magazine determined their idea of culture as much as Russian symbolism, mysticism, and decadence influenced the taste of the Yiddish writers from Russia and the Ukraine. Skeptical of both the efficacy of art and the possibilities of a refined literature in an immigrant vernacular, they attacked the two sides alternately and initiated their own publications to avoid dependency on either.

This schematic description of the three major trends in the youthful literature does not begin to assess its achievement—which was often unrelated to these divisions. Some writers were never associated with any faction. Herman Gold's deliberate bohemianism, his disheveled beard and shabby unrespectability, earned him a reputation as chief among the "schnorrers." The Yiddish literary community was never certain whether he was a genius or a fool; some found his stories simple to the point of banality, while others declared their staccato narrative style to be an early example of Yiddish modernism. Gold appeared in the magazines of the group, be-friended its members, corresponded with them and wrote about them, without ever becoming an intimate.[30]

Joseph Rolnik smarted from the refusal of *Shriftn* to publish his work and, despite his artistic affinity with Mani Leib and Ignatoff, became one of the major contributors to Opatoshu's rival miscel-lany. His long poem cycle "Hafiz," which appeared in *Di naye heym* (based loosely on Richard de Gallienne's English translation of the odes of Hafiz), presents the poet as an outcast whose only protection against the world's calamities is his ability to set his suffering to music.[31] Whereas Rolnik was denied inclusion in *Shriftn*, Lamed Shapiro, who was far less compatible with the aims of the group, was welcomed. Shapiro's small vegetarian restaurant temporarily became the writers' favorite meeting place (their patronage is what made it temporary). He produced several brilliantly crafted stories during the period of *Shriftn* and is therefore represented in its pages by some of his finest work. But soon he drifted away from the group and left New York for Los Angeles.[32]

If the cohesion of the Yunge in the years immediately before the war was largely illusory, their vitality was not. The handsome vol-umes of *Shriftn*, filled with stories and poems about America and carrying the portrait and the poems of Walt Whitman as if he were its patron saint, impressed Jewish literary circles in Europe. It was now clear that, in addition to their commercially successful theater and press, the American immigrant community had generated a literary movement that was free of the shtetl, the insularity that had characterized Yiddish literature in its early phase. As traditional Jews had always regarded America with suspicion, justifiably ner-vous about its effects on the Halakhic Jewish way of life, so too many educated secular Jews believed that life in America was inherently materialistic and coarse. The volumes of *Shriftn* and, on the eve of the war, *Di naye heym* provided contrary evidence of a vigorous culture. Far from vulgarizing their instincts, America seemed to have given a whole community of young writers the opportunity to create a bold autonomous literature that still remained linked to its European roots. In Warsaw some of the most respected Yiddish writers, such as I. L. Peretz, Jacob Dineson, and the critic Bal Makhshoves (Eliashiv), were beginning to read the Yunge with cautious approval.[33] Until this time it had been taken for granted that the lines of influence flowed in one direction only, westward from Warsaw to New York. *Shriftn* was the first signal of a change of course.

World War I cast a sudden pall over the buoyant immigrant community. There was a halt to immigration and no access to a world that had until recently been but a ship's voyage away. American Jews grew frantic about the relatives they had left behind, who became the first casualties of the warring armies. Since Jews were fighting in the armies of both sides, it was difficult to anticipate any satisfactory outcome of the war. The news of atrocities brought home to the young writers the terrible finality of their break with Europe. Also, with the interruption of communication between the literary communities of Europe and America, local publications had to rely exclusively on local writers for their material.

One small immediate consequence of the war was the passage of the prestigious magazine *Literatur un lebn* (Literature and Life) into the hands of Mani Leib and Reuben Iceland. The magazine had been established in 1913 under an apparently sensible plan: the sociopolitical half was edited in New York by Carl Fornberg; the cultural section, drawing on major European writers like I. L. Peretz, David Bergelson, and Jacob Fichman, was prepared in Warsaw under the supervision of Nachman Mayzel. The New York editors expected the stature of the Europeans to win a wider readership for their own political analyses. But when the outbreak of the war in October 1914 made this trans-Atlantic project unfeasible, one of the financial backers of the magazine, who had befriended several of the Yunge, invited them to take over the reins.

Ready or not, the Yunge were now on the editorial side of the American Yiddish literary scene. Ber Borochov, one of the main ideological formulators of Labor-Zionism, expressed his mixed feelings over this sudden aggrandizement of the American community.

> Since the outbreak of the war, the spiritual level of both the local Yiddish press and the entire American Jewish mass has risen apprecia-

bly: they realize that the world is experiencing a moment far too seri-
ous, and the Jews a crisis far too tragic, to allow them to continue with
their empty-headedness, their bluff, and their boring trash.[34]

This damning praise conveys the European's prejudice against the
frivolity of the New World, along with a grudging acknowledgment
that on this branch of the Jewish nation the future of the whole may
increasingly depend. By the same token, Borochov deplores the
"feminine" sensibility of the Yunge, now more inappropriate than
ever.[35]

Overwhelmed, like Borochov, with their own sudden coming of
age, the Yunge reacted to the challenge in impulsive and contradic-
tory ways. They chose this moment to dramatize their originality.
When I. L. Peretz died suddenly in early April 1915, *Literatur un
lebn* devoted a commemorative issue to this most influential of all
Yiddish writers, whose magazine of the same title had been the
model for theirs. The issue contained at least one brilliant item—a
fierce threnody by Moishe Leib Halpern that extols the fallen gran-
deur of Peretz by calling into question the meaning of every lesser
life.

What attracted most notice, however, was Iceland's denial of
literary influence, whether of Peretz or anyone else:

> We didn't learn anything from him directly, nor from Mendele Mo-
> cher Sforim or Sholem Aleichem either.
> We have no grandfather. We have no father. We never even had a
> teacher.
> We came on the scene like bastards spawned in the dirt.[36]

This symbolic patricide was aimed at the idea of a literary tradition
that Sholem Aleichem had ingeniously formulated in the 1880s.
Younger by twenty-five years than Mendele Mocher Sforim, and
taking up Yiddish fiction when it was still fairly raw, Sholem Alei-
chem had attempted to create a genealogy by crowning Mendele the
"grandfather" and dividing contemporary writers into generations,
with himself as part of the third. By means of this sobriquet Sholem
Aleichem suggested a tradition with strong roots and healthy
prospects.

One might say that Iceland's rebellion offers inadvertent proof of
Sholem Aleichem's success. The denial of paternity and influence

recognizes that the myth is in place. But beneath the bravado there is also a sad awareness that the tradition of Yiddish poetry was very slight; the pioneering work of the classic prose masters had yet to be equaled in verse. Peretz's death in Warsaw during the first year of the war, followed in eerie succession by the deaths in New York of Sholem Aleichem in 1916 and in Odessa of Mendele Mocher Sforim in 1917, seemed to lay to rest the classical basis of the literature, and the way of life to which it had been consecrated.

Along with their embrace of orphancy, the Yunge turned as never before to the past. Zishe Landau, who worked during the war in a munitions factory, wrote laments for the destroyed communities of "Mother Vilna, Kolomei, and Brod." He wept not only for the holy places but for the Jewish brothels:

> For every dirty Jewish alley,
> Each dingy hole with goods for sale;
> For every pawnshop, tavern, alehouse;
> For our false measure, weight and scale.[37]

The irony of this nostalgia, which would later be heard in the poems of Leivick, Halpern, and Jacob Glatstein, balanced the imperfections of the life they had abandoned against the greater imperfections that were destroying it.

It was also during the war years that Iceland composed his elegy on his native city, Tarnov, and Isaac Raboy began his novel *Bessarabian Jews*, which he considered the best of his works, his "song of songs." David Ignatoff wrote legends about the Hasidic master, the Baal Shem Tov, and Opatoshu his historical novel about a Hasidic dynasty, *In Polish Woods*. Mani Leib completed a book of ballads and another of old-country Jewish and Slavic folk motifs. Halpern wrote his only epic poem, an apocalyptic vision of the destruction of Europe's Jews entitled "A Night." "We considered ourselves Americans," Ignatoff confessed with a sense of shock, "but World War I left me unnerved, broken. Our life had been torn apart."[38] To be sure, the Americans felt this impact from a considerable distance, but the ruin of Jewish life decisively aged them. They were still close enough to their native lands to feel personally bereaved.

To the decline of artistic solidarity and the disturbing effect of the war must be added the strain of personal life. During their early years of bachelorhood the young writers had reveled in their freedom, in the carefree detachment they felt from their surroundings.

> In the fading afternoon light they strolled along the streets with their elegant canes, their long hair and their wide, sweeping hats. The streets were full of workaday people doing workaday chores. Mothers pushing baby-carriages. Loaded wagons pulling goods. Jewish tradesmen arguing with Jewish housewives. The scent of oranges fusing with the smell of herring. East Broadway was overflowing with stores, many of them advertising their wares in big Yiddish letters. The Yiddish dailies were there too. Yarmulkes and *tsitsit* could be seen down the whole length of the street. And in the midst of it all, a gang of young men with canes and long hair.[39]

This picture captures the determined dissociation of the group from what they called "tsholnt Jewishness," after the heavy traditional Sabbath stew that weighs down body and spirit.

By the prewar years, when they had themselves become family men and could no longer parade through the crowds, they set themselves apart in more sedentary fashion in the cafeterias, which provided the new group with its only stable "address." Sholem's coffeehouse on Division Street was the longstanding gathering place of literary types, but the Yunge took over the smaller basement restaurant of Goodman and Levine's:

> There were two reasons why the Yunge chose to carry on by themselves in a separate cafe. One was purely financial. The coffeehouse on Division Street was too dear for young writers, most of whom either were poor workers in a factory or had no job whatever. To spend these hours at Sholem's they would need at least a quarter in their pocket and—in those days, for these young men—this was a sizable sum. If even ten cents were lacking—which was not unusual—they would order a glass of coffee or tea with a cookie or roll and would sit there the same number of hours for no more than a nickel. The other reason was snobbish. Our spokesmen simply felt that it was beneath us to pass the time in the same cafe as our elders.[40]

As the tension between ordinary life and artistic life increased, it was ever more difficult to keep moving back and forth between the coffeehouse table and the kitchen table. As modern men, the writers could not accept the Old World custom of a wife's supporting her studious, intellectual husband. They felt full responsibility for wife and children and sometimes also for parents and relatives they had brought from overseas. Behind the dreams of high culture being spun in the cafés were some very harassed householders:

> people with homes that have double beds, cribs, chimney stoves, who must lead the raw gray life of the tasteless masses. They get up in the morning, put on their work clothes, take the subway to work. They arrive at work as part of the flood of hundreds of thousands that blackens the streets at dawn, and they leave in the evenings as part of that same dark current. They wash their hands and change their clothes, eat a homey supper and take their children on their knees. They listen to the wife complaining about the neighbor's children who picked a fight with theirs, about the soup that burned and the landlord who came demanding the rent.[41]

This kind of pressure took its toll. Meir Blinken was already a family man with two children when he died suddenly in 1915. He had managed, between work as a carpenter and later as a masseur, to publish over two dozen stories, including several psychological studies in the manner of Arthur Schnitzler. He was among the first to single out for his subject the bourgeois housewife who, having no further need to work in the sweatshops or tend her pushcart in the market, was dangerously tempted by other occupations and distractions. Blinken's frequent absences from his own home suggest that at least some of the descriptions he gave of illicit love affairs and romantic triangles were drawn from personal experience. He was one of the most highly touted of the American Yiddish prose writers, and his unexpected death was attributed to the strain that his artistic ambition exerted on an already difficult life.[42]

During the years 1914–1917 no one had yet begun to make a living from writing; literary work was still a holy task to be performed after a long day's physical labor. The flight to the cafés was a retreat to a higher intellectual realm, made even more attractive by occasional physical rewards. From among the swarms of young women who frequented the cafés in the evenings, women attracted to literature and to literary men, it was not hard to strike up an amorous adventure, which put even further distance between the poet and the mundane. The artistic rivalry among the writers was often spiced by rivalries over the affections of a pretty woman, and a writer's reputation rose and fell in this competition as well as on the basis of his latest work.

One of the handsomest men among the Yunge, Mani Leib had more than his share of amorous encounters. For a time he tried to maintain a balance between home and his attraction to other women. Working long days in the shoe factories, he was able to move his family from their cramped quarters in Williamsburg to a considerably larger apartment in Boro Park. But the strain of meeting his paternal obligations strengthened the need he felt to escape, and the balance kept tipping farther and farther away from home. Reuben Iceland, whose memoirs provide vivid accounts of these years, describes his own discomfort when his friend's marriage was about to disintegrate. Iceland's wife had contracted tuberculosis and was sent to the mountains to recuperate. With the children packed off to relatives, Iceland saved money by giving up his apartment and became a temporary boarder in Mani Leib's home.

His wife, Chasia, had felt for many months that something was wrong with Mani Leib, and that this "something" was of a different quality from other similar "somethings" he had experienced. Silent by nature, she had kept silent. But her expression was eloquent. Everything about her spoke: the way she neglected her house; the baby crawling on the floor, leaving little pools everywhere that were never mopped up; and her eyes that fell on me sorrowfully, with an unspoken plea. It so happened that I had to spend long hours in my room every day because I was then translating several volumes of Heine's prose for Sheliubski's Yiddish Publishing Company. She had me constantly in view, while her husband, whenever he did come home, crept in during the wee hours of the morning so that she should not hear him. But she did hear, and in small ways let it be known that she heard. Sometimes he would crawl into bed with his oldest son, but the bed was too short and narrow for him, so he spent several nights in my bed. At first Chasia swallowed this behavior as she had weathered all Mani Leib's other adventures. But one morning she could stand it no longer and as soon as the older children had left for school, she flung open the door of my room.

Mani Leib sensed that a dramatic scene was at hand. He jumped out of bed and tried to slip out of the room. But the small, ever-silent little wife had suddenly found her tongue and began to scream that she had had enough! She would not take any more from him! With whom was he crawling around all night long?[43]

According to Iceland, Mani Leib fled from this outburst, leaving his hysterical wife and crying infant for a woman whom he passionately loved and with whom he soon quarreled. But in 1917 he met Rochelle Weprinski, a young admirer of his poetry and herself a budding poet, who left her husband and, temporarily, her child as a consequence of their stormy romance. Then began a lifelong liaison, marked by guilt, nomadic homelessness, financial troubles, periodic illnesses, and the ebb and flow of affection. They never married because Chasia would not agree to a divorce. Mani Leib remained his family's sole support until the five children were grown.

By his own account, Iceland was no ideal husband either. He recalls one Saturday afternoon when he dropped in to Goodman and Levine's for a few hours to join in the talk. "From a sea of faces and clouds of smoke emerged the figure of Mani Leib—one finger swaying in front of his nose like a pointer—his penetrating green eyes squinting at the homely, freckled yet vibrant and insolent face of Moishe Leib Halpern." Whatever it is they were discussing, Iceland grew so absorbed in the conversation that he forgot he was expected home in mid-afternoon and did not return until dawn. The grocer in his building, who was just opening his store, greeted him with the news that his wife had gone to the police looking for him. Iceland's memoir preserves the irresponsible joys of that afternoon, but we are not surprised to learn from other sources that his subsequent divorce was bitter, that his children were permanently estranged from him and even after his death showed their anger by destroying his manuscripts.[44]

Not long after Mani Leib left his wife, Iceland made known his own involvement with Rosa Lebensboym, a tempestuous woman who had already had a succession of literary lovers and had abandoned the son of her marriage to the writer Moishe Stavski when she came to settle permanently in New York in 1914.[45] A gifted writer, she had a weekly column in the daily *Der tog* and wrote fiction and essays on women's issues under several pseudonyms. Iceland claimed that once they became involved her threats of suicide forced him to divorce his wife and in 1919 to marry her, but she seems to have attracted him primarily as an artist, as one who could stimulate his creativity through her appreciation and intellectual companionship.[46]

From an artistic standpoint, the marriage initially worked in their favor. Iceland published in 1920 a thin but very fine volume of lyrics. His new wife, to whom the book was dedicated, began to publish her own poems under the name Anna Margolin. She was an original, bold and disturbing:

> Once I was young, hung out
> in doorways, listening to Socrates.
> My closest pal, my lover
> Had the finest chest in Athens.
>
> Then came Caesar, and a world
> glittering with marble—I
> the last to go. For my bride,
> I picked out my proud sister.
>
> At the late-night bashes, soused
> and feeling fine, I'd hear
> about the Nazareth weakling
> and the exploits of the Jews.[47]

Of the many inversions in the poem—the woman as man, the modern as ancient, the poet as ruler—none is so daring as the concluding statement of the Greco-Roman on the Jew, puny and primitive when seen from the hedonistic couch. Rabbinic Judaism had tried with all its power to turn the Jews against just these pagan and incestuous practices. Now here was Margolin looking at the Jews from a shockingly alien position. She had turned to poetry rather late in life, but whereas many of the Yunge experimented for years before finding their own voices, hers was immediately recognizable: confessional, tough, and precise. Margolin's strong command of language made her a formidable critic too, but these qualities, when combined with neurotic possessiveness, did not make it easy for Iceland to retain his old friends. As she became sicker in the years that followed, her body swelling to such proportions that she no longer wanted to be seen in public, both she and Iceland stopped writing poetry and withdrew from the literary scene.

These intense love affairs, as well as flirtations between some wives and their husbands' colleagues, deepened already existing divisions and antagonisms among the American Yiddish writers. Mani Leib and Anna Margolin distrusted one another. As Rochelle Weprinski took up more of Mani Leib's attention, she was regarded with suspicion by his friends. There was now less energy and opportunity for all-night walks through Brooklyn or for animated discussions at Goodman and Levine's.

By the end of the war, as the writers passed into their thirties, there was no longer the same need for a literary movement. If the Yunge had banded together to consolidate a new literature that would let them write as they wished, the movement had accomplished its purpose. They now wrote as they wished. They were now able to put out their own books and magazines in respectable editions of between several hundred and several thousand copies. Their collective publications—*Fun mentsh tsu mentsh* (Person to Person), 1915; *East Broadway*, 1916; *Velt ayn velt oys* (World In, World Out), 1916; *Der inzl* (The Island), 1918—were noted and reviewed, sometimes even in the daily press. As the war drew to an end, the Americans discovered how well known they were overseas to young Yiddish writers, who wrote to invite the Americans' participation in new magazines and to strike up collegial contacts. Especially telling was the rise in 1919–20 of a younger group of local Yiddish poets, the Inzikhistn or Introspectivists, whose very revolt against the Yunge revealed the importance of their influence.[48]

In fact, by the end of the war, the sensibilities of the Yunge had begun to be absorbed by the press they had first mobilized to oppose. When Mani Leib needed extra work to support both his first family and his new second home, he found it in the daily newspapers. Abraham Cahan, editor of *Forverts*, was no fan of the Yunge, but his attachment to Russian literature attracted him to Mani Leib, the most Russian of the Yiddish poets and a devoted translator of Russian literature. Cahan hired Mani Leib to provide a poem a week for the literary supplement—either a translation or an original work—and he appointed him one of the editors of the popular *bintel briv*, where his function was to select, ghostwrite, edit, and answer the letters that came in, mostly from women seeking counsel. In the years that followed, all the writers made some such accommodation with one or another sector of the press.

It was their ripeness above all that obviated the need for a group.

A Little Love in Big Manhattan

Some writers outgrew the chorus. They began to dislike being lumped together, whether as the Yunge or under any other name. Instead of miscellanies, they wanted to produce books of their own.

In 1918 there appeared simultaneously, in identical format, three books by Mani Leib—*Lyrics, Jewish and Slavic Motifs,* and *Ballads.* The first was a selection of his best published lyrics and some previously unpublished love poems; the second contained adaptations of Yiddish, Russian, and Ukrainian folksongs; the third, inspired in part by the English and Scottish ballads that Zishe Landau had discovered, became the cornerstone of Mani Leib's worldwide reputation.[49]

Mani Leib was one of the first among the Yunge to realize that the goal of personal poetry was easier to pronounce than to achieve. The declaration of artistic independence from the collective identity of Jews, sufferers, workers, or revolutionaries might allow the use of the first-person-singular pronoun, but the idea of individualism was itself borrowed from other Western models—to deny one's culture in favor of imported standards of selfhood was merely to substitute one kind of influence for another.

In addition to the lyrics he continued to write, Mani Leib began to turn to the folk imagination. In *Jewish and Slavic Motifs* he shaped an entire repertoire of "anonymous" singers, the pious young wife praying before Sabbath candles, the weeping bride whose groom will never come, the lonely son of a distant mother, the joyous traveler on a winter voyage, the Ukrainian cossack setting out for battle, and a host of lovers, Jewish and gentile, blessing or mourning their fortune. It was this book that the Soviet Yiddish critic Dobrushin credited four years later with having performed an historic mission. Mani Leib, he said, was the first to elicit in modern Yiddish poetry the architechtonic and rhythmic-pictorial character of the folksong after many had attempted it and failed.[50]

Dobrushin's excitement over the quality of these poems was not misplaced. Underlying the apparently artless style is vigorous experimentation with lines of two, three, four, and five feet, rhythmic schemes variously dominated by trochees, iambs, dactyls, and amphibrachs, rhyming arrangements of many kinds in couplets, quatrains, and stanzas of different lengths and patterns. Working for his own poetic pleasure, Mani Leib seems deliberately to have reduced diction and theme to the simplest level of utterance, in order to explore the full range of what a modern Yiddish poet can do.

The ballads tried for something more. These too, told by an apparently anonymous folk narrator and quite at variance with the ideal of personalism, employ an unexceptional Yiddish without any of the exotic wordplays and effects of Mani Leib's early lyrics. If he knew Wordsworth, Mani Leib might have been taking for his text the poet's preface to the *Lyrical Ballads* of 1800:

> The principal object . . . proposed in these poems was to choose incidents and situations from common life, and to relate or describe them, throughout, as far as was possible in a selection of language really used by men, and, at the same time, to throw over them a certain coloring of imagination, whereby ordinary things should be presented to the mind in an unusual aspect.[51]

Wordsworth and Coleridge were reacting against predecessors who had brought verse to such a fine polish that any further cultivation seemed impossible. Heralding a major revolution of taste, they wanted to turn back to what they claimed was a simpler and more spontaneous way of life, expressed in more natural diction. The Yunge inherited no such burden of exhausted refinement. Indeed, they had tried to play a catch-up game of artistic sophistication. But the more they patterned themselves on Verlaine or even Heine, the more they came up against the shortcomings of their own language, which, deriving as it did from quite another kind of tradition, had a very different vocabulary and tone. Lacking a healthy diction, the lyrics grew anemic. Correspondingly, as soon as the poets strayed too far from the social base of their language, their observations became inauthentic. Landau studied British, Scottish, and American ballads and began translating them into Yiddish.[52] Then Mani Leib found that by adapting rhythms and forms of the Yiddish folksong, as well as its legends and themes, he could use the impersonality of the folk form to great expressive advantage.

His most winsome ballad, "Yingl tsingl khvat," which means something like "Young Tongue Scamp," appeared in *Shriftn*, in the same remarkable issue of 1914 that contained Moishe Leib Halpern's ten-part poem, "In der fremd." It is the joyous tale of a shtetl boy who bears a resemblance to the young Mani Leib of Niezhin.

As his name indicates, Young Tongue Scamp is never at a loss for words. One winter evening, as the boys are about to set off for home after their long day at the cheder, they light their lanterns in order to navigate the thick mud of the marketplace. Although it is already deep winter, frost has not yet hardened the paths, nor has snow softened the landscape. Fearless Tsingl alone refuses the indignity of carrying a lantern and even when he falls, predictably, into the mud, shows no concern:

> Lodged in mud up to his head
> Does Tsingl show the slightest dread?
> He simply takes account of things:
> —I'll wait to see what morning brings,
>
> Meanwhile I will fall asleep . . . —
> But Tsingl's sleep would have to keep:
> A nobleman riding through the square
> Caught sight of Tsingl from afar.[53]

The nobleman pulls the boy from the mud and dries him with his blanket. But Tsingl shrugs off his benefactor's attentions. So impressed is the nobleman with this intrepid scamp that he offers him a choice of magic treasures: Tsingl may take either the nobleman's horse, which can fly thirteen miles a second and transport him to the ends of the earth, or the nobleman's ring, which when turned seven times brings a snowfall to cover the earth. After weighing the choice, Tsingl blurts out that he wants both. And since this is the poet's own legend, the boy with the gift of gab and the temerity to use it wins both horse and ring, the power to soar above the world and the ability to shower it with blessings. Tsingl gives the town the snowfall it has so long needed and then rides off forever, leaving behind his tearful mother. And whenever gray winter withholds its softening blanket, Young Tongue Scamp may appear with his magic ring to transform earth's harshness to beauty.

Beneath the charm of the tale, which made it a favorite of the Yiddish school curriculum, we can detect here the newfound confidence of the artist. Mani Leib is presumptuously insisting on both heaven and earth—the disagreement with Iceland and Landau is, in effect, resolved. In the young scamp's chutspa there appears the poet, fortunate in the gifts that elevate him above ordinary mankind, benevolent in his ability to bring joy and beauty to those below.

David Ignatoff was later to claim at least some of the credit for prodding Mani Leib toward ballads. He recalled that when he was organizing *Shriftn* in 1912, his first foray on behalf of the new project was from his apartment in the Bronx to Brooklyn to see the poet to whom he felt closest. Ignatoff told Mani Leib that he himself was writing a series of stories using the frame device of a grandmother who sits by an ancient stove in the old country, spinning out tales to the children gathered around her.[54] Whether it was Ignatoff's example or coincidence, Mani Leib also undertook a series of ballads using the same organizing device of a storyteller by the fireside, with the blustery wind painting its wreaths and blossoms on the outside windowpanes.

Only Mani Leib's 1918 book of lyrics presents the modern poet in New York, or at least a trace of him. He culled them carefully from his published poems after 1910, adding at the end a series of love poems that are the high point of the book.

> I am the creeper, the wild one,
> Climbing your garden hedge,
> Reaching, a red one, a wild one,
> Up to your window ledge;
>
> To inhale your dress' rustling
> As on your floor I lay,
> To pale in the light of your eyes,
> To sorrow at what you say;
>
> To lurk among your lamps,
> Autumnal and green as a moth
> To rise transfigured like lamps
> Ashen in flames of your hearth;
>
> To lie pale, a dead one, against
> Your window-pane in the snow,

Snowy in snow, a snowman,
To moan to you from the snow.[55]

ikh bin der vaynrib der vilder.
gey oyf bay dem ployt fun dayn heyf.
kleter a reyter, a vilder
biz dayne fenster aroyf.

oyf dayne diln zikh leygn,
heykhn in shorkh fun dayn kleyd;
bleykhn zikh in dayne eygn,
troyern fun dayne reyd.

loyern fun dayne lompn,
harbstik un grin vi a shpin;
oyfgeyn farklert vi di lompn
ashik in flam fun kamin,

lign a bleykher, a teyter,
oyf dayne shoybn in shney,
shneyik in shney a farshneyter,
veynen tsu dir fun dem shney.

There had been nothing before in Yiddish to approach this single breathed movement of a lover (and a poem) from ecstasy to death. The dynamic pace of Mani Leib's ballads seems to have overtaken the static stillness of his earlier lyrics, so that along with the lover the poem itself soars in one sustained sentence to its climax and penetrates the window that had once separated the poet from the world. It is worth noting that Itsik Manger, the outstanding lyric poet of the generation that followed the Yunge, considered this one of the finest lyrics in the language.[56]

The "climbing-vine" poems certainly fixed the image of Mani Leib as a romantic poet. But if his characteristic themes of yearning and the artistic urge to transcend reality mark him as a romantic, his disciplined study of the craft of versification is a sure sign of the classical disposition. Mani Leib proceeded as a poet much as he had once learned bootmaking. First he chose literary models; then he separated poetry into its various kinds; and after experimenting with the different materials suitable for each, he shaped them according to the requirements of each genre and type.[57]

Moisei Olgin, a critic who reviewed these volumes when they appeared, noted that to read Mani Leib's lyrics as they were published one at a time was far more satisfactory than having them in a collection, since the reappearance of the same moods and motifs was disappointingly monotonous. To prove the poet's failure of inspiration and skill, he counted recurring words: night, 91 times; cry or crying, 57 times; child and children, 41 times; mist and cloud, 22 times—in a book of just over 100 pages.[58] Yet the same evidence can be used to demonstrate the poet's cultivated variety of treatment. To compare similar themes in the three books is to see the different levels of vocabulary the poet uses in each; alterations of rhythm and verse form; shift of narrative voice from high to low, intimate to anonymous, active to passive; differences in grammatical structure and imagery; shifts of time and place. Together the books are proofs of mastery. Although contemporary critics differed on the respective merits of the three books, preferring one to the other—often on ideological grounds—there was no one who did not recognize Mani Leib as a significant innovator, the first real evidence that Yiddish belles-lettres did indeed exist.

It would be good to report that, having attained this level of artistic maturity, Mani Leib went on to write poems of ever greater beauty and strength. Unfortunately his progress was troubled by every kind of obstacle, some of his own making. During the summer of 1918, having left his wife, he was without an address, shuttling from rented rooms to his brother's house or to the home of his friend, the writer David Kozanski, in Far Rockaway. His separation from Rochelle, who was spending the summer in the Catskills with her daughter, means that there are many letters from this period. Though the uneasy status of their love is their most prominent subject, they also provide a glimpse of the poet's unstable existence:

We played cards at Kozanski's so I forfeited my letter to you. But at least now we're about to enjoy the ice cream that was bought for the winnings . . . Yesterday I decked myself out in my Sabbath best to go to Dr. Kling's where I had been invited [for a party]. I stayed very late. The singer Yasinovsky was there. He sings well, and sings my songs splendidly! I spent the night at Dr. Kling's. It grew very cold and I was sleeping on the examining table in the doctor's office. The high and narrow table was a hard place to sleep and cold besides. I was shivering. Everyone says I look very handsome, and I boast that I look well because I've been sleeping normally for the past few weeks—now that it's cool in town! Listen, I don't want you to be lonesome. Take care of yourself, and don't worry about practical matters. Everything will be all right.[59]

Or from another letter of the same period:

After work I dropped in at the café. Today is Friday. I spoke to so-and-so and to so-and-so. I haven't eaten, which makes me now, 10 o'clock at night, very tired. And listen: it's been six days since I've seen you. Luckily I'm kept busy at work. Monday I start a job in Brooklyn, near Bedford. I'll have to work and guard my place from 8 A.M. every day; in return, brood that I, a poet, have been stranded in the damned sweatshops; I'll have to restrain myself every minute from quitting the work; then, working for myself, revise many poems without writing them down (there isn't time)—eat in the Bedford Diner . . . and save enough money to move to Far Rockaway . . . It's sad, but cry? No, no. I've already cried ninety-two times according to Olgin's statistics.[60]

With glints of humor alternating with flashes of self-pity (some of them acknowledged, others camouflaged as solicitude), the letters have a breathless quality, written as if on the run, at café tables, at work, on evenings during a break between card games. They are restless in a deeper way as well, hurtling from boasts of artistic self-confidence to dispirited complaints about the lack of time, spirit, sleep, and money. In one note there is anxiety over $50 left in the pocket of a suit he had brought in for repair, and then relief at recovering it; in the next is a poem he wrote about the women whose letters he received at *Forverts* and answered with embarrassment. Most poignant of all are the letters about his brief visits to Rochelle in the country, where the passion of the lovers is chilled by their lack of privacy and trust. (These moments in the Catskills were Mani Leib's first ventures into the countryside since arriving in America.)

On the whole, the letters show a remarkably serious poet, who knows that out of the given limitations of his life he will either have to make his art or fail. There is no letter, no matter how tender in pursuit of his mistress, that does not stiffen with practical details of work, schedule, money, and above all concern for poetry: one poem came out better than another, one poem is to be published in *Tsu-kunft* instead of *Forverts*, one poem promises to be a little better than its predecessor. Even in this stormiest period of the affair, the stolen hours for poetry were as jealously treasured as those for courtship. Still there were not enough hours, and for a long time it appeared that Mani Leib would never surpass his early triumph.

The Street Drummer

This scene from an autobiographical novel by Rochelle Weprinski dramatizes her lover's mood at the time of their first meeting:

> In the noisy shop, where he sits at the high shoemaking machine, stitching the instep of a ladies' boot, Niezhiner's mind often burns with the thought: what is he doing here? What does this ladies' boot in his hand have to do with him? Why do his long, thin fingers chase so obediently after the flashing needle? Damn! He mustn't daydream! The needle has just stabbed the fingers that are aching to get at lines of poetry.
>
> How often he envies those of his colleagues who didn't let themselves be yoked to a machine in a shop and who don't care where their daily sustenance may be coming from, as long as they can stay free. He could never be like them. He is too proud to ask for a handout, and poems can't provide his children with the bread they need.
>
> His friend, Jacob Shore, once tried to persuade him that his confinement from childhood on to the shop and the gray factory had determined the direction of his talent—it helped him become the great original seeker and celebrator of beauty. By contrast, their highly talented colleague, who snatches freedom from the world with both hands so that he can spend his days with nothing to do but sit for hours at a time in the cafés—he sees the world only in its ugliness and falsity. He has become its profaner, its rebel, its cynic.
>
> "Yes, well," Niezhiner replied, "you can play around with that idea

74

if you like, but the reasons for a poet's development in one direction instead of another are much more complicated than that." To be perfectly honest, though, he often found himself thinking about that colleague of his with the white hands of a non-workingman, who plays the poet all day long at café tables . . . He thinks about him with contempt, but also envy. Sometimes these thoughts draw him so powerfully to the café table that he quits work at noon and appears suddenly in the doorway of the café, trying to mask with a smile on his lips the urgency that brought him there.[1]

Weprinski makes her characters transparent so that readers can identify the originals. The bootmaker Niezhiner, obviously Mani Leib, is imagined as a man torn between responsibility and art. Jacob Shore, Niezhiner's artistic comrade-in-arms, is Reuben Iceland, whose interpretive studies of the Yunge always accorded Mani Leib the highest place in the poetic pantheon. The rival genius, approached by Niezhiner with a mixture of admiration and disdain, is recognizably Moishe Leib Halpern, the single-minded artist. Although Mani Leib actually cut the more romantic figure of the two, it was he who submitted to the pressure of steady employment and domestic responsibility, while Halpern remained free for a decade from the mixed blessings of either.

Moishe Leib Halpern, three years younger than Mani Leib, was born on January 2, 1886, in the city of Zlochev, then part of the Austro-Hungarian Empire. Its population of about 10,000, just over half of them Jews, and its location on the railway line between the major Jewish centers of Lemberg and Tarnopol, made Zlochev a fairly lively place. To the same degree that the Jews of Niezhin, some 1,200 miles to the northeast, were exposed to Ukrainian customs and Russian influence, the Jews of Zlochev, particularly those with Western inclinations, were exposed to German influence and Polish culture (Zlochev had been part of Poland until the first partition of that country in 1772).[2]

Halpern's parents were relatively well-to-do. His mother came from a family of innkeepers, his father from a family of merchants in Odessa. The only boy and eldest of three children (a younger brother had died in infancy), Halpern was sent to one of the best cheders in the city and to a Polish-language school. In deference to his higher social standing as the son of a dry-goods merchant, Moishe Leib was the last of his classmates to be awakened each morning as the boys made their way together to school.[3]

Halpern, who inherited his father's combative temperament, liked to tell stories about the odd behavior of Reb Isaac, as he was known in the city: the way he drove haggling customers from his store or insisted on pulling the rotting teeth of peasants who came to buy from him. One favorite anecdote that he later adapted for a poem described the visit of several German creditors from Lemberg, who came to seize the goods of the bankrupt merchant next door. When the Germans began to pack up the merchandise, Reb Isaac broke into the store and, pretending to be a madman, drove the men away by threatening to bite off their noses.[4]

Despite the considerable differences in their social standing, Mani Leib and Halpern had one thing in common: both were apprenticed at an early age. Halpern's father, who was aware of the precarious economic situation of a Jew in Eastern Europe, wanted a practical education for his son. He took the twelve-year-old to Vienna, where he was apprenticed to a commercial artist. Moishe Leib stayed in Vienna, far from his family, until he was over twenty. The young Halpern showed promise as an artist, and it may have been some early manifestation of this talent that prompted his father to investigate this area of training. But once in Vienna the boy developed an even stronger attraction to literature. He sat in on German literature classes at the university and began to write German verse himself. In the manner of contemporary intellectuals, he spent a good deal of time in the cafés, especially those where young Jews gathered to argue the merits of the emerging Zionist and socialist movements. Halpern didn't like to talk much about this period in his life, except to recall his proficiency at football, biking, and swimming.

By the time he returned to Zlochev in 1907, he was a cultural stranger to his birthplace. Halpern's former schoolmates complained about his Germanic Yiddish, which was difficult to understand. His preference for German had been determined by his extended stay in Vienna and reinforced by his exposure to many writers he admired—Detlev von Liliencron, Richard Dehmel, and Heinrich Heine. But apparently the cultural ferment he found at home impressed him sufficiently to change his mind. There were several budding Yiddish writers in Zlochev who persuaded him that he would be wiser to use his native language, which was undergoing an artistic renaissance. With that kind of encouragement he began to write Yiddish poems.

Halpern's beginnings as a poet became the stuff of legend. It seems that when he submitted his first efforts to the Lemberg *Tageblatt*, its editor Moishe Kleynman returned them because they were too mature to be the work of a beginner. At this point Halpern took to submitting work under the name of his little sister Frieda, hoping that a woman's name would account for their romantic polish. The new poems were accepted, and this story became the cornerstone of Halpern's reputation as a genius and prankster.

The memoirs of his friends credit Halpern's renewed interest in Jewish culture entirely to their own influence, but there is an odd item among Halpern's early writings that offers a more complex explanation. During his first years in New York he published a feuilleton on gentile-Jewish relations in which he undertakes to explain to a friend the reasons for his Jewish identification.[5] There follows an account of an important incident that took place during his student years in Vienna.

The narrator is in his final years of study at a teachers' seminary. It is early spring, and he is sweating over a difficult math problem.

> At that time in my life I didn't yet feel the pain of the Jews, but my healthy blood was tormenting me in the worst way . . . I was twenty-one years old, living among non-Jews. My friends were two strong gentiles, Shani and Franzl, and it was this Franzl who first taught me who and what I was.

The narrator with his healthy blood only daydreams about a woman in his arms. Franzl, however, of a more practical turn of mind, hands his roommate his last krone and tells him to bring him back a "girl from the quay." (He would go after her himself, but his cheek is so badly swollen that it has closed up one eye.) The Jewish roommate dutifully undertakes this mission of mercy and, when he meets Shani downstairs, invites him for a walk without telling its destination. Unfortunately the way to the prostitutes' quarter passes the Café Hofmeister, and "even if you blindfolded me, I would find my way there for its delectable tea with rum." He invites Shani in for a drink, deciding that he will have to find a girl for Franzl for less money. By the time the café clock strikes eleven and Franzl's entire krone is gone, the narrator confesses to Shani that he is afraid to go back to face Franzl's anger. Slightly inebriated, the two boys hit upon a plan. They go to Shani's house and dress him up in one of his sister's prettiest outfits, returning at last to the impatient Franzl, who welcomes the lady and in the dim light invites her to undress. "The lady," convincing up to this point, here loses his nerve and falls back whooping with laughter. Franzl takes in the hoax, remains silent for a moment, then shouts: "That's how it is when you deal with a Jew!"

Though the incident is narrated in a tone of light-hearted mockery appropriate to the humor magazine in which it appeared, it rings with unmistakable resentment. Halpern's return to Jewishness —and to Yiddish—as he confesses to his friend in this letter, was at least in part a reaction against antisemitism, his hatred of being hated. This aggrieved anger against Christians was ' .usual in liberal Jewish intellectual circles. It was, for example, wholly at odds with Mani Leib's myth of Jewish and Slavic harmonies, which Halpern was provoked to parody in the 1920s. Deeply suspicious of any nationalist inclinations in himself, Halpern, like Heine, balanced this self-contempt with an equally strong distaste for his enemies.

No matter how little we know of Halpern's eight-year sojourn in Vienna, we do know that it shaped his artistic tastes, his idea of literature, and his views of himself as a Jew in the world. In turn-of-the-century Vienna he was exposed to the showcase of European creativity, more and more of which appeared to be passing into Jewish hands. The example of a poet like Hugo von Hofmannstahl, whom Halpern admired and later translated, must have beckoned. Hofmannstahl's Jewish origins were as prominently acknowledged as Heine's, and both men had become recognized German classics. There must have been a time when Halpern dreamed of making his mark in German literature, since his abbreviated Jewish education and limited exposure to Jewish culture were too rudimentary to provide an alternative model. He could have become one of the many Galician Jews who passed successfully—at least as writers —into the German mainstream.

Yet to anyone so proud by nature, the manifestation of antisemitic prejudice, whether casual or institutional, would have been unbearable. Side by side with the assimilating German-Jewish writers and intellectuals of Viennese society were active groups of young Zionists and Jewish socialists, formulating a nationalism of their own. It was to these groups that Halpern gravitated even before his return to Zlochev at the age of twenty-one. The Jewish literary ferment he then discovered in his native town contributed to his metamorphosis. The example of other young German-educated Jews voluntarily turning to Yiddish as the language of personal and national self-expression proved the final link in his evolution into a Yiddish poet.[6]

The fortunes of Yiddish were then at their highest. Halpern's adoption of the language during his year back home was part of a wide-ranging linguistic consolidation among modern Jews. The formal recognition of this social fact came at a Yiddish-language conference held in Czernowitz at the end of August 1908. The leading organizer of the conference, Nathan Birnbaum, was himself a German-speaking Jew who provoked a good deal of mirth among opponents, since his enthusiasm for Yiddish was not yet equaled by his knowledge of the language; he had to give the opening address in German. Nonetheless, and despite many administrative gaffes, the Czernowitz conference underscored the new status of Yiddish among Jewish intellectuals, including many, like Halpern, who were fluent in German or Russian and still chose Yiddish.[7]

The very fact of the conference, more than any specific resolution or accomplishment, constituted its significance. The organizers had as their political goal the creation of a strong nationalism among diaspora Jews, an alternative to the Zionist insistence on the reconstruction of a homeland. Yiddish was the natural vehicle of such a program, since it was the chief diaspora language, the vernacular of most European Jews and now also of the offspring communities in North and South America. For secular nationalists, who could no longer accept the religious, Halakhic, definition of the Jew and who resisted the primacy of Zionism, the Yiddish language and the emerging Yiddish culture were touchstones. And even among the Zionists, there were members of Poale Zion, the Labor-Zionist branch, who championed Yiddish because it was the language of the working class.

The conference emphasized that, because of the dispersion of the Jews, Yiddish did not receive the kind of natural reinforcement that other vernaculars get from their governments. "Other tongues . . . are guarded like precious children" whereas Yiddish has no dictionary, standard orthography, or defined grammar. True, the sense of inferiority attached to Yiddish in the past was waning, but some sort of official protection for the language would have to be provided to ensure its proper cultivation and appreciation. Unfortunately, arguments over the status of Yiddish vis-à-vis Hebrew consumed much of the delegates' energy and even more of the subsequent attention of the Jewish press. But the meetings must have made an impression on the younger participants, if only because of the presence of such forceful personalities as Chaim Zhitlowsky, the linguist Noakh Prilutski, the writers Sholem Asch, H. D. Nomberg, Abraham Reisin, and of course I. L. Peretz. That Peretz was not entirely comfortable with the direction of the conference, the negative attitudes expressed toward Hebrew, we know from contemporary references and the conference records. But his conviction that the delegates were initiating an historical event, "opening a new wellspring of fresh living water in God's vineyard," communicated itself to the gathering. Peretz proclaimed that the nation, not the state or the fatherland, was the major force of contemporary life:

> Weak, suppressed nations now awaken and fight against the state for their language, for their identity, and we, weakest among them, have also joined their ranks. Let the state no longer distort the culture of its peoples, or destroy their individuality and particularity . . . we are a Jewish nation and Yiddish is our language. In our language we wish to live, and to create our cultural treasures, and never again sacrifice them to the false interests of the "state," which is only the protector of its ruling, dominating nationalities and the bloodsucker of the weak.[8]

The emphasis on legitimate diaspora nationalism and on Yiddish as its legitimate tongue invested authority in the Yiddish writer.

Halpern appears to have attended the Czernowitz conference, either as a delegate or as an observer. He came with a group of young Yiddish writers from Zlochev, the most established of whom, Shmuel Jacob Imber, had already published his first volume, *Vos ikh zing un zog* (What I Sing and Say), a slim book of highly sensuous verse that was a strong influence on Mani Leib when he read it several years later in America. The novice in the group, Halpern seems to have caught the attention of Peretz, who by one account asked him to read a poem to the assembly. Despite the attention he was beginning to get among his fellow writers, Halpern must have known by now that he would be leaving shortly for New York; unlike his colleagues, most of whom had already served in the Austrian army or were then still in uniform, he had no intention of submitting to the draft. So his passage through Czernowitz in August 1908 may have been merely a stage of his journey to the United States.

Halpern's resolve as a writer was evidently strengthened by the ideas and personality of Peretz, even if he could not take seriously all the heated backroom politics. We know that seven years later, when Halpern learned of Peretz's death, he alone among the Yunge expressed genuine grief in an ode, as if the meaning of his own life were being called into question by this death.[9] Peretz had pronounced the dawn of a new cultural age of the Jews at the very moment Halpern was launching himself.

By the time Moishe Leib Halpern arrived in New York, the little magazine *Di yugnt* had already appeared, and with it the humor magazines. It was not long before Halpern was absorbed into these literary circles and recognized as one of the most talented writers. From the first he felt more comfortable with the Galicians, who were prominent in the humor magazines, than with the "Russians" and their aestheticism. The considerable romantic strain in his own writing was always subject to a counter-impulse of self-mockery, where the humor magazines excelled.

There was something special about Halpern that set him apart even from the other individualists and eccentrics of the nascent literary community. For one thing, he resisted employment. He worked as a window washer ("seeing the life of the 'upper stories' from the outside"), as a waiter and a presser, but very briefly. There is a Yiddish theater song in which a series of artisans and workmen boast of their incompetence—the baker of charring the bread, the tailor of ruining the pants. Halpern took similar pleasure in his inability to succeed at a regular job. The financial consequences of this were no laughing matter, but it was a point of pride for Halpern to translate even his penury into negative proof of his artistic worth.[10]

In the early days of his bachelorhood, which lasted until 1919, Halpern also took pride in antagonizing his potential literary employers. There are many accounts of his deliberate rudeness to editors who could have been useful in furthering his career. The ostentation of this rebellion impressed everyone. Shmuel Margoshes, a fellow Galician immigrant who became a good friend, recalled attending one of Halpern's first public appearances, which took place under the auspices of the Galician Literary Society. Such evenings were organized to provide newcomers some support in the new country and perhaps even a modest fee. Margoshes attended in the same fraternal spirit, hoping if not to discover a great new writer at least to assist a brother. But instead of courting the audience, Halpern set out to shock, reading poems of excessive bombast, one of which concluded with "Tomorrow a black sun will rise!" Margoshes was mortified by this "sophisticated primitive" from his native region.[11]

Even Halpern's physical appearance appears to have been startling. His "Mephisto smile" frightened one observer, who thought he looked not like a rising star of the literary establishment but more like a bum from Butchers' Row.[12] His good friend and literary partner, Moishe Nadir, who had come to America much earlier, described Halpern's discomfort in polite society: "You sat—an awkward proletarian in a torn gray sweater, like someone whose body is so hard and stiff it has torn through the skin—in the 'fine society' into which I brought you, and of whose English vocabulary you understood only the ripening lips and golden curls on the heads of the ladies present."[13] Pugnacious and an untamable womanizer, Halpern was perceived to be always somewhat apart even in the company of his fellow writers, hardly the most convivial of companions. A column in *Der kibitser* of 1911, suggesting alternate professions for its writers, noted that Halpern could find employment as a bogeyman.[14]

Mani Leib was particularly touched by this quality of aloofness in Halpern. He recalled that the first and the last of their meetings took place on streetcorners, where Moishe Leib stood leaning against a lamppost, watching the people go by. The first time they were introduced, Halpern asked with a crooked smile: "What do you all do, devil take it, here in America? Turn the machine wheels?" "Yes," Mani Leib replied, "we work in the factories, each of us at something else. Where do you intend to work? Do you have anything in hand?"

> Work? My relatives want to make a butcher or a waiter out of me, the devil take them . . . I'd rather hang myself some night on one of these lampposts. The lampposts here in America are strong enough to hold the likes of me—ho-ho-ho! In Vienna, where lampposts are tall, fragile, and delicate, they would lose their daintiness if a peasant like me were to dangle from them. The devil take it, I hate waiters and butchers.[15]

According to Mani Leib, no one was as outspoken as Halpern, and no one seemed quite so lost.

> We, his friends, were like all other Jewish immigrants, afraid of this wonderful unknown called America. But gradually we compromised, we learned to adapt ourselves, we "ripened" and eventually turned into real Americans. Not Moishe Leib. He couldn't compromise or bend.

Halpern encouraged this notion of himself as an uncompromising rebel, "a wolf that, having fallen accidentally among dogs, is tortured by loneliness."[16] It can be no accident that many of the images of wolves and lampposts that Mani Leib and others use to describe their colleague derive from Halpern's own self-characterizations in his poems. He is the frog croaking in the swamp, the abandoned scarecrow in the field consumed by autumn.

The first poems that Halpern placed in American Yiddish publications were mostly of two kinds: romantic lyrics and parodies of romantic lyrics. The mood pieces are filled with the staples of this kind of verse—moon, seashore, evening song, unrequited love—and are barely distinguishable from the works of any of the Yunge:

> Windows open . . . and piano sounds—purple-red streaks stretch toward the garden, wrap themselves around the trees, around the flowers—

> The trees begin to blossom, all, all the flowers to blossom—
> Stiller, stiller, stiller. In the evening hours my suffering dreams.[17]

Except for Halpern's recognizably longer line, the poem of which this forms the final stanza reads like a variation of Mani Leib's poems in the same magazine. Fortunately he had another outlet.

The humor magazines were popular from the start. They had to fill a minimum of sixteen pages weekly and paid contributors in cash, about $3–$5 for short pieces. This was one of Halpern's steadiest sources of income in his first decade as a writer and gave him an opportunity to experiment. Irreverence and novelty—the requirements of these publications—gave Halpern's fancy a free reign, without the inhibiting requirements of "refinement." The slapdash manner of these magazines and their minimal editorial standards may well have been the ruin of lesser writers; for Halpern their freedom was a boon. Under the transparent pseudonym, Bright Pen (Hel-pen), he could write anything he wished—social satire, occasional verse, parodies, every kind of experimental poetry and prose. Many of the major themes of his mature work are already here in embryonic form. He also translated Heine in bulk for the magazines—all of *Deutschland* between May and August of 1913 and *Atta Trol* beginning later in the same year.[18]

The pages of *Der kibitser* and *Groyser kundes* are the nearest thing we have for Halpern to the diaries or notebooks that other writers have kept of their youthful work. One can see the recurrence of certain social attitudes and the development of favorite literary forms. In the case of several key works, we have a whole string of preliminary variations, showing Halpern's process of trial and error. This is especially intriguing for poems like "The Street Drummer," a boast of devil-may-care freedom from constraint, which was reworked in at least three earlier published versions before the final draft.[19]

> The bird sings free and clear, alone,
> There the king trembles on the throne.
> Trembling is too absurd:
> I sing freely as the bird;
> And as fast

The Street Drummer

As the wind's blast
I dance wildly, blindly past,
Street-out and street-in!
If I'm sick and old and gray
Who could care, ha-ha-hey!
For only a copper coin, or tin,
As if to break
The drum, I bang
And then I make
The cymbals clang
And round and round about I spin—
Boom! Boom! Din-din-din!
Boom! Boom! Din!

A girl comes along, a sorceress,
A blaze ignites inside me; yes,
I dance more wildly round about
And start to clench my teeth, and shout
As I twirl,
Hold hands, girl,
And grab me round while round we whirl:
Dancing's hotter done in couples.
A girl like you—a killer, though
Left me not so long ago.
My sick heart breaks with pain and troubles,
So as if to break
The drum, I bang
And then I make
The cymbals clang
And round and round about I spin—
Boom! Boom! Din-din-din!
Boom! Boom! Din!

Children laugh in sport and fun
But I don't want to be outdone:
Shake a leg, kids! Hop on by,
One more punch, then, in the eye.
One more spit!
In spite of it

With one jump everything is quit.
Inured to all with an evil name,
From my pocket I pinch some bread
And swig from my flask; down from my head
The sweat pours, and my blood's aflame.
So as if to break
The drum, I bang
And then I make
The cymbals clang
And round and round about I spin—
Boom! Boom! Din-din-din!
Boom! Boom! Din!

That's the way I've torn on through,
Torn my way, and bitten, too,
With my head as through a wall,
Cross-country, over roads and all.
Break the stone
With tooth and bone!
Break the stone and stay alone!
Dog and bum, clod and wind so wild;
Reckless and free, on alien dirt,
I have no coat, I have no shirt,
I have no wife and I have no child.
So as if to break
The drum, I bang
And then I make
The cymbals clang
And round and round about I spin—
Boom! Boom! Din-din-din!
Boom! Boom! Din![20]

In all the versions, the singer is a tramp, a social outcast, a street musician—not a refiner of language and sentiment but a rhythmic noisemaker, pounding his drum before a suspicious or even hostile public. Although Halpern obviously took as much care in perfecting this "recklessness" as Mani Leib did in forging his lyrics, one can almost feel his joy in inverting the ideals of his fellow poets and in rebelling against literary gentility. The street drummer was to remain at the core of his artistic identity, as he taunted the high cultural aspirations of Yiddish, which paralleled the attempt of the Jewish masses to achieve American respectability.

Halpern enjoyed confrontation. He lashed out against cant in private and public affairs: religion was just a convenient mask for human greed, and "manners" the equally spurious coverup for lust. Romantic camouflage comes in for repeated debunking: a girl dreaming of her beloved in the garden feels a tickling at her breast and playfully slaps what she thinks is the hand of her pursuer. In so doing she kills at a single blow two flies, a male and a female, who have carried their lovers' chase into the warmth of her bosom.[21] This kind of juxtaposition is a standard motif in Halpern's contributions to the humor magazines. Later his playfulness evolved into a much deeper anxiety about man's real and imagined place in the universe, and these same buzzing flies become examples of irritation without purpose, of cosmic mischief. So too many of the themes of social disparity and moral imbalance that are treated lightly in *Der kibitser* assume a much more somber mien in his later work.

Since the Yiddish humor magazines were the province of East European Jews, barely loosed from their traditions and still in a mood of rebellion, the lampooning of Orthodoxy necessarily occupied a place of honor. The Jewish calendar was observed by the humor magazines as rigorously in parodistic form as it was in earnest by newspapers like *Tageblatt*. Halpern was one of the many staff writers who wrote regular "holiday" features—a poem about Passover as it might be celebrated by a gentile and as it is in fact celebrated by a Jew; a piece on mothers in the old country who used to fill the house with the aroma of blintzes on the holiday of Shevuot, and about their American counterparts—the waitresses who serve the blintzes in the dairy restaurants of the Lower East Side. Halpern seemed to enjoy this internal Jewish mockery, especially when Eros is pitted against the stern Jehovah. In one poem an old Jew asks a young immigrant whether he remembered to put on his phylacteries that morning, as every adult Jewish male was expected to do. What need for *tfilin* on my forehead and arm, asks the young man, if my mistress makes good their absence with a kiss each morning on just these holy places? In another, gentler poem that appeared for the holiday of Simchat Torah, the beadle's daughter, who has been frolicking with a boy in the old house of prayer, cannot get out in time when the men come in for their prayers and tries to avoid discovery by hiding in the ark. The poem ends on the reader's anticipation as the rabbi and cantor open the curtains to take out the Scrolls.[22]

The delight the magazines took in such heresies reminds us just how closely bound the writers still were to their origins. But even in these early works, Halpern complicates the heresy by striking out simultaneously in two directions, showing as much contempt for the lapsed Jew as for the religion he had abandoned. "Hey, you up there!" shouts a petitioner in one of Halpern's Yom Kippur poems, who is fed up waiting for the villa and the beautiful bride he has long been praying for. To spite a tight-fisted God, he determines to fall in love with a toothless old maid who sweats and snores. He will start the Yom Kippur day with a shot of whiskey, eat a blintz or two, follow them up with fish and meat and soup, and may God split a gut!

> You'll not play the Lord with me, Daddy—No!
> The synagogue's where all the milquetoasts go![23]

The man's mean-spirited commercial calculations come under sharper attack here than the old religion. It was typical of Halpern to ridicule both sides of an issue whenever he could. A little satire, written during the height of the New York mayoralty campaign of 1909, shows two Jews in the bathhouse—the standard literary setting for Jewish political debate—arguing over the respective merits of Hearst and Gaynor until both men fall off the bench and burn their buttocks.

From some of Halpern's occasional verse we also learn what he was doing during these years. One brief but interesting chapter unfolds in the pages of *Der kibitser* beginning at the end of May 1912, when Moishe Leib takes leave of his New York colleagues and sets out to join the staff of the *Folkstsaytung* (Folk Newspaper), a Yiddish daily that was being established in Montreal by a coalition of left-wing groups. He was by then so firmly part of the *Kibitser* family that an editorial note assured readers that Halpern would continue to contribute from Montreal. Over the next few months, poems and short items of mock reportage give a taste of some of Halpern's activities in the "half a Paris" of North America.

The spring of 1912 was the time of a large-scale strike in Montreal's garment industry. The labor dispute was complicated for the Jews by fears of antisemitism. English-speaking Protestants held the financial reins of the city, but the work force was largely French Catholic; the Jewish immigrants, many of whom gravitated to the industry because of previous experience in Europe, tried to steer an economic path between the two. Jewish socialists felt it was their duty to help improve the conditions of the French Canadian workers, despite the opposition of the Catholic Church, while Jewish manufacturers felt it was their responsibility to avoid conflict with authority. Since the local Yiddish paper, the *Keneder adler* (Canadian Eagle), was considered an establishment tool, friendly to the interest of the business community, union leaders and members of socialist organizations decided to launch a rival paper.

Moishe Leib Halpern's poem "Strike," on the front page of the *Folkstsaytung* of June 7, stands directly in the tradition of the sweatshop poems: it is a summons to action, rhetorically charged, and its position on the page, side by side with the strikers' statement of aims, dramatizes the strength of the cause:

> Arise. Arise. You've slaved enough!
> Endured enough of hunger, want,
> Of selling off your blood for bread,
> Arise and gather strong!
> Shut down the wheel. Thrust out your chest
> And come to battle with the best.
> Quit the shop—the cage of slaves
> Stand up to strike![24]

Four such sonorous stanzas call upon the workers to leave their machines and join the strike, the "sword of labor." Halpern was there to help sharpen the weapon.

In the pages of *Der kibitser*, by contrast, he describes his Montreal adventures in the tone of a bemused visitor, far more interested in his exploits with the girls he can pick up than with the success of either the workers' movement or the newspaper, of which he gives the following account:

> Montreal's anarchists wanted to put out a paper for pure anarchism. So they invited the orthodox Marxists to found a single association. Then a nationalist-socialist asked to join them, so they discussed the matter for three months, night after night, and having decided that admitting him would be against the idea of individual anarchism— admitted him. They then looked around for a real anarchist to serve as editor, and found—the Labor-Zionist, Chazanovitch . . .
>
> By this time seventeen issues of this anarchist-socialist-nationalist-Labor-Zionist paper have appeared and the gentlemen are still not satisfied: "It isn't sufficiently anarchic!" One member suggested that every complete issue be taken to the *mohel* for circumcision; another countered that it be taken to the priest because he is a passionate proponent of free love. When challenged by a third gentleman to explain this allegation, he swore that he had seen a lovely nun emerging from the priest's house just the previous day . . . a committee was formed to investigate the issue.[25]

The Catholic mood of Montreal may have provoked Halpern's anticlericalism, but what emerges even more clearly from the Montreal sojourn is his repudiation of any sort of affiliation, even with those whose aims he supported. It was not that Halpern lacked political passion; the "Strike" poem was only the first of many such expressions of partisan engagement. Two years later, when the socialist Meyer London was elected by his largely Jewish congressional district of the East Side to the House of Representatives, Halpern was quick to hail the "Red Rooster" who would stir up the black nest of reaction in the capital.[26] But Halpern could not believe in politics as a panacea. Behind the strikes and the ideological statements, he could always make out the roving eye of the shop girl, the personal ambition of a union leader, the rhetorical mannerism of an orator, all the quirks of human personality that defied comprehensive definition. His distrust of overarching explanations extended to politics no less than to religion and left only the discriminating artist as the purveyor of something like truth. The works he translated while on the *Folkstsaytung,* a story by the nineteenth-century German-Jewish writer Leopold Kompert and a story by Chekhov, are a key to his taste for fiction of painstaking accuracy. The *Kibitser* contributions, despite their sophomoric humor and lack of polish, show a fine eye for significant detail.

When the *Folkstsaytung* folded in less than a year, Halpern returned to New York and the humor magazines. It was here that he had launched his first attack on Morris Rosenfeld, singling him out as the model of all that was weakest in Yiddish verse. Ironically, Halpern probably accorded this honor to the older poet at least in part because of the resemblance between them. He recognized a lyrical poet torn between the wish to withdraw from public themes and a concern for human misery. Halpern's friend Eliezer Greenberg later wondered whether, even at this early stage in his career, Halpern did not sense that he would share Rosenfeld's destiny as a lonely and misunderstood Yiddish poet.[27]

By 1910 Rosenfeld had become angry and bitter: Yiddish literary circles did not accord him a place of honor, and the younger poets repudiated him as old-fashioned. One sign of his annoyance was a satirical piece he published in *Forverts* called "Berl the Piececutter Becomes a Decadent," which was clearly a gibe at the Yunge. Reviving a comic character he had created several years earlier, called Berl the Proletarian, Rosenfeld shows him in his latest form as a decadent rhymester. The author declares himself afraid to enter the Decadents' Café where Berl holds forth because, as one who writes and talks so as to be understood, he will be pilloried by Berl and his friends as an enemy of art. The mockery of Berl's antics is meant to discredit the forced modernism of the young writers.[28]

Halpern's rejoinder, "An Open Letter to Morris Rosenfeld," was sharp to the point of cruelty. It shows the side of Halpern that upset so many of his contemporaries. Instead of replying to Rosenfeld's accusations by taking up the subject of the Yunge, he tells the story of a tin clown in the Wurstelprater, the Vienna amusement park, that would roll on the ground and squeal like a pig when you fed it a coin and pushed the "pig" button. This tin clown was once a prime attraction, but when the author comes back to the park after a year's absence, he discovers that the button has turned rusty, and though the clown still rolls on the ground when you put in your penny, he can no longer squeal. Halpern does not bother to spell out the point of the tale, but it would be hard to imagine a nastier picture of the poet performing for pay.[29]

When Halpern returned to the same subject several years later, both he and his criticism had matured, and he was able to offer a somewhat more balanced assessment of Rosenfeld's work. His article on "The Old and the New Morris Rosenfeld" (1915) was actually the first convincing exposition of the aesthetic ideals of the Yunge, demonstrating the distinctions between good verse and bad. The Yunge are Halpern's models of authentic verse, and Rosenfeld exemplifies the best that the sweatshop school had been able to achieve.

> Who, twenty years ago in the Yiddish milieu, ever dreamed of pure artistic creation? The whole Jewish people was then delighting in the jingles of Eliakhum Zunzer, may he forgive me where he now rests in paradise. And the better element (the so-called Enlightened), if they did not quit us outright, fell upon the great-awakening-cry of those years like a bear upon a fat beehive. Even the great Peretz (of the turn of the century) felt that his Hasidic *shtreiml*, his fur hat, would not be festive enough unless he decorated it with a red ribbon . . . Everyone in those days, particularly Bovshover, Edelshtat, Winchevsky, wrote rhyming bugle calls: "Awake! Awake!"—and naturally a temperament as passionate as Rosenfeld's simply electrified this movement. He had to achieve its highest form of expression because he was its very flesh and blood. And here our complaint against him evaporates, because how can we hold Rosenfeld responsible for his bad lyrics if he never appeared on the scene as a lyricist to begin with?[30]

Changes in literary sensibility, in other words, are the products of their time. But now that the lyrical impulse has been liberated in Yiddish poetry, Halpern insists that one must learn to recognize it. With schoolmasterly patience he brings examples of successful and failed verse, showing the differences between predictable rhymes and true rhymes that contribute to fresh statement; between clichés of unproven assertion and "real human experience" rendered as if for the first time. All the energy of the original *Kibitser* assault on Morris Rosenfeld as a panderer to popular taste is rechanneled here into an argument for a new appreciation of poetry that will require more from its readers but offer them much greater satisfaction in return.

Thus it was Halpern who provided the first defense of Mani Leib and Zishe Landau—of the artistic core of the Yunge.

> The true artist has only to let his light shine over scenes of ordinary life—the light that God granted him, His divinely elected one—and the world is enriched by a new masterpiece . . . And like the starry sky of a summer's night in a clear lake, the moral worth of such a masterpiece is reflected in the eyes of those lonely people who take the poet's soul with them and carry it through eternity from generation to generation like a shrine that can never age.[31]

No one among the Yunge ever spoke more ardently than this about the mission of the artist. Yet when the Yunge split into factions in 1914, neither side could claim Halpern for theirs. Far too raucous for the earnest reformers of *Di naye heym*, he was not comfortable either among the poets of quietude. One of his parodies shows the Yunge in a café listening enraptured to a pair of lines that one of their number has just composed:

> If I lack for a horse, my God
> How then shall I ride?[32]

By altering only slightly the opening lines of Zishe Landau's recently published poem cycle "Scales" ("I would buy a horse if I could ride / and quickly set off on my way") Halpern exaggerates the unreality of this kind of poetry, turning its wistfulness to foolishness and its simplicity to banality. His own occasional inclination to just this mood of self-indulgent melancholy made him all the more adept in puncturing its excesses.

The talents of Mani Leib and Moishe Leib Halpern seemed to blossom at almost the same moment in time. The third volume of the miscellany *Shriftn*, containing the poems "Shtiler, shtiler" and "Yingl tsingl khvat," reveal Mani Leib's narrative control and evocative musicality, sweeter than anything yet heard in Yiddish verse. Halpern's first major work appeared one issue earlier and is no less proof of ripened ability. "In der fremd" (On Alien Ground), an autobiographical poem in ten parts, is the first sustained exposition in American Yiddish literature of an individual's actual voyage to America and of his corresponding inner transformation. The Yiddish phrase *in der fremd* refers not only to place but to the condition of estrangement in which the foreigner finds himself.[33]

In later years Halpern's exploration of his own emotional landscape became more gnarled and opaque, but in this first of his long works the images and the speaker's communication of his thoughts are fairly direct. Since the ocean voyage takes many days, the traveler has time to brood over the significance of his crossing from Europe to America. One of the first things he notes is the familiarity of this sensation of uprooting. He had left his father's house when he was very young, so that his experience of solitary wandering is really the touchstone of his identity. He recognizes a continuity in being cast adrift. The Jewish motif grows organically out of these personal musings. It was as a Jewish child in a Polish school, forced to kiss the cross by his classmates, that he learned the meaning of social isolation. Jesus thus becomes the ironic symbol of his own lonely torment, except that he cannot learn to love those pious folk whose faith in Jesus' blood expresses itself in a call for his own.

At the beginning of the poem, on the eve of his departure from Europe, the young man takes playful leave of his sweetheart as if nothing more than an inconvenient separation were at stake. Out at sea, the throbbing engines and churning waters force a much higher seriousness on the traveler and his poem. The ocean crossing is not an interlude but a sentence. Chased out of Europe like dogs, he and the wandering Jewish masses will become squatters in an alien city that looms in frightening, gigantic images. Now the immigrant realizes that he had no home to leave and even less of a welcome ahead in the canyons of stone and steel. The exhausted newcomer to New York summons up the memory of his distant beloved to help him escape the reality of which he is now a part. If Mani Leib yearned for harmony in a world where there is so much discord, Halpern by contrast had come to accept tension as the very condition that poetry must recreate.

Halpern cultivated the public posture of someone *hefker*, unclaimed. Homeless he certainly was. Yoel Slonim remembers that Halpern wrote "In der fremd" while he was a boarder at his mother's house, in concentrated absorption at the kitchen table.[34] Moishe Nadir and Halpern loved to trade stories of these years, when they roomed together with a poet who admired them so much that he did their laundry and cooking as well as pay their rent. Nadir's steady job on humor staffs gave him a measure of financial stability that Halpern lacked.[35] This was to remain Halpern's pattern. Unwilling to write for money except on his own terms, he was forced to accept help he was often too proud to ask for. He scorned those who drudged for a living, not merely his fellow poets for compromising their talent but workers of all kinds. Yet since poverty often made him dependent on those he mocked, he spared himself no contempt either. Women aroused in him the same contradictory feelings. The more he craved their affection, the less he trusted it or himself for being at its mercy.

Halpern's intense reaction to World War I was similarly based on his ability to see both sides of a coin. Unlike most of his fellow writers, he had never been a conscript and had come to America with the express intention of avoiding the required service in the Austrian army. Now, under the impact of the war news, Halpern turned into an ideological pacifist. He was not only opposed to America's entry into the war on the side of the British, like so many European Jews; he also formulated his opposition as a moral principle. Somewhat later, when David Ben Gurion and Itzkhak Ben Zvi came to New York to recruit men for a Jewish legion in the British army (with the hope of ensuring support for a Jewish homeland in Palestine), Halpern furiously attacked his friends who enlisted in its ranks, and this despite his once strong sympathy for Labor-Zionism. Set equally against both sides of the war, he concentrated on the destruction itself. The result was a fevered work of apocalyptic doom in which all of European civilization disintegrates with the Jews in its midst. "A Night" first appeared in 1916, then in a revised version as part of Halpern's first book of poems in 1919. Its twenty-five sections, metrically varied to convey violent shifts of mood, range in length from a dozen to almost three hundred lines. In its epic scope and force of emotion, it is Halpern's most ambitious poem.

"A Night" has been described as the conflation of two night-mares, one personal, the other historical.[36] The collapse of European civilization appears through the haunted inner eye of one of its survivors. Nightmares unfold before the survivor like a vaudeville show. The brilliant master of ceremonies is a *mentshele* (a little man), so nimble that he actually executes all the routines he introduces.[37] Disguised as a magician, he summons up a severed head that can now do duty as a bust; a cracked *tsholnt* pot that can double as a vase now that there are no more Jews to cook the Sabbath meals; a prayer shawl so decoratively splattered with its wearer's blood that it can be used as fancy tablecloth. A sentimental balladeer, he sings of childhood, lulling the sleeper with images of his murdered family. He performs dance tunes and organ-grinder ditties, with a squeaking mouse to pass around the collection box because "Charity saves you from death." The mentshele is even able to masquerade as a priest and to assume a stern Jewish conscience. He mocks everything equally: claims of family sentiment and those of tribe or nation, religious sanctity and modern secular ideals, the authority of the past and hope for human improvement. The hokum of the little man is more chilling than the barbarism he describes:

> Your own brother, poor thing,
> lost both his hands at war.
> Now he doesn't sleep at night
> since he can't scratch himself anymore.[38]

The ascendance of the mentshele is the triumph of nihilism, a denial of all human possibility.

Jewish literature is filled with national laments, from the Bible through the historical poems of the Middle Ages to such powerful modern outcries as Chaim Nahman Bialik's "City of Slaughter," written after the Kishinev pogroms. But these great expressions of mourning kept alive the essential kinship of the Jews and the image of their greatness in suffering. Halpern's vision denies religious and national meaning to the current devastation, which exposes the mendacity of earlier inflated messianic claims. The dead cannot forgive the survivor the rhetorical web of deceit that has been spun around them, and they curse their would-be elegist:

> May the earth remain forever waste
> where you have spun your dream.
> May there hang, every night, without reason or cause

a fresh corpse under your tree.
And should you stretch your hand to it in longing
may your hand forget its cunning.
May you choke to death mid-word
if you invoke The Land.
And as you are dying, may you wander too
and never meet your death.
Because you drag us with your kingship-dream
eternally, from land to land.

Jewish memorialization is accused of having reinforced the false myths of Jewish survival.

The poet seems to divide his identity in the poem into two conflicting parts: one is the speaker, a genuine mourner, a submissive Jew. The other is the homunculus, the mentshele, who is assigned the skeptical voice that Halpern cultivates in the humor magazines. The mocker is the principle of energy, the mourner of impotence and death. The mocker is protean, vivid, inventive. The mourner is passive, helpless, leaving earth without even a trace of his presence.

Let's just say a dream of fear
has been, and is no longer here.
No one has seen me here.
I was never here at all.

In thus dividing himself and the function of poetry between the elegiac and the discordant, Halpern makes it clear which posture is viable in the wake of the war and which is doomed. If there is to be life at all—poetic life—it will have to follow the example of the mocker. Destruction, the vital force of the age, is also the crucial ingredient of any modern aesthetic. *Mentshele* is all that survives of *mentsh*, of man as we have known him, and antipoetry outlives the impulse of poetry.

The intensity of its disillusionment notwithstanding, *A Night* was the personal epic the young American Yiddish writers had hoped to produce. The poem takes on a very large subject, dramatizing Halpern's antiwar convictions. At the same time, the war was a vehicle for Halpern's dark personal premonitions. It had been hard for him to find matter great enough to absorb the power of his rage. In writing about disillusioned love or religious hypocrisy, he was conscious always of stunted actuality—his own and that of the Jewish immigrant community. Through a war that took over a world, he could express his own impotent grief.

We have noted how others of the Yunge adjusted to their situation by making a virtue of necessity. They cultivated the idea of containment as protection against what they could not attain. With their belief that less is more, they could accept a small reading public and few publishing opportunities as the condition of their art. Toward the end of the war, some of the Yiddish writers began to contribute regularly to newspapers and journals, Mani Leib to *Forverts*, Iceland to *Tog*, others to *Morgn zhurnal* or to the leading Yiddish monthly, *Di tsukunft*. In finding these small, not altogether satisfactory niches for their work, the writers grew less oppressed by their isolation from the immigrant mainstream.

Halpern spurned all such associations with newspapers and journals, except the humor magazines for which he wrote whenever he was hungry. He turned down a job on *Forverts*, unable to accept the kind of hack work Mani Leib did. Some of his friends thought he went out of his way to antagonize prospective employers or editors. He publicly insulted Morris Winchevsky, the influential editor of *Di tsukunft*, shortly after he had been paid the enviable sum of $25 for the poem "Pan Jablovski." The quarrels and fights he picked with Sholem Asch, Kolye Teper, and others raise the question whether his pacifism of these days was not an intellectualized restraint on himself.[39]

Miscellanies and little magazines were still the favored form of publication, although often the distinction between them became clear only when the second issue of what was to have been a magazine failed to appear. At the same time that Reuben Iceland and Mani Leib were launching their American-based edition of the magazine *Literatur un lebn*, Halpern started a poetry magazine called *Fun mentsh tsu mentsh* (Person to Person), which did not survive its first issue. Somewhat later, in 1916, he consigned the first version of *A Night* to a second such collective volume, *East Broadway*, which he coedited with Menahem Boreisho, recently arrived from Poland. This lively anthology has the stamp of Halpern's artistic independence, but apparently the very qualities of devil-may-care expressiveness that brighten his verse conflicted with the editorial responsibilities he had undertaken.

Halpern's attitude toward the mechanics of publication is recorded in the memoir of his devoted admirer Zishe Weinper, who accompanied him one day to the printing plant of Dr. Fornberg, in Newark, where the miscellany was being published. The long train ride to Newark on that hot summer's day inflamed Moishe Leib's resentment. "Damn this miserable life of ours!" he complained to Weinper, "as if writing were not enough! We have to read the proofs ourselves and ride the stinking trains!" At the printer's, Halpern was outraged by the mistakes he found in the proofs: "They turn 'sky' into 'golliwog' and 'horizon' into 'salamander,'" he fumed. When Dr. Fornberg came to greet his editors and to ask about the money still due him, Halpern's self-control snapped: "You, too? Why you yourself are a Yiddish writer! Here we bring you our blood, and all you want are our copper coins!"[40] Weinper found the scene very funny, but not Halpern. Schnorring, putting the touch on others for money, was an intolerable affront to his dignity. On another occasion, when David Ignatoff had designed an issue of *Shriftn* containing reproductions of contemporary artwork, he asked the Yunge to devote an evening to gluing them in at the printer's, since he had no more money to pay for the job. Everyone came, with varying degrees of enthusiasm, except Halpern. He could accept poverty, but not demeaning labor.[41]

Halpern's testiness during the years 1916–1919 may have been aggravated by the difficulties of courtship. He had fallen in love with Royzele Baron, a shy and pretty girl with four older brothers; the eldest, Aaron Leib, was a colleague of Halpern's and himself a writer. Aaron Leib Baron's work appeared regularly in the humor magazines and in the Yiddish press, and he published his first book of poems in 1910, several years before Halpern.[42] Though he was off to a fast start, Baron turned to the production side of publishing. He became the general manager of *Forverts* at the time when it was reaching its peak of circulation and was assured a very comfortable living. He could not have welcomed a brother-in-law with a reputation for coarse behavior, an ungovernable temper, and bohemian irresponsibility. Resentment of Moishe Leib's superior ability may also have played a part in Baron's disapproval and in the strained relations that always existed between him and Halpern. Nonetheless, the marriage of Moishe Leib Halpern and Royzele Baron took place in 1919, the same year Halpern issued his collected poems. It is conceivable that the preparation of this book, which instantly confirmed his position as one of the most talented poets in the language, gave him the necessary confidence to press for the marriage.

The idea for a book of poetry that would interpret the new Jewish community of New York had occurred to Halpern at least as early as 1911, when he published in the pages of *Der kibitser* several sections of a work called "De la Hester," which he intended to develop into an epic.[43] The poem's ambitiousness immediately struck the eye: its eight-foot trochaic lines running across the space of half a page were quite a change from the magazine's customary trimeter or tetrameter that allowed for four columns on a page. Yet as the title indicates, the high expectations of European grandeur are to be exploded by their transposition into the milieu of Hester Street, the crowded market hub of the Lower East Side. The work is addressed to the writer's muse, a pretty fellow worker of his in a shoe factory. Their place of rendezvous is not the Place de la Concorde, as it might have been had they been Parisians, but a pathetic New York park of seven trees and a dry water fountain (Rutgers Square), with a watchman to supervise local squatters. "De la Hester" is a debased version of all that European culture had invited one to emulate, and the Yiddish writer-turned-shopworker, an uprooted and diminished European, is a mock hero of a mock epic. Halpern dropped the poem after a few installments because he could not seem to find a dramatic framework large enough to sustain it.

The book he did publish eight years later included many features of this earlier poem, but it was called *In New York* and reflected a considerable adjustment of aims. In place of a single long poem about the city, the book is composed of almost one hundred short lyrics and narratives that together provide an introduction to the immigrant's experience of the "golden land." This fragmentary approach served the poet well. Halpern never ceased to aspire to a great sustained opus, but if it was his tragedy never to be able to complete it, at least he turned that handicap to advantage.

In New York opens with a short poem about a garden indisputably modeled on Hester Park. It is a scrawny Eden:

> What a garden, where the tree is
> Bare, but for its seven leaves,
> And it seems it is amazed:
> "Who has set me in this place?"
> What a garden, what a garden—
> It takes a magnifying glass
> Just to see a little grass.
> Is this garden here our own,
> As it is, in light of dawn?
> Sure, it's our garden. What, not our garden?[44]

One hears here, even in translation, the characteristic lilt of Yiddish speech because Halpern was using a level of colloquialism that cannot be altogether neutralized in English and that was about to penetrate American usage in any case. As Mani Leib was discovering a wellspring of natural language in the Yiddish folksong and ballad, Halpern was the first to adopt the spoken idiom, challenging readers to recognize it as poetry. The brash newcomer unsatisfied with the garden of his exile must know better than to expect anything more. And if the Yiddish reader is not altogether satisfied with poetry that echoes his daily speech, he too will have to learn not to expect anything fancier.

Halpern did not simply collect his best work in this book but shaped the volume according to the hours of a single day, beginning with this urban aubade, a morning song, and concluding with the dark phantasmagoria of *A Night*.[45] The phases of the day correspond broadly to the "ungreening" of the immigrant, who arrives full of dreams and must be progressively stripped of them. There is a motley cast of characters—drunks, derelicts, loose women, and other lonely souls—but the liveliest parts of the book are the personal lyrics in which a character called "Moishe Leib" laughs, mocks, challenges, stabs the air for emphasis, and shrugs off what he does not care to confront. When he occasionally drops the bravado, his musings are uncommonly soft:

When people enter with large and muddy feet
ask no permission, and push doors open,
begin to stroll around your home
as though it were some alley whorehouse—
the heart's best prank would surely be
to take a whip in hand, and like a Baron
teaching his slave to say good morning
simply drive them all away like dogs!

What's to be done, though, with the whip, when people enter
with hair as blond as sheaves and sky-blue eyes,
as agile as small birds in flight
pretend to cradle you in lovely dreams
and steal, the meanwhile, deep into your heart,
and sing while taking off their little shoes,
and bathe, like children in summer water-holes,
their lovely little feet in your heart's blood?[46]

Fearful of his own susceptibility to tenderness, Halpern made fun of his lingering romantic notions and camouflaged his deepest anxieties in humor:

And if Moyshe-Leyb, Poet, recounted how
He's glimpsed Death in the breaking waves, the way
You catch that sight of yourself in the mirror
At about 10 A.M. on some actual day,
Who would be able to believe Moyshe-Leybl?

And if Moyshe-Leyb greeted Death from afar,
With a wave of the hand, asking "Things all right?"
At the moment when many a thousand people
Lived it up in the water, wild with delight,
Who would be able to believe Moyshe-Leybl?

And if Moyshe-Leyb were to swear
That he was drawn to Death in the way
An exiled lover is to the casement
Of his worshipped One, at the end of the day,
Who would be able to believe Moyshe-Leybl?

And if Moyshe-Leyb were to paint them Death
Not gray, dark, but color-drenched, as it shone
At around 10 A.M. there, distantly,
Between the sky and the breakers, alone,
Who would be able to believe Moyshe-Leybl?[47]

un az moyshe-leyb, der poet, vet dertseyln,
az er hot dem toyt oyf di khvalyes gezen,
azoy vi men zet zikh aleyn in a shpigl,
un dos in der fri gor, azoy arum tsen—
tsi vet men dos gleybn moyshe-leybn?

un az moyshe-leyb hot dem toyt fun der vaytn
bagrist mit a hant un gefregt vi es geyt?
un davke beys s'hobn mentshn fil toyznt
in vaser zikh vild mit dem lebn gefreyt—
tsi vet men dos gleybn moyshe-leybn?

un az moyshe-leyb vet mit trern zikh shvern,
az s'hot tsu dem toyt im getsoygn azoy,
azoy vi es tsit a farbenktn in ovnt
tsum fenster fun zayns a farheylikter froy—
tsi vet men dos gleybn moyshe-leybn?

un az moyshe-leyb vet dem toyt far zey moln
nit groy un nit finster, nor farbn-raykh sheyn,
azoy vi er hot arum tsen zikh bavizn
dort vayt tsvishn himl un khvalyes aleyn—
tsi vet men dos gleybn moyshe-leybn?

How well Moishe Leib, Poet, knew those moods of suicidal
yearning that weighed down the poetry journals of his time, and
what delight he took in exposing them to the light of a Coney Island
summer's day! He called this poem "Memento Mori," using the
Latin alphabet, to emphasize the incongruity between the literary
tradition he had adapted and the everyday reality into which he had
introduced it. The playful internal rhyme on his own name,
Moishe-Leibl (which the translator made diminutive for the sake of
the rhyme), the spoof of the death longings of the Yunge, the chum-

miness of Poet and Death—all of this lightens the subject, almost robbing death of its sting. Yet just as an ocean wave gathers force when it approaches the shore, the poem accumulates such momentum by the time it hits the penultimate line, "Between the sky and the breakers, alone," that we are persuaded of its serious intent.

Halpern's *In New York* drew such quick attention to its novelty, to the colloquial style and antipoetic swagger, that its thematic struggle over true value and selfhood was overlooked. Even Shmuel Niger, the most perceptive critic of the new literature, censured the crude language without considering its function. Halpern wrote to him in disappointment: "The very decorative surface of a poem is like an overly ornate ark of the synagogue. You become so impressed with the decoration that you overlook the Scrolls of the Law inside. So I opened the doors a bit."[48] Halpern was trying to explain that he was cutting away not at the Scrolls but at the pretty overlay that detracts from the real thing. He was the essential moralist whose exposure of grit and mud in the streets of gold was a means of reintroducing the discovery that must stand at the center of art no less than of religion. His frequent images of nakedness were not intended to outrage puritans but to make them face what they preferred to avoid. Halpern's outbursts of contempt and shows of impatience with fools were the other side of his seriousness about the responsibility of the artist, who now alone was keeper of the Scrolls.

Mani Leib (left) and Reuben Ludwig, about 1920.
All photos courtesy YIVO except as noted

Seated left to right: Halpern, M. J. Haimovitch, Moishe Nadir, Yoel Slonim.
Standing: Sh. Fox, Zuni Maud, I. J. Schwartz, Joseph Bank

Seated left to right: Menakhem Boreisho, Abraham Reisen, Halpern.
Standing: A. M. Dilon, H. Leivick, Zishe Landau, Reuben Iceland, Isaac Raboy

Self-portrait by Halpern, 1930

Freheit, 1922. Second row, from left: William Gropper,
Abraham Reisen, Melekh Epstein, Moisei Olgin.
Third row, standing from right: Halpern, Menakhem Boreisho, H. Leivick,
P. Novick. Fourth row, standing second from left: Michael Gold

Mani Leib and Rochelle Weprinski, 1936

Itsik Manger, Reuben Iceland, Mani Leib, 1951

Mani Leib's grave, Workmen's Circle
Cemetery, Mount Carmel
Photo by David G. Roskies

Halpern's grave, Workmen's Circle Cemetery,
Mount Carmel
Photo by David G. Roskies

Cartoon by Foshko, "Literary Café." Standing: Sholem Asch.
Seated to his right: Joseph Opatoshu and Halpern

The King of Freiheit

The years 1918 and 1919 marked a turning point for the Yunge, confirming them as the dominant figures of Yiddish literature inside America and beyond. The simultaneous publication of a number of group anthologies and individual books demonstrated their energy at a time when European writers were silenced by the war. Mani Leib's three volumes of poetry, Moishe Leib Halpern's *In New York*, and H. Leivick's poetic drama *The Golem* were as distinct from one another as from anything that had preceded them in Yiddish. Taken together they affirmed the variety and maturity of a group at the height of its powers.

In a letter of September 1919 from Brooklyn, Mani Leib listed for his slightly younger fellow poet Melekh Ravitch, in Vienna, twenty-four books of poetry and prose by his American colleagues that had recently appeared or were on press. Such an account of vigorous output must have overwhelmed Ravitch, who had just been demobilized after service in the Austrian army and was only starting out as a poet. Little wonder that he declared his interest in coming to New York, which appeared to have taken over from the European cities, at least for the duration of the war, the artistic leadership of the Yiddish world.[1]

The books confirmed the existence of a type of literature that had been heralded by these writers only a decade earlier. Zishe Landau's *Anthology of Yiddish Writing in America before 1919* dramatized its modernity by introducing twenty-eight poets, all but four still in their thirties or younger. In his bold revisionist introduction, Landau insisted that everything before the Yunge was merely a chapter in the history of the labor movement: until the advent of the Yunge "the Jewish national and social movements had had their own rhyme departments." His anthology would demonstrate the "lively immediacy of the Yiddish word" instead of its rhetorical powers.[2] Landau admitted that Yiddish poetry was a worldwide phenomenon and that the American nature of the book was dictated more by the pragmatic difficulties of obtaining European selections than by any programmatic dedication to a localized Yiddish culture. Nonetheless, once having decided to make the volume American, he included only those poets whose work was shaped on this continent.

The prominence of American subject matter in the early works of the Yunge contributed to their seeming novelty. Mani Leib gathered the work of forty-six local Yiddish poets in a collection called "New York in Verse" for the miscellany Der inzl (The Island) of 1918.[3] The series opens with the bitter testimonies of the labor poets and continues through the discoveries and self-disclosures of the Yunge, but the final poem in the series—noting the "rich autumn shades / as the Hudson runs beneath the drowsy Palisades"—hails the city for both the splendor of its gifts and the depths of its disappointments.[4] By the end of the world war, New York was as artistically familiar as the shtetl or Warsaw.

In other contemporary publications, Isaac Raboy and David Ignatoff wrote about cities and farmlands. The characters of this fiction —Jewish and Christian farmhands, Jewish convert-missionaries, disillusioned schoolteachers, restless young women—were struggling with a new set of problems that were born of local social conditions. Ignatoff's troubled hero, who warns against attractive gentiles, and Raboy's shy hero, who inspires the construction of a new road in a New England village, may have expressed different attitudes toward the land around them, but they were both part of a new atmosphere and of a literature that had come of age.[5]

Yet, as often happens in the history of cultural movements, the most brilliant year also carried intimations of dimming prospects. By 1919, with families to support, the writers were scattering to the

Bronx and Coney Island and to places as far afield as Kentucky. They could no longer meet every evening or weekend. Instead of the stimulation of the cafés, the writers were absorbed by the domestic atmosphere of their homes, where it was often hard to find a table let alone a room of one's own. During the 1920s self-publication became costlier, and the physical isolation of writers from one another made it harder to collect the manuscripts and the few hundred dollars each project required. Responding to Ravitch's enthusiastic wish to come to New York, Mani Leib warned that the best of times was probably behind them and that the cultural outlook for Yiddish in America was bleak.[6]

The writers were also affected by changes occurring in the larger Jewish community. The war had changed the whole course of Jewish history. The revolution in Russia overthrew the hated authority of the tsar, introducing an untried system of government. Britain's Balfour Declaration, which looked with favor on the establishment of a Jewish homeland in Palestine, galvanized the Zionist movement and, by turning the vague dream of haven into a potential reality, demanded a political response of Jews. Poland's emergence from the war as an independent country and President Wilson's stated desire to protect national minorities invited Polish Jews, at least theoretically, to constitute a vocal minority in their native land. While Jewish writers and thinkers in Russia, Palestine, and Poland exploded with energy in response to these new challenges, American Yiddish writers had to adjust from a distance to changes of which they were not an essential part. A decade earlier they had pioneered a cultural revolution. Now they were established writers and householders; the revolutionary force was elsewhere.

The local political atmosphere was also dispiriting. The open-door policy of the United States was modified after the war. Immigration restrictions voted by Congress in 1921 were tightened by the quota law of 1924, which seemed to be aimed at Jews although they were not singled out specifically. The decline in the number of Jewish immigrants from that time on, combined with strong nativist pressure to prove one's American loyalty, resulted in a progressive decline in the number of Yiddish speakers and more reluctance to maintain a separate Jewish language. Many intelligent and cultivated Jews who might otherwise have shared the audience for modern

American Yiddish literature were drawn instead into the English milieu. "Publishing houses are closing and the public isn't buying any books," Opatoshu complained in the summer of 1921.[7] "This is not a crisis," wrote Leivick two years later. "A crisis is temporary; this is expiry, decline."[8]

In their first publications the Yunge had emphasized the cultic nature of their association, boasting of how few readers they had across the country. The little magazines they published between 1908 and 1920, "cultivated by a minority for a minority," tried to ward off the leveling-down influence of literature in an age of machines. Withdrawal from the mass market that treated words as just another commodity seemed the first necessary step in the preservation of good writing. But since the writer, no less than the machinist, is a man or woman with a body to feed and shelter, this aristocratic approach to art implied an aristocratic method of patronage—for how else could writers live to write? If a paying public could not sustain them, they would have to depend on patrons with a dedication to quality that matched their own. The evenings of Mabel Dodge that became a staple of Greenwich Village life from 1912 until after the war represented just such a social contract between a wealthy woman of taste and the writers and radicals encouraged by her money. Before the government and the universities stepped in to fill this role, patronage was the avant-garde's alternative to a paying job.

An artistic cult is predicated on the existence of a sophisticated minority that can respond to its standard of quality. Like their counterparts in other languages, the Yiddish writers longed for this kind of appreciative support. Shortly after his arrival in New York, the poet Menakhem Boreisho wrote a description of the Yunge in their cafés in which he speculated how liberating it would be if a patron were suddenly to appear on the scene to rescue them all from their gnawing poverty.[9] But in immigrant Jewish circles such patronage was unlikely. As a low-status language, Yiddish could not confer on its benefactors the high status that usually accompanies cultural patronage. The potential patrons of Yiddish were likely to be workers themselves, cultural nationalists, or simply lovers of their own language, who were willing to forego a certain degree of advancement in America because of their attachment to nation or class.

They were seldom wealthy by objective standards, and because their attachment to Yiddish derived from their social or national passions, they often craved the very sort of writing their protegés were trying to put behind them. The social limitations of the Yiddish milieu set severe limits on the development of a viable Yiddish avant-garde.

Since Yiddish writers, then, could hope for no wealthy patron to support them, no government to honor them, and no institution of higher learning to sponsor them, they were forced, if they wanted to earn a living by the pen, to work for the press. Fortunately, by the end of World War I, the young writers and poets were famous enough by the standards of Yiddish readership to attract the notice of editors and theater directors who were looking for a higher level of entertainment and for prestigious, recognizable names. This was to prove one of the critical differences between the artistic life of Greenwich Village and its Yiddish counterpart only a few blocks away on the East Side. As the gap between high and low culture widened throughout America, the best Yiddish writers were absorbed by the organs of mass appeal. The Jewish writer in a non-Jewish language could, if he wished, pass into the general culture, as did Anzia Yezierska, Ludwig Lewisohn, Samuel Ornitz, Edna Ferber, and many others. But the Yiddish writer was organically bound to the Yiddish-speaking Jews. Living as he did among Jews, appearing and being reviewed in Jewish publications, he was dependent on the fate of the language and its speakers. Few Yiddish writers had anticipated this condition, and they adjusted to it with varying degrees of enthusiasm.

Moishe Leib Halpern seemed in a particularly good position. *In New York* made his reputation as a controversial poet, and with its appearance in 1919 he became a local celebrity. The figure he cut of an unhappy castaway on strange shores had a strange appeal: here was an uncompromising individualist who would *not* make all the required adjustments to the new country.

Halpern's marriage to Royzele Baron added urgency to his search for income. Like his friends, he tried to tap the Yiddish press and theater for money, but he was too prickly to take a job and his get-rich-quick schemes were rarely grounded in practical considera-

tions. Shortly after his marriage, he received from his friend Moishe
Nadir an invitation to come out to his place in the country for a brief
honeymoon. Nadir later bought a large farmhouse in Loch Shel-
drake, New York, where he ran a profitable summer colony for
writers, artists, and cultural hangers-on, but at this time he and his
wife Ida were renting a summer house and he was looking for a
literary collaborator. When the Halperns arrived, Nadir took his
friend on a long hike to reveal the real reason for his invitation.

> Nadir (after a three-mile climb uphill, with a sigh): Well, here we are,
> two mature literary men.
> Halpern: But what are we to do? How will we make a living?
> Nadir: We're going to write a play.
> Halpern: Who will?
> Nadir: You and I will. Now let's get back to the house to telegraph.
> Halpern: To whom?
> Nadir: To the theater.
> Halpern: What for?
> Nadir: To say that we have a play, and that we're prepared to come
> into the city to read it to them if they pay for our trainfare.[10]

From this light-hearted bit of literary history, one might imagine
that the play the two men tossed off on their way back into town was
a frothy comedy in the style of some of their *Kibitser* articles and
satires. Perhaps such an item might have turned into a theatrical
success. Instead, their play *Under the Burden of the Cross* was a grim
treatment of the postwar mood of American Jews, a dramatic ver-
sion of Halpern's obsessive nightmare of destruction.[11]

The play does start out as social satire. In response to the news
from the war front of devastation and pogroms in Europe, a group
of American Jews forms a relief committee and decides to send a
representative overseas. This part of the plot clearly derived from
current events. The American Jewish Joint Distribution Committee
had been founded in New York at the outbreak of the war, gradually
drawing together sections of the community in a common relief
effort. In 1919–20 it sent a staff of social workers overseas to help
refugees and to allocate the millions of dollars collected for aid.
Nadir and Halpern recognized in this mission the dramatic kernel of
a play that could combine two issues that disturbed them: the fac-
tionalism of American Jews and the European curse of antisemi-

tism. In their drama (which, though it was never performed, did earn its authors a little money in advances), the joint committee chooses as its delegate an intense, neurotic, and idealistic young physician, David Herbst (the name means autumn), whose mother was caught in the pogroms. The rest of the family, having reached America, lives together in a large apartment that constitutes the set of the play for the full five acts. The main plot revolves around Herbst and his Christian nurse assistant, Lucille Baranowski, who partly out of love for him and partly out of compassion for the victims of war, decides to go overseas with the Red Cross. Of several subplots, the most important is the parallel love affair between Stephan Baranowski, Lucille's brother, and one of Herbst's sisters, emphasizing the paradox that even as the American Jewish community responds to the bloody slaughter of its coreligionists by Christians in Europe, individual Jews in America are finding it hard to resist the attraction of gentiles.

Halpern worried throughout the war over the fate of his mother and sister in Europe, and in the figure of Herbst he was able to give voice to some of his guilt and fear. Autumnal in spirit as well as name and burdened by responsibilities, Herbst cares nothing for social or economic advancement but works tirelessly for the good of his patients. When he agrees to undertake the mission to Europe, he insists that it be at his own expense. The straightforward social criticism of the opening scenes, where several Jewish organizational types use the noble cause as a means of advancing their own interests, turns much more complex once the "burden of the cross" begins to impinge on the action. Attracted though he is by his nurse, Herbst distrusts both her love and her charity: "That's what you all do. First you come with the black cross and split our heads open and cut open our stomachs. Then you come with the Red Cross and bandage up our heads and stitch up our stomachs."[12] The doctor burns with the kind of anti-Christian rage that Halpern sometimes gave vent to in his poetry, and he resists the liberal plea that each "goy" be considered on individual merit.

Later, when Lucille is killed in Europe during her mission of mercy by pogromists who mistake her for a Jew, the tables are momentarily turned. Now it is her brother Stephan who blames the Jews for his sister's death. But the moral scale is hardly balanced in this equation, and while Baranowski simply breaks off his engagement with the Jewish girl by mutual consent, Herbst suffers a fatal breakdown. In Europe he learned that his mother was murdered when she left her hiding place to bring water to some thirsty children, and he sees in her death the symbol of Christian love in the name of which pogroms are invariably launched. Maddened by guilt and grief, he determines to reclaim Jesus from the Christians who befoul his name:

> We dreamed up a messiah for the world. The world is blind. We must open its eyes. Don't kill in the name of the cross . . . If you carry the ax along with the cross we will take the cross away from you— because he who hangs on the cross belongs to us. He is ours, our martyr, the sacrificial victim of our messianic dream . . .
>
> Since when did Christ become yours? He is our flesh and blood. When you killed him he became yours. You claim all the Jews once you have put them to death. Jesus my brother! Drunken goyim cheapen your faith. Strangers disgrace you and your own people doesn't recognize you. I swear: let the whole world hear—I swear that you are ours.[13]

(These passages appear on the typescript of the play in Halpern's handwriting as inserts to the original script.) Inspired by the vision of "Jesus, my brother," Herbst tries to convert the local New York Jews who, however, failing to grasp the subtleties of his proselytizing, turn him into the martyr he seeks to be by pelting him with insults and blows. The play ends with Herbst on his deathbed, facing the same phantasmagoric procession of horrors that the poet-dreamer sees in Halpern's epic "A Night."

In writing of the cross, Nadir and Halpern were not exactly breaking new ground. Lamed Shapiro had sent shock waves through the Yiddish literary community in 1909 with a story called "The Cross," a Nietzschean study of a young Jew who transcends the pogrom violence and becomes a new type of man by showing himself equal to violence.[14] The cross haunted the Jewish imagination as symbol of a theory of love perverted into the practice of hate which the Jew was somehow challenged to redeem. The subject was of potential popular interest, especially in the anguished postwar atmosphere. Halpern's revisions, which pressed the action inward, away from the dramatic events into the confusion of the protagonist's mind, clearly ruined whatever chances the play might have had for theatrical success. By collapsing the distinction between himself and the world, a technique that characterized expressionist poetry, Halpern turned the drama into a poetic medium, a condition for which the American Yiddish stage of 1920 was not yet prepared. The internalization of violence also ruined whatever chances the character might have had of regaining his psychological balance: there was no way out of the dilemma that the Christian world had forged for the Jew. If he is simply a Jew, he is killed for his sin, and if he tries to be a real Christian, practicing selfless love, he is victimized by forces that cannot tolerate a prophet of goodness. The conclusion of the drama, like that of "A Night," shows the depth of Halpern's demoralization in his struggle with this painful theme.

The founding of the Communist newspaper *Freiheit* (Freedom) in the spring of 1922 was for Halpern the answer to a dream or, more accurately, the end of this nightmare. The presence of a radical Yiddish newspaper meant that he would no longer have to choose between the destructive and creative impulses but could unite the two in an outlet that represented just this combination. As a prorevolutionary paper, *Freiheit* invited criticism of capitalist society in the name of the new world order that would emerge from its ruins. As a meeting place for radical intellectuals, it determined to appeal to the better sort of reader, the same audience that the little magazines of the Yunge had targeted for themselves. Thus, for the first and only time in his life, Halpern was able to enter into an economic arrangement with a newspaper without compromising his integrity, and to yoke the idealistic and iconoclastic elements in his character to what seemed to him healthy artistic goals.

Freiheit opened an entirely new chapter in Jewish cultural history. The newspaper was established following intense factional rivalry within the American Left between outright supporters of the Bolshevik revolution and other supporters of socialism who wanted to pursue the class struggle within their own national frameworks. In practical terms the argument came down to how much power would be accorded the Comintern, Lenin's Third International, which ruled that its decisions must be binding on all constituent parties, and how much autonomy would be maintained by local

American organizations. When *Freiheit* was founded, its sponsor, the Jewish section of the Workers' Party of America, still upheld an open policy of collaboration and cooperation with non-Communists, and the first editorial board was composed of equal representation from Communists and non-Communists. During its first eighteen months, when the newspaper remained editorially independent of Moscow, writers with broad sympathies for the movement were invited to contribute without having to adhere to the party line.[15]

The Russian revolution exerted a powerful influence on American Yiddish writers and intellectuals, Halpern among them. Though most of them remained unaffiliated with the Communist Party, they were attracted by the promise of the new state in Russia, which at least claimed to be striving toward the perfectibility of human society. They were also grateful to Lenin for outlawing antisemitism and to the Red Army for smothering the Ukrainian pogroms that had claimed an estimated 100,000 Jewish lives by 1921.

The editors of *Freiheit* offered other cultural inducements for joining their group. They boasted of their "high regard for Yiddish" as confirmed by a decision to use modern Yiddish orthography and to strike a higher literary level. One of the editors explained their appeal: "The seeming resurgence of Yiddish culture in Russia, actively supported by a friendly government, helped induce in the American Yiddish poets and writers a feeling that they were actually cooperating with the cultural efforts in Russia. They regarded their work on *Freiheit* as a bridge to reach the isolated three million Soviet Jews."[16]

Halpern's early association with the newspaper coincided with and was a contributing factor to the happiest period of his life. He had a small and, at least in theory, steady income—$30 every two weeks—and a constant incentive to write and publish. The editors, for their part, knew that the reputation of such an unreconstructed individualist as Halpern would stimulate interest in their paper, advertise its openmindedness, and lend it literary prestige. Halpern's importance to the paper is demonstrated by the prominence given to his poem, "Jew, My Brother" (an echo of Herbst's "Jesus, my brother") in its first issue of April 2, 1922.

—Jew, my brother, tell me if you know
what is noble?
—Goy, my brother,
not the child and madonna on canvas paint
nor the golden robe on priestly saint
but the forever-grimy-laboring hide
of you, of you and your wife and child—
that is noble.[17]

In this homey catechism, the morally informed Jew teaches his brother gentile that the body is nobler than the soul, the peasant than the mighty king, the laborer than the cleric. He parts company with the social ideologues, however, in the final stanza, which responds to the gentile's unlikely question, "Is killing allowed?"

—Goy, my brother,
when you have the enemy in your hands,
turn your sword away from where he stands.
But if your brother turns from you instead
when the enemy's sword hangs over your head,
give him to the wolves to devour.

Is this Communism or Christianity? Perhaps Halpern's vision of the good man owes something to nineteenth-century communitarian idealism, but not to the Leninist vision of the urban proletariat. The very juxtaposition of the words "Jew" and "Goy" must have made the editors very nervous, recalling as they did the national divisions and racial stereotypes that the Left was doing its best to minimize. From the beginning, Halpern confounded the expectations of the newspaper at least as vigorously as he served its purposes.

It was hardly unusual for intellectuals of Halpern's generation, especially those discouraged by the carnage of the world war, to yield to the bright vision of hope emanating from the Russian revolution. Perhaps the most talented prose writer among his contemporaries, David Bergelson, became a convert to the new ideology. A decade earlier, when he first appeared on the scene as a Yiddish writer, Bergelson used the decline of the Jewish shtetl as the literary representation of his pessimism. In 1918, still in this vein, he wrote a novel investigating and justifying the suicide of a young Russian Jew who could find no philosophic meaning in his life. Then in the early 1920s Bergelson experienced a change of heart. The model of Soviet society, as he observed it from his expatriate outpost in Berlin, persuaded him that the transformation of mankind was a reasonable prospect, requiring the wholehearted participation of the writer. Declaring himself "in harness" to the Communist program, he wrote a novel that justified the harsh application of the "letter of the law" to the process of collectivization in Russia. He eventually acted on these principles by moving back to the Soviet Union in 1933.[18]

Bergelson's conversion may be attributed, at least in part, to the exhausted writer's search for a new source of creative energy as a way out of numbing despair.[19] The same can be said of Halpern. He did not harness himself to any political ideal, and he stopped far short of expressing enthusiasm for the Soviet system—the rational faith of Communism could not tempt a spirit so skeptical as his. Yet he too was attracted by the destructive energy of Communism, which gave negation a sense of higher purpose, inviting the writer to rid civilization once and for all of false flags and causes.

The first casualty of the campaign for truth would have to be poetry itself, or at least the kind of poetry that sought to raise the human spirit to a nobler range of consciousness. Beauty, refinement, enchantment—these chimerical allures were a wicked distraction from reality. The poet lies when he tries to purify the common functions of life, as Mani Leib and Zishe Landau and the poets of quietude had been doing. Halpern wrote:

> There are people who maybe go on bragging
> That it's not nice to crowd around a wagon
> With onions, cucumbers, and plums.
> But if it's nice to schlepp in streets after a death wagon,
> Clad in black, and lament with eyes sagging,
> It is a sin to go on bragging
> That it's not nice to crowd around a wagon
> With onions, cucumbers, and plums.
>
> Perhaps one should not be so pushy, so attacking.
> One can, perhaps, crowd quietly around a wagon

With onions, cucumbers, and plums.
But if you cannot chase them even whip wagging,
Because earth's tyrant, our belly, nagging,
Wishes so—you must be evil to go on bragging
That it's not nice to crowd around a wagon
With onions, cucumbers, and plums.[20]

Dragging into his poem the cacophony of the marketplace, the poet hawks his wares like any vegetable monger who has to keep himself and his customers alive. How can the artist, because of his thin-skinned intolerance for noise and rudeness, deny the dominion of the stomach? The poet may be disheartened by the barbarity of the material struggle, but it forces its terms on him and on anyone who pretends to deal in truth.

Halpern's sense of reality coincided at this critical point with the newspaper's editorial thrust: the first step toward the realization of a new social order is the destruction of false beliefs. Having earlier resisted the withdrawal of the Yunge from *di masn in di gasn* (the masses in the streets), he now turned even farther away from idealism and its aesthetic goals. His poetic vocabulary, always plain, turned cruder. His poetic voice grew rough and loud in its passion for "justice" and "honesty." Halpern used his space in *Freiheit* to attack enshrined clichés with an inventiveness and anger that had never been heard before in Yiddish verse.

Zlochev, O my home, my town,
With a steeple, *shul* and bath,
Wives who sit in the market place
And little Jews who scramble like dogs
Around the peasant who's coming down
With a basket of eggs from the hill—
How life in the spring wakens in me
My poor little bit of yearning for thee—
My home, Zlochev.[21]

After World War I, with so many of the home communities fatally overrun by the invading armies of both sides, immigrants saw the chasm widening between themselves and their native lands. Expressions of yearning became a standard feature of Yiddish cabaret songs, fiction, plays, and the new art of film. Among poets, too, the lost life of the shtetl was a compelling subject.

Halpern's "Zlochev" tore away the gossamer veil of memory. If the Jews recalled the Jewish sanctity of their towns, Halpern's poem reminded them that the church always took precedence over the synagogue, which enjoyed no more privilege in the shtetl than it does in its undistinguished place in the second line of the poem. While other poets might linger over the figures of the miller and the rabbi, Halpern recalls the frantic tradespeople, the profiteering synagogue stalwart, the hypocrites and the sinners. Using the reference to his actual birthplace to establish his credentials as a truthteller, he clinches his denunciation of the double-dealing town with a revelation about the narrator's dubious origins:

> You are my witness. It really was so.
> When grandfather, helped by the police,
> Put my mother out of the house,
> My grandmother, on widespread feet,
> Simpered almost as honey-sweet
> As a peasant girl with two soldiers—
> Cursed be that hatred in me
> Which reminds me of her and of thee—
> My home, Zlochev.
>
> They stood in a ring, like naked Jews
> Around a scalded man in the bath
> Shaking their heads, stroking beards,
> At the thrown-out packs
> The rags and tatters in sacks
> And the broken remains of a bed—
> My mother still is crying in me,
> As that time, under heaven, in thee—
> My home, Zlochev.

Through broad hints and suggestive metaphors, the poet recreates the primal scene: his mother is thrown out of her parents' house and publicly humiliated for having stained the family honor. His grandparents seem to enjoy their daughter's shame. The embryonic child, a bastard, lives to bear witness to the ugly conditions of his birth and to avenge his parent by exposing her tormenters to the world.

> Yet the world is a wonderful thing.
> With horse and wagon over a field
> We dragged ourselves to a train
> That flies like a demon over the land
> Till it reaches a steerage that goes
> To downtown New York—
> This is the only solace to me:
> That I won't be buried in thee—
> My home, Zlochev.

The poet's only relief is that the society that spawned him cannot claim him. The songlike stanzas, with their refrain "My home, Zlochev," create the expectations of nostalgia, as in the popular Yiddish song "Mayn shtetele Belz," but only so that the anticipated pleasure can the more effectively be undercut.

Despite Halpern's allusion to his actual birthplace and his assurance that "it really was so," this episode conveys neither the facts nor the atmosphere of his home as he and others described it elsewhere. In a literal sense the scene is not true. And yet Halpern credited this episode with determining his literary role and the direction of all his future work. In a speech about himself that he took on the road to a number of Jewish communities, he again evoked this scene of a dispossessed pregnant woman. He was haunted, he said, by a cluster of words that demanded animation: *on, the ground, was, gentile, bride, infant, flax-merchant, beard and sidelocks, evil-spirit, trial, evening-red*. These terms—thirteen in Yiddish, including some contractions—claimed him as their mouthpiece, and despite (or because of) the offense to others, he had no choice but to tell their story:

> On the street outside, wearing a white dress and with large red paper flowers in her hair, sat a gentile bride weeping, with a circle of people around her.
>
> One of the onlookers, the hunchbacked tailor who did minor alterations for everyone in town, tried to comfort her.

"Don't cry," he said to her, "your fiancé will come back. He won't abandon you with that large belly."

My mother said nothing, but slowly helped the girl to her feet and holding her by the arm brought her into our woodshed where she gave birth. When she was asked whether someone should go for help to the flax-merchant in whose house she had served since childhood, the girl crossed herself and made a cross over her infant and cursed the merchant.

The town's fool, Tsemakh, a witness to all this, ran outside and began stopping strangers in the street, pleading with tears in his eyes that they wait for the child to grow a little older to see it acquire a beard and sidecurls, like the flax-merchant. Once the evidence was visible, they could summon him to a *beys-din* for trial.

And every time Tsemakh ended his story, he gave himself such a resounding thump on his naked breast that I began to fear him as much as I did the evil-spirit who, my mother told me, would come to choke me if I forgot a section of my prayers before going to sleep.

And from then on—

Like a beggar with fists full of coins, who begins to lose them when his memory fails, I have lost all the psalms I used to know by heart and all the prayers and blessings, and wherever I find a scrap of paper I write on it those accursed thirteen words: on the ground was gentile bride infant flax-merchant beard and sidelocks evil-spirit trial evening-red.[22]

Actual or not, this drama of injustice became Halpern's litany in place of all the old teachings. The pious flax merchant's seduction of his maid led to the destruction of the boy's faith. Quite a number of Halpern's scenarios seem to come, like this one, straight out of the pages of Haskalah satire, bridling with the discovery of iniquity and the assurance that the hypocrisy still present in a religious civilization is virtually bred by it. As Tsemakh pounds his breast in anguish, so Halpern in his poem on Zlochev transposes the tale of deceit, ascribing to his own kin the callous eviction of the pregnant woman and to himself the bastard's fate.

But Halpern is more than the conscience of the Jews. If the scene is of such importance to him it is because he can identify with every role. The pregnant humiliated bride served the poet as warning never to be taken in by the romance that obscures practical consequences. Both poetry and religion have in common the striving for perfection. Both create verbal representations of that perfection—

psalms, prayers, blessings, romantic verse—and ensnare innocents in their embrace. The betrayed bride is the symbolic mother of the Yiddish poet, who suffers the fate of a seduction similar to hers.

At the same time, Halpern can also identify with the flax merchant who exploits a girl without having to take responsibility for her. Poetry, too, is promise without obligation. The writer takes people in, both as subjects and as readers, without carrying the blame for any hardship that might befall them as a consequence. An active womanizer, before and after his marriage, Halpern incurred the seducer's guilt in his life and in his writing. If he was Tsemakh, the town fool, bearing lifelong witness to the hypocrisy of religion, he was also the abandoned bride and not least of all the flax merchant, fully implicated in the evil he was exposing. It is doubtful whether the *Freiheit* audience caught all the facets of this autobiography, but since his attacks on false religion, and on nostalgia for it, bolstered the forward-looking posture of the movement, Halpern's work was at first welcomed with little scrutiny.

Under informal contract to the newspaper to produce a couple of items a week, Halpern felt free to try his hand at everything. In theater and book reviews he lashed out at the failures of his contemporaries, trying to establish criteria for a strong culture by exposing weakness. An inferior item he would dismiss in a few scathing lines; he complained that a folk tragedy called *Oaks* constituted an insult to trees.[23] But whenever a play or poem threatened to seduce its audience into some form of idealism, Halpern became alert to the danger, as if he feared its corrupting powers.

Indeed, much as he tried to camouflage his intensity, Halpern was charting an independent moral course through one essay after another. Since he always exaggerated and interrupted himself, used common language, and otherwise drew attention to his irresponsibility, he did not satisfy the expectations of either contemporary literary criticism or political debate, and almost invited dismissive disregard as Moishe Leib the Takhshit, the bratty showman. But like Tsemakh the fool, he could more easily say what he wished if he avoided being taken too seriously. Through comic keening—a little like Kolye Teper's "zigzaging" and very much in the style of the Viennese turn-of-the-century satirists—Halpern's style was a weapon for puncturing pretensions and dangerous illusions. In the autumn of 1923, for example, when the editor of *Freiheit*, Moisei Olgin, published a favorable review of the new Maurice Schwartz production *Shabtai Tsvi*, Halpern used the bulk of a tiny independent magazine he was editing at the time to attack both the reviewer and the play. Here Halpern certainly yielded to the compulsion to bite the hand that fed him, since Olgin was at least nominally his employer and Schwartz had hired him to do translations and occasionally lent him money.[24]

Maurice Schwartz, one of the most talented actor-directors in Yiddish theater, had taken over the Irving Place Theater in 1918 with an artistic platform that echoed the Yunge's principles of a decade earlier: "The theater must be a kind of holy place, where a festive and artistic atmosphere always reigns . . . a company of young artists who love beauty must strive to bring Yiddish theatre to beautiful fulfillment."[25] But Schwartz also understood box-office pressures, and he staged historical dramas like the story of the false Messiah, Shabtai Tsvi (who before converting to Islam in 1666 had inspired a wave of hope), because he knew that the tragic grandeur of the Jewish past would attract Yiddish theatergoers looking for some national satisfaction as part of their entertainment. The compelling faith of the messianic figure in the imminent return of the Jews to Eretz Yisroel was bound to remind the viewers of the political struggle of the Zionists in their own day.[26]

Halpern did not attack Schwartz's production for its artistic failure but rather for its success, fearful that its neomessianic appeal might become a new opiate of the people. He begins with disarming praise for Schwartz. Only the other day this great actor was treating him to French pastry and coffee at a café on 23rd Street, and then just a few blocks away, at the corner of Madison and 27th, he transforms himself into a God-intoxicated hero. Schwartz's artistic brilliance only adds to the problem: by breathing new life into the false idealism of the past, the actors may well resuscitate it. "So what if a man uses himself to symbolize a messianic figure like Shabtai Tsvi? What skill does this require if even a piece of wood, representing Jesus on the cross, does the same thing?" If wood can be worshiped as symbol of the Christian Messiah, then Schwartz ought to be ashamed for using himself to represent the Jewish Messiah, and

Olgin should certainly be embarrassed for having greeted Schwartz with almost the same enthusiasm that Christians show for Jesus:

> We must be hooligans, vandals—with stones in our hands if necessary—to drive out the Shabtai Tsvis. We must destroy those who cry, "Higher, and ever higher!" We must do just the opposite: bend the church-and-synagogue steeples till they point downward to the ground rather than up into the blue void. We don't want to soar or to win eternity in the world to come. We only want to prevent the dead from stealing the air we need to breath.[27]

If Maurice Schwartz's theatrics stir up a longing for grandeur, for missions and flags, then it is doubly culpable because it stimulates exactly what it should be helping to destroy.

Halpern's gibes against the Yunge were of the same order. In a piece called "What Do the Aesthetes Want?" he has their spokesman say, "I want the words that we sing out of ourselves to be as delicate as church carvings in the Middle Ages and as pure as the yearning of a flutist in the evening." Halpern locates this conversation between himself and a delicate colleague on a subway train punctuated by noisy stops and starts, and by repeating the aesthete's remark to a housepainter sitting beside him in overalls smudged with brickdust and soot, he points up its contextual absurdity. The housepainter moves nervously away along the bench. Halpern says he would have done better to ask the man whether he was looking forward to a hot bath.[28]

The desperation of Halpern's argument with the aesthetes and the theatrical fabricators can only have had its source in his own susceptibility to illusion. It was he who dressed as an aristocrat on a pauper's budget. It was he who could never stoop to the ordinariness of a steady job or family life. But if he could not make his peace with drabness, neither would he contribute to the corruption of men by urging upon them a myth of noble labor, perfect beauty, national reawakening, or human perfectibility. The flax merchant would never again be able to mask his lust once piety and propriety were made permanently suspect.

In the political climate of the time, Halpern's belligerent anti-idealism made him the leading example of the "proletarian poet," and it was in this role that *Freiheit* sent him on a series of speaking

tours to the major Jewish communities of North America: Roches-
ter, Boston, Philadelphia, Detroit, Cleveland, Chicago, Winnipeg,
Toronto, Montreal. In each city Halpern was welcomed by groups
or committees of readers and party enthusiasts who sponsored his
official lectures and organized informal gatherings in his honor. The
income from the lecture tours helped to pay the rent and support his
family, which expanded with the birth of a son, Isaac, in July 1923.[29]
The tours were also an important outlet for his restlessness: he
could play the gay blade, and his well-attended lectures confirmed
that he and his poetry were awaited by a vital young readership. In
New York, though he was eagerly welcomed whenever he did make
his way to the literary mecca, the Café Royale, he sometimes could
not get into the city from his home in Coney Island for weeks at a
time. On the road he could stay up nights among admirers, dis-
cussing poetry and politics, flirting, enjoying a respite from poverty
and domesticity.

From the point of view of the audiences, the periodic visits of
Yiddish poets helped to create the sense of a living American Yid-
dish culture as the printed word alone could not have done. Sitting
in a crowded hall, listening to Halpern lecture on "Modern Yiddish
Literature" or "The Proletarian Poet," ordinary Jews felt them-
selves part of an organic linguistic community that had taken root in
America. As the Jewish preachers, the *magidim*, were once the peri-
patetic interpreters of tradition, so the Yiddish writers were now the
traveling promoters of the texts and ideas of an emerging secular
culture.[30]

Halpern was fortunate in finding warm supporters in a number of
cities—an architect in Detroit, a builder in Chicago, and the owner
of a shoe store in Cleveland. The latter, Yosl (Joseph) Drost, was an
immigrant with no formal education beyond the cheder, but he
loved literature with an intensity that occasionally eclipsed even
family and work. From their first meeting in 1922, when Halpern
paid his first visit to Cleveland, Drost looked after the poet, sending
him money, shoes and clothing, and sound advice. He undertook
the publication of Halpern's second book of poetry, *Di goldene pave*
(The Golden Peacock), which was paid for and handsomely put out
by Drost's cultural committee. Halpern reciprocated as he could,
inviting the Drosts to stay with him in New York and drawing

Drost's portrait. When Drost occasionally complained that he didn't understand a poem, Halpern replied with far more patience than he ever showed his critics or editors. And it is to Drost that we owe most of what we know about Halpern's life during the 1920s. He collected Halpern's letters, certain that he was preserving greatness for posterity, and through them we catch a glimpse of the difficulties in which that greatness sustained itself.

In the person of Drost, a typical *Freiheit* subscriber at the time of the newspaper's founding, Halpern had an inspiring example of his potential reader. The product of a religious upbringing who brought to secular texts the reverence he had been taught to show the sacred, Drost shared with Halpern the conviction that the poet was the most trustworthy interpreter of values in the modern age. The seriousness of his expectations could also pose a problem: Drost was occasionally baffled by what he considered to be unnecessarily difficult in Halpern's work. Why did Halpern have to complicate verse beyond the understanding of a fairly intelligent Yiddish reader who felt an uncommon devotion for poetry? And if Drost, who admired and loved Halpern, took offense at the incomprehensibility of the work, one is not surprised by the resentment of other readers and editors.

The first open clash between Halpern and *Freiheit* came not over his politics (though his anti-Christian sentiments made the editors uneasy) but over the nature of his art. In the spring of 1923 the newspaper ran a public forum on the question of Halpern's *grobe reyd*, his coarse diction, which seemed to insult readers and overturn the decorum of poetry. As a proletarian organ, the paper said it welcomed literary realism and considered Halpern's plain speech proof of his working-class solidarity. Although the moderator of the symposium, editor P. Novick, distinguished his own misgivings from the attacks of bourgeois critics, "those professional connoisseurs with fish oil in their veins who accuse Halpern of writing poverty-row verse," he too raised questions about his contributor's vulgarity, wanting to know why the poet had to stretch the definition of earthiness to include its refuse.[31]

Novick did not note specific examples of Halpern's insulting language, but he could have taken his pick from almost any poem, such as this one that had appeared a short time before:

So this bird comes, and under his wing is a crutch,
And he asks why I keep my door on the latch;
So I tell him that right outside the gate
Many robbers watch and wait
To get at the hidden bit of cheese,
Under my ass, behind my knees.[32]

The poem, to which Halpern later gave the title "The Bird," is a trenchant parody of the immigrant condition. It recounts the conversation through a keyhole between a bird, crippled during his recent trans-Atlantic crossing in steerage, and the nervous local resident whose hospitality he has come to seek. By the time the poem ends, ten stanzas and seven years later, the bird is still trying to force his way in, and the barricaded proprietor is still guarding his precious hoard in his special hiding place. Compressing fantasy and social reality, the poem slips toward the scatalogical in its dramatization of human greed.

Halpern organizes his playful scenario with great ingenuity. This immigrant Jewish bird vulgarizes two literary traditions at once: the haunting power of the native American tradition of poetry, as it can be heard in Edgar Allan Poe's "The Raven," and the softer music of Yiddish folksong, whose symbol is the Golden Peacock. Raven and Peacock, splendid emblems of two mighty streams of music of the past, are here reduced to a crippled mutation. The poem offends its noble antecedents and the bird his would-be host with just the same cranky chutspa. The nasty image of the hoarder, hiding his treasure under his ass (more pronounced in the original where the word always falls in the final rhyming position of the stanza), is indeed an instance of vulgar usage, but the intention is to disturb the reader. The crude diction belongs to a coarsened people. It marks the reduction of civility to this grotesque stand-off between two deracinated creatures.

In the newspaper's forum of 1923, the debate over Halpern's language was carried on in general terms with no such contextual considerations. Where was the poet's higher vision of man? Why did the poet have to upset his readers? Although the editor tried to distinguish his criticism from the aestheticist pretensions of critics, the Left proved quite as prudish as the Right, objecting in the name of class discipline to what bourgeois readers labeled bad taste. Halpern struck the kind of pose he often assumed when talking about poetry and railed against those who wished to tame him: "I refuse to be a poet if poetry is synonymous with beauty . . . If a poem can't justifiably express disgust or hatred—who needs it?!" When you live among deafening elevated trains and tenements that blot out the sky, you cannot be expected to sing of the holy temples and fairy princesses. The early Hebrew and Yiddish poets wanted to prettify their dismal lives with flowery language, but that was false, and whatever is false is truly vulgar.[33] In the context of this debate, Halpern published one of his most provocative poems, "The Moralizer and the False Poet," in which he writes:

> I know they will say, Moishe Leib is coarse,
> If he were to mention an unclean place
> But—God forgive him—what is he to do
> If their shouting does give off the true
> Stench of an unclean place?[34]

The debate brought a flood of mail from readers. Halpern was becoming something of a household name as a result of his newspaper connection. Even the painter who came to touch up his apartment turned out to be one of his admirers. But despite their strong identification with his work, readers did not always grasp its quality. "Halpern is the true workers's poet," said one, and "Let him keep telling the truth," said another, "since all the poets before him obviously failed to elevate mankind." "There is no vulgarity," granted a third, "but why is Halpern's work so hard to understand, sometimes virtually incomprehensible?" "Let him punish us, by all means," agreed a fourth, "but the poetry is so difficult. Who can tell what it is that he is flogging?"[35]

Almost without exception, readers were prepared to accept literary coarseness on the grounds of honesty ("Tolstoy said that the more we devote ourselves to beauty, the farther we get from truth"). They could not justify, however, the difficulty of the verse that put it beyond their reach. The insult, as readers perceived it, was not the poet's vulgarity or his rage but his literary modernism, the development of a private, disjunctive, and intricate web of images that did not present a clear sequence of thought. In fact, the poetry that Halpern published in *Freiheit* was considerably denser than anything he had published before. A visionary with a sharp pictorial imagination, he had begun to give freer rein to metaphors and similes that had an existence almost independent of the "plain meaning" of the text. In even a relatively simple work like "The Bird," the knot of fantasy and reality was daunting: it represented some kind of social commentary, but what in particular?

While the *Freiheit* editors couched their nervousness in questions of social value, some readers realized that Halpern was moving away from them. Because the words and the rhymes were simple, the tone so chatty, and images drawn from such familiar objects, it was all the more painful to acknowledge that one could not really understand what the poem meant. The debate over poetic diction confirmed the exceptional intimacy of American Yiddish culture of the 1920s. One can hardly imagine Ezra Pound trying to justify himself in the pages of a local daily for writing poetry beyond the grasp of its regular subscribers. But it showed too that no modernist poet could take his readership along with him, not even when he was otherwise so much a part of their way of life and so accessible to them on a daily basis.

Halpern's attitude toward modernism was painfully complex. Worried about losing touch with the housepainter in his spattered overalls, he was also mindful of the introspective (Inzikh) group of American Yiddish poets who announced their appearance on the literary scene in 1920 with a full-blown modernist manifesto. College-educated in America, familiar with Freudian theory and contemporary English poetry, and a decade or so younger than the Yunge, the Introspectivists were self-conscious about everything that separated them from the generation of Mani Leib and Halpern, and they challenged their elders in great theoretical detail.[36]

The early poetry of Jacob Glatstein, Aaron Leyeles, and N. B. Minkoff, closely linked to their program of *in zikh* (in the self), championed free verse and imagism. Associating received rhymes and rhythms with insincerity, they could not understand how a real poet could write one poem about the subway, another about the sand at the seashore in summer, and a third about his love for a girl —all in the same rhythm. In their attempt to articulate the poet's innermost voice, to filter reality through the prism of the psyche, they undertook to be as "kaleidoscopic, contradictory, unclear, and confusing" as would be necessary to achieve their artistic purpose.

Halpern's response to Jacob Glatstein's first book of poems records his ambivalence to modernist theory and practice. Attacking Glatstein with the gusto of a fighter who had finally found a worthy adversary, he points to certain foolish excesses. Pontius Pilate had only to wash his hands to show that he was through with someone, but Yankl, son of Reb Yitskhok—Glatstein's traditional Jewish designation—must go to much greater lengths: "I am the rustle of your mantle-hem / O Brahma / The echo of your melody at sunset / Your dream in a night of mist." The pretentious word specialist, the poet, is contrasted with the shopkeeper who sells a herring, perfectly sure of the words he utters: "It says on his register the herring costs seven cents. How coldly and calmly he speaks the words, the herring costs seven cents." The same technique Halpern used to deflate the aesthetes is here applied to their Introspectivist successors.[37]

But the reduction of Glatstein is not Halpern's aim. Once a few objections are out of the way, it is clear that he had discovered a genuine poet:

> I once read a story somewhere about an artist who lived in a forest. He showed a savage his life-sized painting of a man and asked for his opinion. The savage replied, "Dear sir, what will you do when you reach heaven after death and God asks you why you copied his creation without giving him a soul?" Yankl the son of Reb Yitskhok painted himself alive in the middle of the world with his whole bloodied soul: fire, blood, the rays of a dying sun for the light that burns around his eyes and heart.

As opposed to people who try with their whole beings to be poets and manage to produce only words stuck to paper, Glatstein is the real thing, although it is doubtful whether many readers understood Halpern's extraordinarily indirect way of saying so.

Halpern's approval of Glatstein is apparent not only in his adoption of the poet's fragmented images and the defense of his musical sound patterns, but in the unguarded excitement of this discovery. Here was a poet, one of a school of poets, who knew that the modern soul could only reveal itself in splinters, in contradiction and paradox. While Halpern would never acknowledge the theoretical basis of Introspectivism, his own crowded thoughts and feelings could no longer be rendered either in conventional poetic forms or in the kind of plain speech his newspaper readers craved. The Introspectivists sharpened Halpern's taste for experimentation; the paper tried to dull it.

From a political point of view, Halpern's complexity was a good protective device. As long as the paper tolerated ideological irregularity and he did not openly defy its positions, he could retain both his independence and his job. The official Communist statement on the question of Halpern's vulgar usage came in the form of a letter from the Moscow correspondent, Moishe Taytsh, who declared that Halpern's poems were harbingers of the revolution about to take place in America. Taytsh explained that, just as Russian poetry was coarse and intemperate prior to the revolution, so now in America "the masks are being torn away, the play with silver-paper swords has ended, and the true battle has begun—a battle smelling of real hatred, real enmity, and real blood. Here is the joyous moment when literature almost merges with real life." Halpern was the American Mayakovsky: how could language fail to be vulgar in revolutionary times?[38]

But underlying the intricacy and the belligerence of Halpern's work was an emotional and philosophic complexity that was bound to come into conflict, sooner or later, with the purposeful politics of *Freiheit*. Although the editors were prepared to accept Halpern's deviations and excesses as perhaps a valid expression of the temper of the times, they could not admit the pessimistic appraisal of humankind that increasingly dictated his choice of idiom and subject. Halpern might share his sponsors' distaste for the American system, but his distrust extended to every other political system as well. His ability to hear "the sound of bones rotting in the earth / and the worms digging their way into my heart" induced scorn for all absolute claims and for all schemes of conquest. Here is his "The Tale of the World":

> I ordain the conquering of the world
> —So the great king said,
> And all the people were duly informed,
> And all the mothers truly mourned

Their living sons as though dead.
But the plow in the field,
And the cobbler's leather sole,
And the mouse in his hole,
Laughed without sound
When the news was brought round,
The bad, black news.

Now the world has been conquered at last.
What's to be done with the thing?
The Royal Palace is far too small
—They forgot to measure the world at all
When designing the opening.
But the plow in the field,
And the cobbler's leather sole,
And the mouse in his hole,
Laughed till they cried,
Laughed so hard in their pride
That the king's crown was shaken.

The courtiers, meanwhile, hold that the world
Should be kept out there under guard.
But the king has turned a deathly gray,
Fearing the world will get wet some day
When the rain falls hard.
But the plow in the field,
And the cobbler's leather sole,
And the mouse in his hole,
Laugh till they cry,
Laugh till they nearly die.
The world's still there, outside.[39]

—ikh bafel men zol aynemen di velt,
hot der kinig gezogt.
iz dos land gevoyr gevorn der fun,
hot di mame ir lebedikn zun
vi an emesn toytn baklogt.
ober dos akerayzn in feld,
un di moyz in kamer

un di zoyl untern shusters hamer,
hobn shtilerheyt gelakht
ven men hot zey di bsure gebrakht—
di dozike finstere bsure.

itst hot men shoyn ayngenumen di velt.
vos zol men ton mit ir?
zi kon nisht arayn in dem kinigs shlos.
men hot fargesn tsu nemen a mos
fun der velt—ven men hot gemakht di tir.
ober dos akerayzn in feld,
un di zoyl untern shusters hamer,
un di moyz in kamer,
kayklen zikh far gelekhter shoyn.
se tsitert azh bay dem kinig di kroyn
fun zeyer farshayt gelekhter.

di hoyflayt meynen, di velt zol dervayl
a bavakhte in droysn shteyn.
nor der kinig iz vi der toyt azoy blas.
er hot moyre di velt kon nokh vern nas
ven es vet a regn geyn.
ober dos akerayzn in feld,
un di zoyl untern shusters hamer,
un di moyz in kamer,
lakhn azoy, az es iz shoyn a shrek.
zey shtarbn shir far gelekhter avek,
vos di velt shteyt nokh alts in droysn.

Reality by its very nature defies metaphysical schematization, and the spirit most attuned to nature must be duly profane. In a sense, *Der kibitser*'s art of deflation is ideally wedded in this poem to the political struggle against imperialism. The triumph of the domestic creature over the tyrant seems to represent a clear victory for the oppressed. Yet the king in this tale is laughed off the stage of history not, as we might think from the first stanza, because plow, leather sole, and mouse promise to introduce an improved society but because the timeless biological aspects of life that they embody will forever resist any attempt to "bring them indoors," to fix them inside any theory or social order. While Halpern continued to enjoy the Communists' energy of opposition to kingship and courts, he was never politically reliable, turning his irrepressible mockery against his employers almost as a matter of artistic honor.

After a time, the editors had to acknowledge that they found their prize poet disturbing. His protest against injustice and inequity, instead of stopping at the appointed targets, marched right on, as if drawing attention to its own absurdity.

> The sack is ready. The corn thrives in the field—
> Enough for everyone who labors in the world.
> But when the *porits* exchanges corn for gold
> The sack lies empty in every house.
> And if the peasant has a wife and children
> And if they're hungry but there is no bread
> No wonder that he attends to their need
> And comes to town to steal your bread.
> And when he sees the golden chain
> Aristocratically across your stomach draped
> No wonder that he steals it too.

So far and for a few lines more, we have the prescriptive formula of the revolution's cause and effect: the exploitative and greedy Polish landowner, the *porits*, triggers off the peasant's inevitable, apparently justifiable reaction. These are the simple terms and formulas of Communist agitation propaganda. Having thus presented the issue, however, Halpern extends the argument of cause and effect— pretending to follow the rational sequence to its conclusion, he explodes all our expectations.

> And if the goy has a wife and children in the village
> And if his stove is icy and there is no wood—
> No wonder, then, he comes to you
> And splits open your window and door for wood.
> And if you thrust your hands in the path of his ax
> The wood-hacking goy can't watch out for you.
> And when you lie on the ground, hands severed, dead,
> And your blood on the ground runs flaming red—

No wonder, then, he splits your head
As he would a fallen log in the woods.
And if your screaming child has a head like you—
No wonder, then, he chops off that one too.[40]

The poet and the goy with the ax both refuse to stop at the limits of reason, at the historical consummation of current ideology. They go on cutting away, uncovering with blood the irrational forces that govern man, for which political explanations are so pitifully inadequate. Halpern turns the pieties of the new religion inside out, using the propagandistic language of class conflict to ridicule its oversimplification, the scenario of Communist revolution to show real violence trampling dialectics underfoot, as real peasants deviated from the revolutionary scenario to smash the heads of Jewish infants.

Halpern's aggression could not be contained. The conflict between those who claimed the moral right to power and the entrenched bourgeoisie was for him essentially a battle over a piece of rotting cheese, both sides victimized by different kinds of greed. Halpern could no more swallow the rational claims of Marxism than he could countenance the mystical promise of Jewish messianism. The more dogmatic *Freiheit* became, the more dramatically Halpern sought freedom from its certainties. But the final break was still to come. In November 1923, to celebrate Halpern's fifteenth year as a poet, the newspaper organized a banquet in Arlington Hall, which Halpern considered a great moral success.[41] According to the young poet Meir Shtiker, in these years between 1922 and 1924 Halpern was "the king of *Freiheit*."[42]

By the end of 1923, Halpern was eager to put out a second collection of his poems. With the help of Yosl Drost, he prepared the manuscript and supervised the details of publication, including illustrations by his friend Yosl Kotler. He took most of the poems from the pages of *Freiheit* but organized and revised them carefully, as he had done with *In New York*. As it turned out, *Di goldene pave* was to be his last book: Halpern would never again enjoy the kind of support and composure necessary for such a large project. Pouncing on the shrillest parts of the volume, some critics crowed that Halpern's association with *Freiheit* had ruined him as a poet and turned him into a sloganeer. They pointed to some of the intemperate assaults in the middle sections of the book on "the God-accursed intellectual / with the loathesome pair of white hands / that don't want to work" as proof of his publicistic crudeness. But taken as a whole the volume is much more reflective and personal than the earlier collection. It is consecrated to the singer who has somehow to strum out, on a rough and clumsy instrument, his awakened longing for the abandoned home and the strange rhythms of his new land. There are many representations of him in the book.

Halpern's first book, from its opening parody of the garden of Eden, fashioned a composite review of immigrant life in New York. The title of this second book, *The Golden Peacock*, hearkens back to the traditional splendor of Yiddish verse. It recalls the fabled bird of the Yiddish folksong that flew off to a distant land, losing on the way one of its precious golden feathers, a haunting symbol of yearning and undying love. "The Bird" of Halpern's version is, as we have seen, quite a different sort of creature. He loses one of his legs and eats it during his ocean crossing to ward off starvation. Yet this hobbled beggar does not even arouse our sympathy; his sob story is too glib to be trusted, the song as debased as its subjects.

Halpern's New World bestiary is filled with insects. It is a fly, for example, the lowest mutation of the winged bird, who takes up the ancient national dirge:

> Evening sun.
> And, in evening cold, all the flies
> In the corners of the panes are numb,
> If not already dead.
> On the rim of a water glass, the last
> Is alone in the whole house.
> I speak:
> "Dear fly,
> Sing something of your far-off land."
> I hear her weep—She answers:
> May her right leg wither
> If she plucks a harp
> By strange waters,

Or forgets the dear dung heap
That had once been her homeland.[43]

The evening sun (evening-red, one of Halpern's thirteen haunting
terms) has by now reduced the world, in this grotesque miniature of
it, to a mortuary. In the mouth of this moribund fly the mighty
137th Psalm, vowing eternal fealty to Jerusalem, is unmasked as a
misguided instinct. Generations of Jewish singers were inspired by
the dream of an end to exile, which meant, for some, a return to the
city of David and Solomon, to others the redemptive promise of the
messianic age. But the whine of the fly, a derivative bit of nostalgia
for something that does not bear remembering, casts powers of
memory in a strange evening light. Her sole source of remain-
ing dignity, like that of the Jews in Babylonian exile, is her refusal to
sing on cue. She may thus be nobler than the American Yiddish
poet.

Throughout this disturbing book of Halpern's, the displacement
of the Jew, the immigrant, the poet, unveils the dislocation of man in
the universe, an ontology of homelessness. Estrangement gives the
singer a strange view of what used to be familiar. A starving man
wonders why God should continue laying His daily sun every day,
the way the hen he is too poor to own lays its daily egg. A victim of
violence interprets the Gospels as the story of a little devil who
arranges the fresh corpses of men with the same buoyancy that the
son of God or an ordinary baker sets out his loaves of bread. Inner
distance renders the familiar grotesque:

> Man, that ape, the first time in his life
> He sees an elephant at night,
> In all that darkness, the elephant's
> Wearing, it seems, a pair of pants.
> He broods about this for a while,
> Then from some fig leaves, constructs a pair
> Of pants, a pull-over, and underwear,
> A shirt and shoes and then a hat,
> And a skullcap for wearing under that.
> Man, that ape.[44]

Once they are no longer sustained by faith or habit, human deeds and aspirations assume a farcical shape.

Halpern's imagination worked best in opposition, and there are signs in this book that he was pitting himself quite deliberately against Mani Leib. Certainly Halpern's ballads and the section called "From My Slavic Motifs" recall the very different *Jewish and Slavic Motifs* that were then consolidating Mani Leib's reputation in Poland and Russia. Halpern's themes of cheating and deception, mutual distrust and exploitation, evoke a corrupt past. The neighboring peasant was a lout "who's got himself an alehouse / where he whoops it up and drinks / a churchhouse where he supplicates and stinks / and that's all he needs."[45] His own little portrait of a family by lamplight shows a bloodied Jewish widower and his child among their smashed possessions crying over the murdered woman at their feet.[46] The decorative features of this poem are not *blimelekh krentsel-ekh*, the pretty frost flowers on the windowpanes in the ballads of Mani Leib, but the night seen through broken shards of glass in the crooked windows "that bring to mind nothing—the eternal nothing that waits for us everywhere in the dark."

The most sustained character of this book, subject of a long final section that takes up more than a quarter of the whole, is a certain Zarkhi, also a species of singer, who stands on the ocean shore with a pipe in his mouth, ruminating or strumming out his sorrow on an instrument he fashioned from a tin pan and three rubber bands. The thirty-eight poems of the cycle, "Zarkhi at the Seashore," are divided into twelve uneven sections, beginning with a series, "Zarkhi to Himself," and concluding after Zarkhi's burial in 1923 in the "holy Jewish community of New York." At times Zarkhi appears to be the final manifestation of the diaspora musician, epigone of a tradition that reaches back to the shores of Babylon but is now unceremoniously dying. He is the descendent of those who crossed the Red Sea with Moses into the desert, but Halpern identifies him more with those who danced around the golden calf than with those who stood awestruck before the granting of the Law. T. S. Eliot's diminished hero, J. Alfred Prufrock, retains a whiff of former glory because his creator admires the Christian civilization of which his protagonist is the pallid, late specimen. But Zarkhi lacks even that much fallen grace. Halpern regards Zarkhi's inherited culture of Torah wisdom and martyrology with less than perfect respect.

Halpern had thought of making Zarkhi the leading figure of an experimental novel.[47] In the few extant episodes of this work, Zarkhi hopelessly pursues an unprepossessing woman named Myrtle, who mocks his advances and the holes in his bathing trunks. He blames his woes on the ocean: its saline water has eaten even through its wooly protection. Philosopher and clown, Zarkhi is a familiar Jewish literary type, but Halpern did not seem able to develop a romantic plot to sustain a long work of fiction. Instead, abandoning the prose experiment after several chapters, he made Zarkhi the cornerstone of his longest cycle of poems.

The Zarkhi of Halpern's poem cycle, no longer a suitor, is a poet, who tries to build a bridge of longing across the ocean in his first song and, in his last, listens from beyond this life to the waves washing up green slime on the shore. In between, he imitates and parodies the whole Jewish literary inventory, from the biblical narrative as he learned it from his grandfather, through adventure tales and prayers and samples of Talmudic exegesis, to modern Yiddish poetry. Zarkhi's range of feeling is as wide as his repertoire; he is reverent, pious, childlike, wistful, angry, despondent, funny, tired. The final word is never uttered because Zarkhi is never sure of himself, not even in his mockery:

> Or maybe—who knows?
> Maybe it means something altogether different
> And my tongue will roast in hell
> For not interpreting it well.[48]

Halpern obviously invested a lot of himself in this troubled figure, but he also kept a humorous distance from the character, whose improbable name he may have borrowed from one of the Coney Island neighborhood peddlers or from a story about an "extra man" that Herman Gold had published years earlier in *Literatur*.[49]

Humor, as always, is one of Halpern's major sources of relief from basic sorrow. Rage is another. Critics who drew attention to the book's shrillness failed to note the welcome relief provided by these punctuations of anger. At least in the heat of his anger, the speaker seems connected to the world. Some of the poems are indeed unpleasant, and their vulgarity is not always justified by the artistic use to which it is put, but the speaker's passion reestablishes the possibility of human engagement, which is frighteningly absent elsewhere in the book.

Yet a third form of relief from the book's climate of exile is the quiet presence, here and there, of the poet's wife, one of the loveliest depictions in Yiddish poetry, and of his son, a fixed point of affection. The wife of the poems is very much like the descriptions we have of Halpern's wife Royzele—diminuitive, blond, gentle, and loving. The son is an obvious projection of the poet's fears and ambitions, barely out of the cradle and already, in a poem Halpern wrote not long after the boy was born, the addressee of an ethical will. While it is always dangerous to infer from an artist's work any facts about his life, Halpern obviously chose to present his family as a *mokm miklat*, a sanctuary from the inhospitable world outside.

Those who knew Halpern only in public as the rakish seducer or the rude artist could never understand what he had in common with the shy and delicate woman he married. His friends observed his extraordinary tenderness toward this apparently fragile woman and the pleasure he took in protecting her. Halpern designed clothes for his wife and decorated their household objects—chairs, wooden bowls, crates—with saucy pictures of Eden and naughty nuns. He tried to shield her from his own failings as much as he was able, and made sure to be home at difficult times, as when she was weaning the baby.[50] When he fell sick once during an extended trip to the Midwest, he invented an elaborate lie so that Royzele would not know he was in the hospital. Halpern took his role of provider seriously and fretted when he could not fulfill it as he should. "I don't worry much about myself," he wrote from the hospital, "sooner or later —it's all the same. But I love my wife and child and I can't bear even the thought that they will have to suffer."[51] From the moment of his son's birth, he loved the boy intensely, observing him at close range since his desk was for a long time in the baby's room. As Isaac grew, Halpern treated the boy as a companion, taking great pride in the liveliness of his mind. Friends joked that a simple inquiry about the boy would elicit an unbroken monologue on his latest achievements.[52] Isaac figures as the conscience, or the redemptive possibility, in some of Halpern's best poems.

Whenever wife and child appear in *The Golden Peacock*, the possibility of "home" is momentarily established. So it is when the poet writes a letter home from the road, describing his loneliness and expressing his impatience:

> Soon, soon, as I told you. Now I am more
> Than a thousand miles nearer you than before.
> Give my best to New York—a lousy town
> But not too bad, if you have someone there.[53]

These rare expressions of tenderness serve to remind us that the unruly and coarse figure who dominates the book has only adopted the wolf's disguise so that we should not see him trembling within it.

It is with the evocation of his wife that Halpern concludes this book of poetry and the cycle "Zarkhi at the Seashore," summoning her in as a partner in his work.

> So I ask my dear wife
> How to finish the affair
> Of my little booky—
> Says she: Let happiness leave on a train
> And wave back with a hanky.
> Says I: Hanky-panky
> Says she: Booky-shmooky
> And asks me whether I'd like
> With my coffee a cooky.
> Says I: Cooky-shmooky—
> And tell her to put a case on my pillow
> And not to play hooky.
> Says she: Hooky-shmooky.
> And tells me to repair her shoe
> By hook or by crooky.
> Says I: Crooky-shmooky.
> So she jumps up and points at my head:
> I am bald and spooky.

Says I:
Spooky-crooky-hooky-cooky-hanky-panky-booky-shmooky.
But she cannot say it as fast as I can, as fast as I can:
Spooky-crooky-hooky-cooky-hanky-panky-booky-shmooky.
So we laugh together
Laugh so nice.
Till she closes my eyes—
Closes my eyes.
And rocks me with a song of rain and light,
Rain and light,
That you sing to little children at night,
Children at night.[54]

Against all odds, the book's chronicle of homelessness and of a homeless poetry thus concludes in a mood of peaceful intimacy. Poetry is a children's game, quickened by love and laughter.

But it is not only the wife's presence that lightens this dark book in its last few pages. The poetic presence of Mani Leib is also palpable in the rhymes and images of the concluding lines. Whether consciously or not, when Halpern reached for a soothing effect, he found it in the peaceful cadences of Mani Leib's lullabies, his pictures of untroubled innocence and simplicity. Mani Leib's harmonies were as far as Halpern could get from the grating disjunctions of his own verse. The poetry of Mani Leib represented to Halpern the same kind of tranquility he found in his home, and he invoked it, as he invoked his wife, in order to bring his book to safe harbor.

6

Allure of the
Red-Haired Bride

W hen the Yunge wrote their memoirs or engaged in remi-
niscence, they liked to recall their childhood in the old
country and their frisky youth on the Lower East Side, but not
much about their lives thereafter. Dogged by financial worries and
personal problems and illness, they looked back fondly to the early
immigrant days when they launched their artistic revolution with all
the confidence of youth. They preferred to remember the heyday of
their common association rather than the adjustments they had to
make during the 1920s, when Yiddish began to decline in America
and the center of Yiddish literary culture shifted back once again to
Europe.

From a material standpoint, life in the newly reconstituted Polish
state after World War I was exceptionally difficult for the Jews. The
nationalist fervor of the Poles worked against the diverse ethnic
minorities, particularly against the Jews who had sunk deep roots in
the country over most of a millennium. From the peasants seeking
cooperative control over their agricultural output to the profes-
sionals and tradesmen in the cities who wanted to reduce competi-
tion, Poles resented the role that the Jews occupied in the country's
economy. Nationalist politics combined with older forms of reli-
gious antisemitism to isolate the Jews and prevent their absorption
into the now independent nation.

Yet the barriers to their political and economic progress stimulated the internal culture of Polish Jews. While the democratic process in America persuaded Jews to become part of the larger society, and the ideological reconstruction of the Soviet Union drew Russian Jews into the Communist mold, Polish nationalism forced other minorities in on themselves, stimulating among the Jews reflexively powerful national sentiments. The tightened immigration restrictions of the United States and the closed border with the Soviet Union left the Polish Jewish community with few attractive opportunities for emigration. One positive consequence of these social liabilities was a resurgence of Jewish culture, most of it in Yiddish.

Warsaw was the dominant though by no means the only center of Yiddish culture in Poland. In the early postwar years, the capital was flooded with Yiddish writers from Galicia and Russia who came to find out what was happening and to make themselves known. Much as the Yunge had come together after their immigration to New York, the poets Uri Tsvi Greenberg, Peretz Markish, Melekh Ravitch, and the writer I. J. Singer drew briefly together as the Khaliastre, the Gang, to put out cooperative miscellanies and little magazines. The poet Moishe Broderzon hailed this group that would take Yiddish poetry *per aspera ad astra*, and Ravitch himself, who had earlier wanted to come to America, said that to be a Yiddish writer in Warsaw after World War I was "to feel the Redemption at hand and to be at its center."[1]

There was also a surge of cultural energy across the border in the Soviet Union. Though thousands of Jews left Russia after the revolution and many Yiddish writers were driven out by sheer hunger, those who remained vigorously advocated a new literature in the spirit of the revolution. For some of these writers the Yunge epitomized the stale past. As the critic Nokhem Oyslender wrote to Leivick in 1924, describing a process that had already ended, "Our battle here in Moscow was often directed against you, just as your battle was once directed against Einhorn."[2] Leivick had identified David Einhorn as the representative lyrical poet whose personality never engages the reader, never stirs his blood. Soviet Yiddish literature had similarly declared itself in opposition to the unsatisfactory personalism of the Yunge. Now Moscow was feeling its ripening powers.

No one could say the same now for New York where, despite a much higher general standard of living and far greater prosperity, the Yiddish writers were experiencing a decline of influence and opportunity. It is hard to say which of the two poets struggled harder during the postwar decade—Moishe Leib Halpern, at the financial mercy of *Freiheit*, or Mani Leib, whose somewhat steadier income was still not enough to support his two families. Though neither writer was a stranger to feelings of loneliness and isolation, it was the deteriorating cultural atmosphere even more than their poverty that sapped their artistic energy.

Mani Leib's tempestuous romance at age thirty-five with Rochelle Weprinski and his decision to leave his wife and five children created great hardships. While Rochelle tried to support herself and her daughter with help from her former husband, Mani Leib maintained his first household and bore the final economic responsibility for both. During their life together Rochelle had five abortions, not because the couple did not want children of their own but because they knew they could not support any more.[3] (A mournful poem by Weprinski begins: "Unborn children cry from my slender limbs / Through my flesh they want to see the white world / And to blossom under the sun / With their curly heads.[4])

The consequences of their courtship were so dramatic that fifty years later Rochelle was moved to write a roman à clef to protect her memory of it. She wanted to show that both she and Mani Leib had despaired of their marriages long before they met one another, and that the love affair between the noted poet and his much younger admirer united two lonely, unhappy people. Flirtations were a commonplace of the literary cafés, but not the breakup of families with small children. While defending their love, Rochelle did not spare herself in describing the pain caused to parents on both sides, to brothers and sisters who felt that family sanctity was more important than "lust," to the deserted wife and the jilted husband, and above all to the children, the innocent victims.

The most startling scene in Weprinski's autobiographical novel *The Crossing of Hands* describes a visit of the deserted wife, with three of her children to the home of her rival. Miriam, Rochelle's counterpart in the novel, has moved in temporarily with her brother and mother, neither of whom understands or approves her love affair with the older poet. Crying, "Give me back my husband! A decent human being doesn't steal a husband from his wife, a father from his children," the distraught wife appeals to Miriam's mother, alternating between tears and threats in an attempt to win the family's support. (We recognize in this passage the quiet homebody of Iceland's memoir who suddenly erupts in anger.) Miriam's mother looks at her daughter with angry shame.[5] Though she feels no connection between herself and the disheveled housewife who has come to curse her, Miriam sees her lover's eyes staring up at her from the face of his unhappy son. Guilt poisons her love. Mani Leib did not formally divorce his wife, but neither did he visit her. He was always in touch with his children, but these relations were strained by their resentment of his defection and of the woman their mother blamed for all her grief. The new liaison perched precariously over the broken marriage, the shreds of which were never really cleared away.

In the autumn of 1919 Mani Leib fell sick with what may have been his first bout of tuberculosis, an affliction so common in the immigrant community that it was called "the Jewish disease."[6] In the following years, whenever he was well, he worked at two jobs, in the shoe factories and at *Forverts*, where Cahan kept him on a small but steady retainer. Early Saturday afternoons, when he finished the last factory shift of the week, he would meet his older daughters at the foot of the Brooklyn Bridge. He took them shopping for a few things they needed, bought them sandwiches, and gave them the money for rent and food so that he would not have to confront his wife.[7]

Rochelle's health was also poor. Even if she was technically innocent of the charge of breaking up a family, she could not escape the censure of those around her. Her already delicate health was worsened by the practical worries and emotional strain of becoming a poet's unwedded wife. She was also a budding poet, attracted to Mani Leib at least in part because of his literary stature. In a paternal sort of way he encouraged her writing and took pride when she succeeded in getting her poetry published. As she became acquainted with the writers and editors who frequented the literary cafés, she gained access to the pages of local magazines, but this inside track cost her something in independence; later she complained of the problems of women poets who were married to male poets. Her admiration for Mani Leib and her role as the consort of a noted poet conflicted with her own poetic ambitions.

She might have hoped for some help from Anna Margolin, the very talented poet now married to Mani Leib's colleague Reuben Iceland. Margolin expressed her dissatisfaction with the major Yiddish journals for their neglect of serious poetry by putting out a private anthology, *The Yiddish Poem in America, 1923*.[8] She evidently intended to make her own annual selection of the year's best verse. Margolin favored younger poets but among the women she included in her selection only Celia Dropkin, who was associated with the Introspectivists and wrote a much more modern, self-revelatory kind of verse than Weprinski's. Whatever expectations Weprinski may have had of either personal or literary friendship with the older poet were soon dashed, in any case, by Margolin's high-handed treatment of literary wives, from whom she expected not comradeship but homage.[9]

The periodic illnesses of Mani Leib and Rochelle Weprinski complicated their attempt to set up a home. When one of them was sick, the other was forced to give up their rented apartment and find temporary shelter with friends or family. Mani Leib was edgy about not having the time and peace of mind to write. He wrote to Ravitch, "I publish weekly poems in *Forverts* and you can understand what sort of poems it is possible to write on weekly demand!"[10] Many of the poems he did write conveyed the heavy fatigue wearing him down, and his continued belief in poetry as an alternative to suffering:

> The hand fell in pain
> In effort strained and confining
> The patience of an ox is required
> And you are a delicate deer.
>
> So wider flare the eyes
> Sharpen the pointed ear
> Like shafted arrows, cast your feet
> Up over the crags.

And fly through open heights
Catch the stars with your horn like a spear!
And attain—what's in a dream.
And as in a dream—disappear.[11]

As usual when Mani Leib is at his lyrical finest—something the
reader of a translation must take at least partly on faith—the music
of the poem carries its theme, rising from the hard consonants of the
first stanza to broad vowels and assonantal effects of the second and
third, where the speaker resolves to set himself free from burden-
some toil and then, momentarily, succeeds. The poem is what it
expresses—a short, liberating flight.

Nevertheless, Mani Leib never gave up the idea of an integrated
way of life in which the calling of poetry could be united with pro-
ductive labor. In the early 1920s he set up a shoe cooperative, Safran
and Brahinski, where poets would work side by side in a common
economic enterprise, enjoying one another's company as they
earned their bread. He recruited for this effort the poets Al Guria,
who had started out as an Introspectivist, and I. I. Segal, a young
lyric poet from Montreal who came down to New York to be
trained in shoemaking by the poet he most admired.[12] For a short
time the poets enjoyed working together, but the experiment failed
to support all the families that depended on it for sustenance. Segal
eventually returned to Montreal, where he eked out a living as a
teacher, and Mani Leib went back to the larger factories for as long
as his health permitted. On the back of a Safran and Brahinski busi-
ness card he scrawled his thanks to his friend Kalman Marmor for a
$15 loan that may have saved his life: "That's how desperate I was
when you lent me this."[13]

Although he failed in the attempt to integrate shoemaking and
poetry, Mani Leib accomplished just that some years later in one of
his most appealing poems, forging a resolution between the compet-
ing necessities of his life:

I am Mani Leib, whose name is sung—
In Brownsville, Yehupetz and farther, they know it:
Among cobblers, a splendid cobbler; among
Poetical circles, a splendid poet.

A Little Love in Big Manhattan

A boy straining over the cobbler's last
On moonlit nights . . . like a command,
Some hymn struck at my heart, and fast
The awl fell from my trembling hand.

Gracious, the first Muse came to meet
The cobbler with a kiss, and, young,
I tasted the Word that comes in a sweet
Shuddering first to the speechless tongue.

And my tongue flowed like a limpid stream,
My song rose as from some other place;
My world's doors opened onto dream;
My labor, my bread, were sweet with grace.

And all of the others, the shoemaker boys,
Thought that my singing was simply grand:
For their bitter hearts, my poems were joys.
Their source? They could never understand.

For despair in their working day's vacuity
They mocked me, spat at me a good deal,
And gave me the title, in perpetuity,
Of Purple Patchmaker, Poet and Heel.

Farewell then, brothers, I must depart:
Your cobbler's bench is not for me.
With songs in my breast, the Muse in my heart,
I went among poets, a poet to be.

When I came, then, among their company,
Newly fledged from out my shell,
They lauded and they laureled me,
Making me one of their number as well.

O Poets, inspired and pale, and free
As all the winged singers of the air,
We sang of beauties wild to see
Like happy beggars at a fair.

We sang, and the echoing world resounded.
From pole to pole chained hearts were hurled,

While we gagged on hunger, our sick chests pounded:
More than one of us left this world.

And God, who feedeth even the worm—
Was not quite lavish with his grace,
So I crept back, threadbare and infirm,
To sweat for bread at my working place.

But blessed be, Muse, for your bounties still,
Though your granaries will yield no bread—
At my bench, with a pure and lasting will,
I'll serve you solely until I am dead.

In Brownsville, Yehupetz, beyond them, even,
My name shall ever be known, O Muse.
And I'm not a cobbler who writes, thank Heaven,
But a poet who makes shoes.[14]

With its cheerful beat, the verse sweeps us into the wonderland of poetry where conflict can be resolved like rhyme. The jolliest stanza of the original is the one that compensates by internal rhymes and tripping rhythms for its description of the starving poets. Ideally, the poet would like to live in unalloyed service to beauty. Failing that, he tries to use his presence in the world to transform as much of it into beauty as he is able. Poetry was to become for Mani Leib an instrument of harmony, of reconciliation to immanence. But, in the meantime, the decade of the 1920s was burdened by doubt and failure.

The winter of 1922–23 in New York was enlivened by the presence of a notorious couple: Isadora Duncan, the legendary interpretive dancer, and her considerably younger husband, the Russian poet Sergei Esenin, whom she had married in Moscow the previous year. Isadora had returned to America for a dance tour intended to reestablish her artistic dominance in her native land, and Esenin, who described himself as "the last poet of the village," hoped to extend his fame while exploring the country. The tour turned out to be a failure for both and destroyed what had been from the start an unbalanced, stormy union.

Isadora seemed to court controversy as much by her public in-
sistence that "Communism is the only solution for the world!" as
by the daring individuality of her dances, which she performed in
scanty dress and punctuated with commentaries on literature and
art. Yet she, at least, was at the perpetual center of public attention.
Esenin, hailed in his homeland as a lyric genius, felt isolated in New
York by his ignorance of English and belittled by the newsmen and
fans who treated him as Duncan's odd husband. His drinking got
out of hand and, perhaps because of the uneven quality of liquor
during those days of Prohibition, had serious side-effects.[15]

Apart from the Russian émigrés who might have lionized Esenin
if the patriotic poet had not despised them for their defection, his
warmest admirers in America were the Yiddish poets from Russia,
especially Mani Leib, translator of a good deal of Russian poetry
into Yiddish. Shortly after Esenin's arrival, there appeared in
Forverts one of his most famous poems, "The Song about a Dog," in
Mani Leib's somewhat softened translation:

> Once in a corn-lined cowshed,
> Where the bast-mats gleam like gold,
> A bitch bore a litter of puppies,
> Seven ginger-haired pups all told.
>
> Till evening came she caressed them,
> Smoothing their coats with her tongue,
> And the snow beneath her stomach
> All melted because she was warm.
>
> But when the hens that evening
> Were roosting above the track,
> Out strode her lowering master,
> And bundled all seven in a sack.
>
> Close behind him she ran through snowdrifts,
> Only just with the strength to run . . .
> And she saw how the unfrozen water
> Lightly trembled so long, ah, so long.
>
> She was plodding heavily homewards,
> Licking the sweat from her sides,

When the moon rose over the hut-tops,
And it seemed like a pup to her eyes.

Up at the blue heavens
She stared, and whimpered loud,
But softly the moon glided
And vanished behind the clouds.

And sad, as when people mock her,
And throw her not food, but a stone,
In the still of the night the dog's eyes
Fell as bright golden stars in the snow.[16]

Although the stark cruelty of Esenin's work set it apart from his own writing, Mani Leib also remained a "poet of the village," nurtured by the rural landscape and filled with the pitying and self-pitying sorrow of Russian folk culture. Translation from Russian into Yiddish affirmed the cultural affinities of the Jew and the Russian, particularly when the two found themselves together in the American metropolis.

Esenin visited Mani Leib several times during the winter. Back in Russia it is doubtful whether he would have accepted invitations from a Yiddish poet, but here they shared a common exile. When Mani Leib asked him and Isadora to a farewell party in their honor, he was pleased to come to a gathering where he rather than his wife would be the center of attention. The party, which took place at the beginning of February in Mani Leib and Rochelle's four-room apartment in the Bronx, turned into a fracas, though for Esenin it was only one of many. It seems the drunken Esenin began to abuse his wife, and, when some of the guests forcibly restrained him from hitting her he cursed them as *zhids* and accused them of plotting his crucifixion. Others say he shouted slogans of the antisemitic Black Hundreds and almost had to be strait-jacketed when put into the taxi that took the couple back to their hotel.[17] The next day the Russian sent Mani Leib a letter of soulful apology, attributing his behavior to an attack of "the same illness that afflicted Edgar Allan Poe and de Musset," presumably epilepsy. "My soul is innocent in this," he wrote, "and my reason, which has awakened today, makes me shed bitter tears, my good Mani Leib!"[18] He was clearly contrite, but even if the excuse were valid it would not explain why this illness or a lapse from reason should have taken the form of an antisemitic tirade. Esenin's outburst reminded the Yiddish poets that they had left behind a hatred so spontaneous and deep that it could erupt even in fellow poets. Theirs was an unrequited love: Mani Leib might continue for the rest of his life to consider himself a son of Niezhin and to consecrate nostalgic poems to his homeland, but it was certain that Niezhin would never long for him or wish for his return.

Among the Yiddish writers and intellectuals there were those, like H. Leivick, who protested the attention that had been accorded the Russian poet. They felt that accommodation to an antisemite degraded their Jewish culture.[19] Still, the Jewish poet's love could be as stubborn as the Russian's rejection. Though Mani Leib and his brothers had brought their parents to America before World War I, severing their immediate family ties to the Ukraine, he remained attached to it with a passion that went beyond political or practical considerations. For Mani Leib no less than for his undisciplined guest, Great Russia was the landscape and the source of his literary tradition. The tantalizing encounters with Esenin, far from alienating Mani Leib, stimulated his identification with the poet, with Russian verse, and with the land of his birth.

Translation was the most direct expression of this attachment. In 1920 Mani Leib thought of preparing a volume of Pushkin in Yiddish as part of a library of translated classics of world literature. The book and the series fell through, but many Pushkin translations found their way into the daily and periodical press. The same year he published translations of two works by Alexander Kubrin, whose wintry settings and folk-narrative style bring to mind the atmosphere of Mani Leib's ballads and folk poems.[20] Over the next decades Mani Leib translated many kinds of Russian verse, including folksongs, songs of convicts, and Bolshevik songs. He translated, among others, the poetry of Derzhavin, Batyushkov, Tyutchev, Kozlov, Lermontov, Alexei Tolstoy, Fet, Nitikin, Sologub, Gorodetsky, Gumilyov, and Mandelshtam.[21] He admitted that translation could be a matter of relative convenience. Since he had to submit at least one poem a week to *Forverts*, supplying a translation was occasionally simpler than writing a poem of his own. Nonetheless, there were also translations, done as painstakingly as original work, that cost him weeks of effort.

Mani Leib's attachment to his native land was unaccompanied by the rage that governed Halpern's memories of his birthplace, and the massacres of Jews in the Ukraine during the First World War did not disturb his tranquil images. Even when addressing the tension between Jew and Christian, he elicits an underlying harmony from their apparent estrangement. In one of his poems about childhood he describes himself as

> A little gentile among gentiles
> who feed their pigs.
> But you are not a gentile
> you are a cheder student.[22]

> a sheygetsl mit shkotsim
> vos pashen di khazeyrim
> nor du bist nit keyn sheygets
> du bist a kheyder yingl.

The separation between those who feed pigs and those who attend cheder was considered absolute in Niezhin; yet by picking up the aural connection between *khazer* (pig) and *kheyder* (Jewish school), the poet minimizes their difference. Besides, as the poem proceeds to demonstrate, the very texts the boy studies are shaped by his Ukrainian surroundings: the biblical David roams in his mind as a common local shepherd picking flat stones, as the poet himself did, from the dried riverbed. His youth and his Jewish memories are indissolubly bound to Ukrainian landscape and lore.

Actually Mani Leib's translations and poems about his Russian childhood were not at all unusual in the *Forverts* of the 1920s, which continued to highlight Russia of the past and present. At the time of Esenin's arrival, for example, the newspaper was serializing the biography of the fiery Russian revolutionary, Vera Figner, who played a leading role in the assassination of Tsar Alexander II. It was headline news when the Siberian counterrevolutionary government was ousted from Vladivostok. Eyewitness reports from an Odessa correspondent brought gruesome news of pogroms that had been loosed against the Jews in the city and region. On the theater page, under the banner, "Russia! Russia! Russia! in the Broadway Theater World," Cahan reviewed three Russian plays that had just opened locally; there was also a report on the Moscow Yiddish Theater, and an announcement of Maurice Schwartz's forthcoming production of Gogol's *The Inspector General*.[23]*Forverts* differed from *Freiheit* more in its opposition to Bolshevism than in the extent of its Russian coverage.

Mani Leib's poems and translations, which fell in so naturally with this general attentiveness to the old country, were far more than an exercise in nostalgia. His work as a mediator between Russian and Yiddish was part of his need as a craftsman to strike deeper roots for a language that was growing enfeebled in its new soil. Since the Russian poems dealt with situations and scenes that were foreign to local immigrant life, they required that he reach back for idioms from his native region, for terms and expressions that were no longer used in America and could only be reactivated in an authentic context. Though their mood is sometimes dreamy, the poems strive for verbal precision and material substantiveness, and command a far richer diction than that of the earlier poems. Mani Leib often spent hours trying to recall an old-country term that had slipped from memory.[24]

It is thus odd that, although no two associates of the original Yunge were farther apart in their approaches to poetry, both Mani Leib and Moishe Leib Halpern were drawn back to their European roots, Halpern seeking the origins of his estrangement and Mani Leib a remembered harmony. As political divisions deepened during the 1920s, the two poets occasionally appeared to be in the same ideological camp as Mani Leib's search for perfection and Halpern's intolerance for imperfection were often expressed in common opposition to the embourgeoisement of the community. Europe attracted them not in its actuality but as their linguistic homeland and an artistic alternative to the here and now.

During the early postwar years, a similar distaste for Main Street was propelling many young Americans to France and England. Leaving behind a country they felt to be inimical to the arts, scores of writers and artists fled to Europe looking for an aesthetic way of life, insulated from the pressures of materialistic industrial society. Their move temporarily released them from their civic responsibilities and left them free to examine and criticize the world entirely according to personal taste. Expatriation, one of the most powerful influences on American culture of the 1920s, separated many artists from their middle-class lives, from the smugness of Babbitry, of what in Yiddish was called "the allrightnik." This separation eventually awakened in some a refreshed appreciation of their native land; in others the dislike hardened into ideological opposition.

But, coming from Europe, the American Yiddish writers had already exiled themselves in search of a more congenial society. Now, typically approaching forty and immured in family life, they could not uproot themselves again. Nonetheless they were oppressed by the same perceived superfluity of the arts in their community and were correspondingly attracted to another country of greater cultural promise.[25] In one way or another, Russia served the purpose of inner expatriation for many of the writers who were originally associated with the Yunge and currently splintered into factions. It loomed largest for the radicals, those who saw in the Soviet Union the promise of a new world order that contrasted favorably with the inequities of America. As we have seen, Moishe Leib Halpern felt at home in these circles because, although he lacked enthusiasm for one side of the Communist program, its promotion of Soviet politics, he was brilliant in the other, the attack on the American status quo.

Moishe Nadir, Halpern's closest friend and occasional collaborator, progressed from the negative agenda of finding fault with America to enthusiastic support for the Soviet Union after his visit there in 1926. "The bride is a great personage," he wrote in the style of a prospective suitor. "Her crown of red hair suits her saintly, careworn face. She is dearer to me with each passing day. One of her local relatives . . . doesn't approve of me because I proffer my love without dowry or marriage vows. But my heart belongs to her, my sisterly bride. And may my right hand forget, etc. (See the Zionist pledge!)."[26] In applying the Zionist pledge—the passage from Psalm 137 that sacrifices the loyalist's right hand should he ever forget Jerusalem—to the Soviet Union, Nadir is burlesquing its religious and national meaning. His meetings with the Soviet Yiddish intelligentsia, who were being supported and published by the state, his visits to the new Yiddish schools and cultural institutions, foretold a new Zion in Russia where support for Yiddish, to the detriment of Hebrew, would be of particular benefit to the Yiddish writer. And if Nadir complained in one of his letters that a local Communist resented his "loving the bride" without fully committing himself to her welfare, the majority of those he met in Russia encouraged his ardor in the hope that the union would soon be consummated—either by resettlement in Russia or by affiliation with the Communist movement. (Jacob Glatstein said of Nadir that he was the first Jewish Communist: he had the energy to run to the Jewish marketplace every day and to put his artistic wares on view.)

The attraction of the Soviet Union was also powerful during the 1920s among writers less rebelliously energetic than Halpern or Nadir. The poets H. Leivick and Aaron Leyeles and the novelist Joseph Opatoshu tried to affect a reconciliation between the egalitarian principles of Marxism and the way of life of their fathers. They believed that secular Yiddish culture could be the natural heir of the religious culture of the past, and in keeping with their views they created institutions that would encourage the development of Yiddish literature and education. Their work drew heavily on Jewish history and folklore and engaged many central Jewish themes—the tension between chosenness and universality, the conflict of body and soul, the search for messianic perfection. Leivick's play *The Golem*, based on the legends of Rabbi Loew of Prague, and Opatoshu's novel *In Polish Woods*, about Hasidic life in Poland in the eighteenth century, were always cited as examples of American Yiddish writing that satisfied the requirements of a modern national culture.

The political attitudes of these writers to the Soviet Union were naturally influenced by their cultural expectations. Their trips to the Soviet Union and Poland—Opatoshu in 1922 and 1929, Leivick in 1925—established personal ties with writers in those communities and raised their hopes for an international Jewish literature in the Yiddish language. By appearing to do so much for their language, and for the welfare of all its national minorities, the Soviet government contrasted favorably not only with the antisemitic nationalist government of Poland but also with the democratic government of the United States, which promoted public schools and individual liberties but not the collective aspirations of any immigrant group.

Those least affected by the imagined advantages of Soviet Communism were the writers among the original Yunge who remained constant in their aestheticism. Having rejected social usefulness as a criterion for art, they were not susceptible to the idea of social engineering. Jealous of their autonomy, they tried to remain indifferent to popular pressure, whether democratic or proletarian, and they chided Ignatoff, when he published an attack on *Freiheit*, for reducing himself to the same low level of mudslinging. Though this left them with no prospect of public support, they were full of scorn for those popular Yiddish writers whom they accused of courting public affection and dipping into the national charity plate. "Even before he wrote his first poem, he was already planning his national funeral," they said contemptuously of Leivick, who by taking on the mantle of the prophet seemed to have betrayed the calling of poetry.[27]

But it was they who received the brunt of contemporary criticism. From the pages of *Freiheit*, Leivick attacked the remaining members of the Yunge for their reactionary withdrawal from life's battles, for their second-hand Verlainism, slovenliness, and self-immolation.[28] From these attacks Mani Leib was always granted a partial exemption because of his emotional attachment to Russia. He could also claim more authentic credentials as a member of the proletariat than many of those who sang its virtues. Yet even he did not escape unscathed. If the Yunge had appeared to be aloof from Jewish concerns in the early days of immigrant settlement, how much more remote did they appear in the mid 1920s, when the ideological struggle between left and right, socialists and Zionists, assimilationists and nationalists, colored every aspect of communal and cultural activity.

Sensitive as they were to criticism, Landau, Iceland, and Mani Leib, joined by the novelist David Kozanski and often encouraged by their old comrade-in-arms David Ignatoff, knew that they had not yet exhausted the creative impulse of their dream of an independent literature. Landau was prepared to argue that, far from reducing their relevance the world war had made their emphasis on "the dignity of the word" even more important than before. The ideals of precision, beauty, and grace had to be upheld more than ever now that the war had collapsed all standards of decency and devalued the old beliefs as fast as the European currencies. With the slogans of battle drowning out common speech, only the disengaged, the true poet, could control the exact pitch of words.[29] According to Landau, America was as important in the salvation of words as it had been in the rescue of refugees. Perhaps on the other side of the ocean, where "swollen figures and words are a matter of necessity— so many hundreds of thousands for bread and potatoes, so many thousands for a box of matches," words could no longer keep precise meaning. Art, however, cannot abide such exaggeration and forfeits its power when overwhelmed by so much misery.

This idea of rescuing their language from its perverters inspired Landau and Iceland to launch the magazine *Der inzl* in 1925.[30] Theirs being the generation of the flood, threatened by chaos, they wished to secure an island of high ground where human proportions could be maintained. Concerned lest the "epidemic of profound themes" infect all of literature and obscure ordinary men and women, Landau was certain that the new idea-purveyors were more dangerous than the situation they proposed to remedy. The individual had to be rescued from abstractions. Read within this context, Mani Leib's "Ode to Simplicity," which appeared in the second issue of *Der inzl*, invests the original aesthetic ideal of the Yunge with new urgency:

> Come, serene Plainness, with your bare blade cut
> Through my soul's black entanglements until
> My world, from heavy, sullen fetters freed,
> Shines like a burst of sun upon my sill;
>
> So all my eyes found blind, hidden and strange,
> In murky darkness covered and remote,
> Will suddenly grow clear like rainbow light,
> Or like the linen whiteness of my coat.
>
> And all of living, all not living things
> Now severed and apart from me, bring near;

Make them transparent like pure water's flow,
Close like my hands' ten fingers and as dear.

Then from the tight cell of my narrow grief
The voice of all who suffer rising strong
Will cry to me like kin to kindred crying,
Will ring out cleansed, transmuted in my song.[31]

From the cutting knife of the opening lines to the cry of blood at the end, the poem sustains a desperate faith. The petitioner is enmeshed, like Laocoon, in complexities that have dulled the raw edge of sensation, separating him from nature, damming up the well of human sympathy. Once the spontaneous condition of his life and poetry, simplicity (*pashtes*), with its overtones of humility, directness, and serenity, is now the absolute requirement of the artist's calling. A state of grace that cannot altogether be willed into existence, simplicity will allow the poet in progressive stages to liberate his mind and spirit until they are restored to their full powers, readied once more for their task. Like the priest, the poet, though he seems preoccupied with only himself and his altar, actually serves the nation, bringing salvation to sinners and comfort to sufferers, voicing the anguish of his fellow creatures.

Zishe Landau with cogent argument, Mani Leib in this quasi-religious invocation, recognize the social value of their long-standing creative ideals. Only a decade earlier these poets were insisting on their right to uphold the standards of personal truth and artistic excellence regardless of any public application. Now, in the ideological tension of the 1920s, they interpreted their quest for beauty and poetic authenticity as the poet's priestly contribution to the general good.

Reuben Iceland, the main ideologue of the Yunge, provided the most radical new defense of aestheticism, contrasting it with the moralism of traditional Judaism that had been subsumed in secular Jewish ideologies. In an essay on Yaddo Park, the Saratoga Springs resort that was frequented by many of the newly prosperous New York Jews, Iceland notes the inevitable dissatisfaction of his fellow Jews with its beauty: no sooner have they done admiring it than they regret that the garden is not being put to practical use.

Their own "benefit" from the beauties of the park and the pleasures they reap to the point of bursting—these they are utterly powerless to grasp. They will be satisfied only if this gorgeous park would cease to stand idle and serve some useful purpose, like a home for children, a facility for the aged, or a tuberculosis sanatorium.[32]

Iceland notes that, although the reformers castigate these bourgeois vacationers for the attention they accord their stomachs and purses, the radicals and the bourgeoisie are equally incapable of taking simple satisfaction in an aesthetic response. The concentration of both on material consequences precludes their appreciation of beauty —of poetry—as its own delight.

Iceland calls this narrow moralism "a purely Jewish point of view," which the postwar crisis of the 1920s is in danger of extending to all the world. But his fellow American writers had long since been attacking the puritan heritage for its deadening effects on the soul, blaming what they thought particular to *their* religious tradition for the neglect of American literature and art. (Ironically, when Yaddo was finally harnessed to a utilitarian function, it was turned into a colony for writers and artists, who had managed to define themselves as a group in need of a supportive environment.) It was not a particularly Jewish emphasis on morality that set Iceland, Mani Leib, and Landau apart from the American scene; if anything, their impatience with philistinism was in the mainstream of American letters. But the antisemitic pressures to which the Jews were subject did affect Yiddish writers who worked for the Yiddish press, as did Iceland and Mani Leib, or for Jewish organizations, as did Landau and Ignatoff. Within a few years Iceland would be forced to reexamine his favorite poet, Stephan Georg, who had "built for Germany a temple of Art in which he was the high priest" and then turned into an evangelist of Fascism. Iceland had to reconsider his own distinctions between the poet and the prophet, and his desire to maintain a disinterested art, in the light of his mentor, who had moved "from pure art to Nazi messianism."[33]

When *Der inzl* folded after sixteen issues in 1926, the efforts of the Yunge to mount an independent publication came to an end. In the same year David Ignatoff published the final volume of *Shriftn*, the irregular but impressive series of miscellanies that had launched the group fourteen years earlier. The demise of the "aesthetes" caused no great anguish to the literary community. In 1923 Opatoshu was already confiding to a fellow poet that "Landau has been dead for a long time and Iceland was never alive."[34] The high quality of much of *Der inzl* proved him wrong, but his negative judgment represented the general attitude toward these poets. The Yiddish world was contracting much too rapidly to sustain the kind of disengaged literature that they cultivated.

Though Mani Leib's reputation also suffered from the growing antagonism toward the Yunge, he was still a recognized star in the Yiddish literary firmament, and many factions of the local community celebrated his twentieth anniversary as a published poet in 1926. One of the contributing elements to his ongoing popularity was his children's verse, or the poetry that was being read as children's verse in Yiddish schools throughout the world. Wherever secular Yiddish schools were established, from Warsaw to Buenos Aires, the poems of Mani Leib were taught as a basic part of the curriculum. Yoel Entin, one of the original editors of *Di yugnt* in 1907 who then became a pioneer of the Yiddish school movement in America, identified Mani Leib's importance to its development: "My friend Leon Elbe and I were looking for material . . . for the first Yiddish anthology for the Jewish school that had been founded in 1910. When I came upon Mani Leib's new ballad 'Der fremder' in one of the literary journals, my heart began to pound. This was exactly what we had been searching for."[35] This narrative poem, "The Stranger," composed in simple couplets, reanimated the familiar folk figure of the Wanderer, identified by Jews with Elijah the Prophet, who travels anonymously among the poor, correcting injustices and alleviating pain. Entin had reason to exult in his discovery because the poem proved an immediate success in the schools. Mani Leib subsequently wrote many poems about this ubiquitous folk figure. One such Elijah poem he wrote later for a class of Vilna schoolchildren who had written to tell him how much they enjoyed his poems.[36]

Though "The Stranger" had not been written for children, its introduction along with several of his other poems and ballads into the school curriculum decided Mani Leib's role as a children's poet and created its own reality. When *Kinder zhurnal*, the children's journal of the New York Yiddish Sholem Aleichem schools, was initiated in 1920, Mani Leib contributed lyrics, lullabies, and rhymed stories, which he said he was writing for his own children. Their main theme was "wonder upon wonder"—the discovery as if for the first time of black bread and white salt, of water that quenches thirst and fire that warms, and of all the rhymes that unite them.

In one of his children's stories about himself, Mani Leib recalls his visits as a child to the hut of his grandmother, where he would sit curled up against the oven for warmth, staring out the small window at the road that led from the city, and listening to her wonderful stories. The crisp imagery, spare language, and simplicity of these lyrics were a compelling model of what poetry could be.[37] Since this poetry was so accessible and satisfying, it was often set to music, and the songs became a permanent part of the repertoire of the Workmen's Circle and children's choirs.[38] Yet the very popularity of this kind of verse, which turned him in the popular imagination into a folk balladeer, caused the neglect of the grittier, ruminative aspects of his work. In literary and intellectual circles, the complaint of thematic insubstantiality that had been leveled against him since the appearance of his three books in 1918 grew more aggressive. His reputation among the critics declined as it rose among ordinary Jews.

Some of his colleagues held the press responsible for Mani Leib's failure to realize his full potential as a poet. Just as *Freiheit* was blamed for the rhetorical excesses of Moishe Leib Halpern, so *Forverts* was accused of sacrificing Mani Leib's talent on its pages: *Forverts* was portrayed as a bawdy house, where Mani Leib and his fellow prostitutes try to entertain retired field marshal Cahan. Penury drives them into his arms, and he knows that he can treat them as he pleases. Whenever Mani Leib fails to please the old whoremaster, he is sent back to the factory to stitch boots.[39] This is an updated version of the accusation the Yunge had launched against the press years before for not publishing the Yiddish writer in the first place.

Other of Mani Leib's detractors blamed not the press but the hollowness of what was left of the Yunge: without a fruitful idea, without the ability to share in the suffering of his people, the writer simply howls into the wind. Leivick published such a dismissive attack on the "twisted cynicism" of the group that Mani Leib was roused to respond (despite the somewhat softened treatment he personally was accorded). "You go your way, and I'll go mine," he wrote in anger, advising the moralizer to *shvayg, shvayg, shvayg*—in essence, to shut up.[40] Until old age united them in illness, the quarrel between the two poets was not resolved.

Nor was Leivick's the worst attack on Mani Leib. Mocking the poet's anachronistic diction, the critic B. I. Bialystotski told the story of a sinner who, when he finds himself before the angel of death, wants to swear by his beard and sidelocks that he had done his share of good deeds while forgetting that he is cleanshaven.[41] Zishe Weinper published an exceptionally nasty pen portrait in 1928, contrasting the princely figure Mani Leib used to cut every night in the cafés with his current isolation. He was accused of masking the decline of his inspiration by crabbed intolerance for the poetry of others. Although Mani Leib's poetry had often been associated with feminine qualities of softness and coquettishness, this is a picture of a sour has-been whose waning popularity makes him shrill with envy of the younger usurpers.[42]

The attacks on "Mani Leibism" gained momentum over the years. In 1931, in an issue of the magazine *Oyfkum* (Resurgence) ostensibly dedicated to him to mark his twenty-fifth year as a poet, a dozen contributors damned him with faint praise or consolidated their criticism of his work. "All that Mani Leib represents— quietude, refinement, nuance; alienation, solitude, seclusion, estrangement, sorrow; lovely-sounding, little-saying wildvine; Russification, Sologubism; Romanticism, Aestheticism—all this has since 1914 passed into history." "His delicate ear is socially deaf." "Mani Leib is fortunate—he never changes." It is unpleasant to contemplate what the poet must have felt on reading this volume of tribute.[43]

These snide or frankly hostile comments in a collegial celebratory volume alert us to the atmosphere blanketing American Yiddish literary culture from the mid-1920s onward. The intensifying factionalism can be attributed at least in part to a political style that favored this kind of aggressiveness. In 1926 the struggle over control

of the labor unions resulted in a local civil war in the garment indus-
try, when "the methods of the class struggle" were imported into
the union movement and "the Communists fought the old-line
union leaders as if Jewish socialism were their main enemy."[44] The
introduction of violence as an instrument in the fight for social
progress had its parallel in the rhetorical sphere. A front-page box of
two or three columns in *Freiheit* most mornings assaulted the so-
cialist *Forverts* in deliberately inflammatory headlines: "How Do
You Recognize a *Forverts* Socialist, an Idiot, and a Provocateur?"[45]
By the same political token, the Communists afforded writers
license to defame their fellows as part of their higher social responsi-
bility, raising denunciation to the level of *mitsva*, a positive good. Of
course serious quarrels among the Yunge dated from the earliest
days of their association, but ideological justification made them
nastier and public.

This release of rhetorical aggression afforded some writers a new
sense of freedom. As we have seen, Moishe Leib Halpern broke
loose from the proprieties and constrictions of Yiddish culture into
a deeper region of feeling. Moishe Nadir, too, and the saturnine H.
Leivick occasionally thrived in the rough give and take of public
debate. But the polemical years had a very different effect on the
temperament of Mani Leib. The transcendence of poetry, for which
he had once argued so intensely against the expectations of Jewish
moralism, was now being denied, aggressively denied, by former
colleagues. At the same time, his natural identification with the poor
and with the socialist cause, which dated from his apprentice years
in Niezhin, made it hard to defend what others called his egotism
and smugness. Even as he fought off his attackers, he felt guilty for
his own lack of engagement.

On November 6, 1926, a small box on the front page of *Freiheit*
announced that the famous Yiddish poet Mani Leib was joining it.
"By uprooting himself from his *Forverts* exile, Mani Leib will gain
his freedom in the cultured working-class atmosphere of *Freiheit*
and give us the very finest and best of his pen." Mani Leib's poems
began to appear quite regularly at the very time that Halpern had
fallen from favor, and in a few of them he consecrated his "knife" as
well as his sorrow to the struggle of the oppressed.[46] But the poems
of empathy lacked conviction:

> Plain, humble and poor
> Like the clothes we wear
> We bear the burden of the world.[47]

They seemed the warmed-over sentiments of a poet whose real tragedy was the loss of inspiration. And the confessional poems, though fresher and more convincing, bore all the neurotic marks of self-laceration that the "proletarian culture" sought to eradicate. Most of Mani Leib's contributions to *Freiheit* were such a disappointment to the engaged sector of the Yiddish intelligentsia that parodies of his verse began to appear in the pages of the newspaper itself.[48]

This brief attempt to join the ranks of the Left brought on the deepest crisis in Main Leib's life as a poet. When he stopped writing for *Freiheit* in the autumn of 1927, he stopped publishing altogether. For two years he dropped from sight, an apparent casualty of Yiddish literature in America. Whatever had made him quit *Forverts* and think he could serve poetry more honestly on the Communist paper, he forfeited his small income without appearing to gain the least artistic advantage.

It was a bad time for the immigrant culture as a whole. Though the United States enjoyed a general prosperity under Presidents Harding and Coolidge that was "unique in its experience or that of any other society,"[49] this increase in material well-being did not engender a corresponding sense of spiritual contentment among the general population, much less among the New York Jews. And the quickening acculturation of the immigrant Jewish community, at least partly in response to anti-Jewish discrimination, isolated all those who remained dependent on Yiddish. In the same month that Mani Leib fell silent, H. Leivick published a bitter lament over the Yiddish poets whose works resemble stalks of wheat devoured by locusts.

> Sometimes, like frazzled cats, dragging
> Their kittens around, distraught,
> We drag our poems between our teeth
> By the neck through the streets of New York.[50]

An ominous cloud hung over the literary community. The talented young novelist Borukh Glazman, who felt that he had no future in America, decided to leave the country forever and, in a novel called *In the Golden Swamp,* gave fictional justification for his departure to the Soviet Union. The pages of the book resound with the arguments and counterarguments of the literary cafés, where cynical Yiddish writers who now make a comfortable living at journalism mock those who are still struggling over "belles-lettres," where established Yiddish writers mourn their lifetime investment in a literature without a future and the younger generation feels aggrieved:

> —You, older writers, can still put up with it. Because what is America for you? A place where one can live in security and more easily make a living . . . Artistically, America barely exists for you . . . Like old folks you are nurtured by memories—some vivid and bright, others pale and watery—but you live out your lives in the immigrant-milieu . . . and if you sometimes discuss America as you are doing now, it's because you have nothing better to do . . . somewhere, all the time, in a corner of your mind, you surely harbor the comforting little thought, "Well, so what? Let's not take the matter too much to heart because what there is will suffice for our remaining years."[51]

The young writer in the novel angrily rejects advice to leave for Europe if he finds no place for Yiddish in America, but Glazman himself was driven to this solution, at least for a time. Mani Leib's silence coincided with this period of widespread disheartenment.

To Weinper, author of the earlier poisonous pen portrait, Mani Leib may have seemed belligerently aloof, a faded prima donna, but others speak more kindly. Meir Shtiker, a young poet highly regarded by the Yunge, recalled the extraordinary generosity that he and his fellow poet Aba Shtolzenberg were shown by Mani Leib and Zishe Landau when they were much in need of it. The older poets invited their protegés to their homes, taught them how to play cards, and contrived, Shtiker was prepared to swear, to lose small sums of money to them on a regular basis so that they would have enough for food. The young poets were taken up, humorously, as prospective suitors for Mani Leib and Landau's daughters and were hired, more seriously, to tutor the girls in Yiddish as a means of ensuring them a tiny income.[52]

Mani Leib was frankly envious of only one colleague: Halpern. Traveling around the major cities of America, having a good time,

stirring the blood of readers with outrageous—and inspired—
poems, Moishe Leib represented all that Mani Leib could no longer
afford to be in the 1920s. Halpern continued to project the *image* of
the poet, while Mani Leib at his sewing machine felt less and less
able to keep his poetry alive. It was obviously far more difficult for
Mani Leib to arrange a speaking tour than it was for Halpern, who
had no job and for whom the tour itself represented a major source
of income. But once on the road when he could manage it, Mani
Leib felt that he had sprouted wings. The Yiddish cultural world
was so small that he was warmly befriended by the same people who
hosted Halpern. For him, however, the diversion remained just that
and could not be repeated very often:

> I came back from my short trip to Detroit and Cleveland a lazylegs,
> and now must, though I dawdle, return to the shop. I was simply
> transformed, and now all I want to do is set out into the world, to
> far-off cities, to read poems for grown-ups and children and speak of
> higher matters and forget all the cares that each of us must bear. In
> short: I got the urge to live as a poet! Well, try living as a poet! . . . I
> forget that I've lived peacefully for years without seeking the full life
> of a poet. This means, I've grown spoiled. And whether I want to or
> not, I have to take myself in hand, stay at home, and work in the shop
> as all the good and pious folk do and rid myself of all foolishness, such
> as the good times I enjoyed in Detroit and Cleveland.[53]

Mani Leib could not help feeling that he had compromised "the full
life of the poet" by trying to yoke it to a worker's routine. Each poet
thought he saw in the other the solution to his predicament: Hal-
pern associated Mani Leib with the stability of home and hearth.
Mani Leib envied his rival's unencumbered freedom.

Radiant Exile

Romance in the tenements was a natural theme for the American Yiddish writer. The image of lovers jammed in dark hallways assumed a personal significance for the Yiddish poets of the Lower East Side, who were engaged in a similarly uneven contest with their surroundings.

> Near a tenement house on Avenue B,
> A girl in a new silk frock
> Paced the street with deliberate steps
> Her eyes eagerly scanning the block.[1]

In his "Ballad of Avenue B," written in 1913, Mani Leib tells the story of a girl who strolls off arm in arm with a boy friend, followed by her mother's anxious glance, and returns hours later, her silk dress crushed. The young man puffs on his pipe as she sits crying—a familiar tale of sullied dreams, with male predator and female victim. Yet there is something in Mani Leib's telling of the story that belies its conclusion. The balladeer weaves such a gentle spell of romance that he maintains the innocence of the poem even though the girl has to sacrifice hers.

When Moishe Leib Halpern took up this subject a decade later, no doubt with "Avenue B" somewhere in mind, he used the convention of the ballad to shatter its romantic charm. Instead of a silk dress, he shows the dark roots of his heroine's dyed hair and the sorry camouflage behind which the tenement tries to hide its misery.

> There in the shadowy, dank hall
> Right alongside the ground-floor stair—
> A weeping girl, attended by
> A grimy hand in the mussed-up hair.
> —A little love in big Manhattan.
>
> The hair—a whiff of some cheap rinse
> The hand—hard, stiff and leathery
> Two equal lovers, for whom this is
> As good as it'll ever be.
> —A little love in big Manhattan.

Sammy and Bessie, the lovers of Halpern's "Song: Weekend's Over," try to make out in the dark, but the howl "From a million fire escapes / And all the dark ceilings overhead" drown out their attempts to communicate. The poem, like their interrupted romancing, moves fitfully by way of sudden shifts of rhythm, changes of tone, and slang expressions; the imagery fragments what romance generally tries to soften and blend.

> O huge night city, such grim strangeness
> Wraps you up in the darkness here!
> Man and wife sleep by the million
> Like drunks all bloated up with beer.
> —A little love in big Manhattan.
>
> Like monkeys in the trees, the children
> Hang in their fire escapes, asleep;
> Soot drifts down from above their heads,
> Dropped by the moon, a chimney sweep.
> —A little love in big Manhattan.
>
> And the girl Bessie knows "from nothing"
> And Sammy, too, with his open mouth,

And Monday swims up before your eyes,
A desert of dead miles toward the south.
—A little love in big Manhattan.

And even Bessie's poor old mother
No longer asks, "Where is that kid?"
It doesn't matter that black hair
Has all been bleached to blond and red.
—A little love in big Manhattan.

It isn't that he's ill, the sad one
Who contemplates these things at night;
But sick of his own sadness only
He lies and broods, his pipe alight.
—A little love in big Manhattan.[2]

Even the mother in this version of the story holds out no hope for her daughter. The only one still paying attention is the sorrowful poet, who lies awake somewhere in the city, thinking and puffing on his pipe. Is this a deliberate echo of Mani Leib's ballad, where the young man leans back, puffing on his pipe, once he has satisfied his lust? (In a drawing dated about the time this poem was published, Halpern sketches himself in just such a way, pipe in mouth, looking coolly at the world.) Perhaps Moishe Leib was suggesting that the poet, like the rough suitor in Mani Leib's ballad, is also a detached participant, who can do no more than grieve over the situation for which he is responsible.[3]

The two ballads express two different approaches to art. While Mani Leib's poet uses artistic harmony to draw the sting out of hurtful experience, Moishe Leib's poet confronts the impossible choice between mendacity and complicity: either he helps to conceal the ugliness he sees, and thereby contributes to the deception, or he adds to the sum of human misery by describing it. Since Halpern normally elected the second of these options, he had to crush the silk dreams that have no place in the tenement world. But this was hardly the sort of deed that could fill a man with pride.

As much as he played the poet in public, brandishing his cane, peppering conversations with curses, Halpern understood the incongruity of his position. The more he credited materialism as the determinant of the human condition, the less importance could he ascribe to the poet, and the less pleasure could he take in his art. Disgusted with the attempt of other poets to "rise above" their obvious limits, Halpern sometimes went to the other extreme. "He thinks that farting is a joke, a revolt against the purists," one of his colleagues objected, "and he does it on the pages of *Freiheit*." But the disgust with romanticism was primarily a revolt against his own nature, and it left him increasingly helpless to protect the poet in himself.[4]

Halpern was particularly vulnerable in his dealings with *Freiheit*, whose editors felt no such ambivalence about their social and philosophical importance in the scheme of things. When the newspaper stopped paying him, a year into their informal contract, because funds were short, the editors had no trouble persuading Halpern that he had the moral obligation to keep his side of the bargain even though they could not keep theirs. "The *Freiheit* doesn't pay me, but demands that on ethical grounds I continue to submit my promised two items a week. When I hear the word 'ethical' I am lost. I have no excuse—because I did give them my word."[5] He seems never to have been aware of what was going on in the inner editorial circles, though he felt a change in the treatment accorded him whenever control shifted or tightened. Since the real reason for sudden changes of policy, namely, directives or pressure from Moscow, could not be publicly acknowledged, associates of the paper, like Halpern, were left to wonder how *they* had incurred the displeasure of management. During one major editorial shakeup, Halpern was convinced that the editor had resigned on his account![6] At the same time, he distrusted the individuals on the editorial committee. "I've stopped believing them," he wrote as early as 1923. "It seems to me that not one of them is honest."[7] Yet though he often threatened to quit, he went back to his arrangement each time the editors courted him with a fraction of his back pay, ready to forfeit the badly needed money but not the social significance he felt he gained in working for a proletarian paper.

Paradoxically, one of the things that kept Halpern at *Freiheit* was his knowledge that he could get a job at the rival *Forverts* "as easily as picking up a straw from the ground."[8] The great daily, which defined itself as a socialist organ, did not want to lose ground to the radical press and tried through various means, such as upgrading its literary section, to win back the young intellectually oriented reader from its upstart rival. But by radical standards *Forverts* was even more suspect than the avowedly nationalist newspapers, since it siphoned off reformist energy by pretending to encourage it. "*Forverts* let it be known that I could have $50 for only one item a week, or maybe even one every two weeks. Yet I don't know why, something held me back—not because of them, because of me. They are the same scoundrels (*svoleches*) as the others [on *Freiheit*], only with a little more chutspa. But I felt that I wouldn't be able to justify the move to myself."[9] No matter how disappointing the individual Communists or their stiffening orthodoxy, Halpern was still more afraid of selling out to the organs of bourgeois culture than of suffering personal humiliation. Years later one can see this same anxiety in disillusioned party members and fellow travelers who wanted to break with Soviet-dominated Communism without appearing to submit to its bourgeois alternative. A whole generation of intellectuals, susceptible to what Richard Hofstadter describes as the "forced morality of alienation," was similarly inhibited from giving up its ideological opposition to the middle class.

Halpern's fear was of just this kind. He suspected that his own hankering for a bit of financial security and social stability would conflict with the radicalism of the artist. The consequences of this oppositionism were very grave. In the political battleground of the mid 1920s, independence from both the Left and the "Right" (this being the improbable designation for Jewish anti-Communists) meant condemnation to no-man's-land, with support from neither side and with harassment from the Communists. For someone like Halpern, who had no source of income apart from his writing and lecture tours, it was a desperate risk, one that he was obviously reluctant, but as obviously destined, to take.

In the winter of 1925, at the beginning of a major speaking tour that he hoped would net several thousand dollars, Halpern precipitated a crisis. During his first public appearance in Chicago, he defended his friend Moishe Nadir, who had recently run afoul of the Communists. At a large public sendoff, on the eve of his departure on an extended trip to Poland and the Soviet Union, Nadir had suddenly announced that he was a Communist. When the audience cheered, he interrupted their applause and said mischievously, "You see how easy it is to take you in!" The Communists were not amused and censured their undisciplined comrade.[10] Although Nadir made it up with the Left when he returned to America, Halpern's spontaneous support of Nadir cast him permanently adrift. *Freiheit* withdrew its official support and canceled the rest of his tour. Now that they were under the unambiguous control of the Comintern, the editors must have fretted about his unorthodoxy and dropped him after his very first lecture, when they realized that they could not control his speeches. Halpern affected an untroubled air. "Well, thank God, now I too am a *contra-revolutionary*, that is, a revolutionary from the 'country.' Joking aside, they are proclaiming me a petit-bourgeois. How do I please you as a petit-bourgeois?"[11]

But it was no joke because, without the organized attendance of young people from the radical branches of the Workmen's Circle and the unions, he would have a hard time attracting an audience. He decided to continue with the tour, desperately in need of the money and hopeful that his personal popularity would help him raise at least a fraction of the sum he had anticipated. The good services of loyal friends could not compensate for the coordinated support of ideologically motivated institutions. To continue without sponsorship meant facing the apathy of the Jewish public at large and the concerted hostility of its most militant sector. The editors of *Freiheit* did not give up on Halpern. They hoped that like Nadir he too would return to the fold once he had been out alone. Halpern never really did, becoming one of the first victims of the tactical excommunication that the Communists practiced so effectively.

The lecture tour was preceded by a bizarre incident that seemed a kind of evil omen. Sitting one day in an East Broadway café, Halpern was accosted by an amateur poet who punched him in the mouth without provocation, accusing him of having stolen all his poetic subjects and ideas. That the man was subsequently taken away to a psychiatric ward indicated only that he was mad, but it did not explain why he had singled out Halpern for this attack. Halpern was badly shaken and hurt—later he had to have a tooth removed.[12] By the time he reached Detroit, after Chicago and Cleveland, he was also suffering from acute stomach pains, diagnosed as gallstones.

Telling his wife that he was staying on for additional lectures, he entered a Detroit hospital and underwent surgery. The recuperation was made more troubling by his worries over the $600 bill, a sum he could raise only by pleading for help from friends in several cities. "How rotten I begin to seem to myself when I write to you like this [for money] . . . When I get well I'll become a copywriter for a daily paper, or a hatmaker, or whatever."[13]

Once he regained his strength, though, Halpern had to continue with the tour so that he could bring home something to show for his long absence and to tide him over the rest of the year. He had skirted poverty for most of his life. It was something else to feel incapable of supporting a wife and child, to have to seek donations of shoes, winter coats, money for food, the down payment for the next quarter's rent. *Freiheit* was demanding an official apology before it would take him back. Halpern mocked its bourgeois conventions and swore that he would rather "croak" than excuse himself. Nevertheless, he added, if his child had to suffer on account of his stubbornness, he was prepared to write ten letters of apology.[14] Back in New York, Halpern was under heavier strain than before. His wife began to take in sewing to make ends meet. Nadir, one of the few writers who knew the extent of Halpern's difficulties, sent him some money and invited him to spend time at his country place in the Catskills. Halpern was in no position to take advantage of the proffered vacation, unless it could be turned into a working trip. "It would be good if you could arrange a small concert that would bring in some money. But I don't want anyone to know that I'm the one who needs it, the money, I mean."[15] By the end of 1925, Halpern's condition was so desperate that he had to consider moving out of New York to Chicago, where he thought he might find work on a new journal, to Detroit, where he had been offered a small theater to run, or to Cleveland, where he could live with the Drosts.[16]

Whereas Nadir, having made up with *Freiheit*, became one of its star attractions and could count on support from at least one quarter, Halpern was now subject to attack from all sides. The critics treated him only a shade more respectfully than they did the aesthetes of the Yunge, and Halpern's own harsh brand of mockery made him fair game in magazines of every political hue. Sometimes their comments were as biting as if they had been lifted from the master's own book:

Everyone is fighting over the red ribbon.
First Leivick with his victim-Communism thought he had it.
Then Opatoshu-Leyeles with their Yiddishism-Communism thought they had it.
Then along came the magic-tongued sword-swallower, Moishe Nadir, and hocus-pocus he's got the ribbon for his hocus-pocus Communism.
So while this was going on Moishe Leib Halpern was once talking about "our *Freiheit* poet" [Nadir], "our strong proletarian poet," "our revolutionary poet," and then he looked up and wondered aloud— And what about me?
Looking at Halpern then I was reminded of the joke about the men of Chelm in the bathhouse who were afraid to take off their clothes. Why? Because they were afraid that, without their clothes, no one would know who they were and they would get mixed up. So one clever man hit upon a plan. He stripped naked and tied a red ribbon around his foot so that everyone should know that he was Chaim. But as he accidentally lost the ribbon, another man picked it up and tied it around his ankle. When Chaim discovered that he didn't have the ribbon, he was beside himself with anguish, until he caught sight of it around the ankle of the other man.
"I know who you are," he said to its new owner, "but could you please tell me, who I am?"
The moral? Well, it speaks for itself.[17]

Since this little parable was published by the generally favorable critic Bialystotski in *Oyfum*, which was edited by Halpern's most fervent admirer, Zishe Weinper, it should provide some of the flavor of contemporary literary debate in general and of criticism of Halpern in particular. Far from admiring the poet's independence, Yiddish critics took his ideological homelessness as proof of intellectual weakness. He was the fool who could not trust his own identity, the radical without the courage of his conviction.

By his fortieth birthday, in January 1926, Halpern's life had become a fit subject for his poetry. The self-styled street drummer who had proclaimed his reckless abandon for so many years was now feeling the bite of want in earnest. Because of his personal fastidiousness and pride, even his close friends did not fully appreciate the transition he had undergone from the defiant bohemian to the precariously unsalaried husband and father. He himself, however, was well aware that the burden of his artistic independence fell heaviest on his wife and child.

The dramatic quality of Halpern's poetry had grown ever stronger over the years. The voice of the poet was projected into the voices of an assembly of characters, some of them, like Moishe Leib the Brat, bearing an obvious kinship to their creator, but others less intimately related. Already in his first book he had used various members of his family as dramatis personae, but he now consigned to his wife and son a larger role, for it was unjust that they should be subjected to such hardship in the name of his art without being allowed to "speak for themselves." In "From My Royzele's Diary," for example, all the tenderness and protectiveness of her affection do not altogether obscure her husband's failings. Other people wake in the morning and go about their work in the city:

> Yet my husband—
> As the sea will never stop its swell—
> He'll never cease
> To make war against the flies
> In a bathrobe.
>
> With my hat on his head, the one with the red flowers,
> He races about and throws his arms
> Like a hot conductor in an opera.
> He sweats like a beaver (he might, God forbid,
> Catch cold). What shall I do with such a man, my God?
> Shall I scold him like a child,
> Or, with words, put him to play like a child?

Royzele's sweetness is a perfect foil for the darker doubts that assail the poet about his unique occupation, his obsessive ideas, his political sponsors.

> Here, in this country, grown-ups, like children,
> Desire new games every day.

Why shouldn't—I ask—a competition
In fly-catching also be a game?
It's hard for me to think about it,
Because every thought appears as an image
Before my eyes.
Now I see a poster
Where letters big as pillars
Announce the name of my husband,
The fly-catching champion of the nation,—
That's what it says.
Painted with glasses, hair and a bowtie,
With his arms and his legs in the air,
He looks—forgive me for saying so—
Like a madman climbing walls.
But above all, the woman in me is annoyed!
How they've dressed up my dear husband!
Never mind the golden pot hanging on his chest—
He has to drop the flies he catches into it,
So they can count them
When the competition is over.
But what are those
Wide red trousers for?
Are flies wild bulls
That one must tease them?
But maybe they want to attract us—
The women?
Red reminds us of an apple-rosy sunset,
And of the sound of spurs of young officers.
One of them once bowed
To me.
It happened when I strolled
With my girl friend
In Vilna, on Main Street.
Peshe-Gittel was her name.
A *landsman* who just came off a ship
Told me that she killed herself
When soldiers in the middle of the night
Burst into their house—[18]

This comical diary suddenly turns sober as it moves from the husband's apparent immaturity, to the way his profession of fly-catching is dolled up to attract an audience, to the lurking danger behind it. Letting her imagination loose, the wife foresees that his innocent and apparently foolish talent will be used for purposes that are ultimately linked to violence and bloodshed. The red trousers are so clownishly improbable that they resist the notion of their political significance or of the connection between male bravado and wanton bloodshed. Yet far from obscuring the menace, her run-on thoughts lead inexorably to the unconscious realization of what Man is really about—war, rape, brutality—and deadly complications of a life that is no more.

Through his wife's chatter, Halpern mounts a wry commentary on several kinds of innocence, the charming madness of the poet, the caprice of grown-ups "in this country," and the vulnerability of women to the forces behind all this play. The wife wraps the husband in her affections, and his characteristic protest against cruelty and neglect is softened when it is placed in her voice. At the same time, the poet uses this vehicle of tenderness to sharpen the attack against himself. Royzele's readiness to excuse her child-husband, and her inability to speak of her anxieties directly, invite the reader to recognize what she cannot: that an authentic chain of associations will trace the connections between "fly-catching" and "soldiering" and the danger to which she is subject.

In a different mood, Halpern's poetry enlisted the artistic cooperation of his son. Whenever the child joins him in a poem, fantasy springs delightfully free:

> I have a fine little son.
> We play together
> Like small and older brother
> In a pile of sand outside.
> But when he becomes king
> O ho—will things be merry!
> As after a summer's rain
> The roads will all be bright
> No one will fear again
> Demon, robber, crow.[19]

The presence of the child gives his father leave to spin out a redemptive vision of innocent wisdom that triumphs over adult foolishness. Playing with his son in the sand, Halpern was also playing with the tradition of Yiddish poetry, for the opening line, "I have a fine little son," would have reminded every Yiddish reader of one of the best-known verses in the language:

> I have a son, a little son,
> a youngster very fine!
> and when I look at him I feel
> that all the world is mine.
>
> But seldom do I see him when
> he's wide awake and bright,
> I always find him sound asleep;
> I see him late at night.[20]

Like a youngster with *his* older brother, Halpern takes up the famous lullaby by Morris Rosenfeld and shows what he can do with it. Rosenfeld sang of a laboring father who was deprived by his work of even the simple pleasure of playing with his child. In a sense, Halpern remains true to the original because the child's presence reminds us, in his poem as in Rosenfeld's, that children suffer most from adult failures. Yet Halpern's poem breaks away into the completely different atmosphere of the child's kingdom, where toy drummer bears thump so loudly when they go to welcome their new king that they punch holes in their instruments and set all the birds to laughing. Children have senses so keen that they can hear the stars singing in the new king's crown. Halpern's child is not simply the occasion for an adult poem; he temporarily frees the burdened father from his bitterness and grants him license to hope.

Some of Halpern's "children's verse" may have been written especially for the children's magazines. The Yiddish poets, whether or not they made formal provision for their children's Jewish education, had to face the prospect of a new generation that might not know, or care to know, their work. Through the Yiddish children's magazines, which were used in the classrooms of the Workmen's Circle and the Labor-Zionist schools, and adopted also in other

parts of the world, the poets felt that they retained at least some
contact with the younger readers. By this time in the mid-1920s,
Mani Leib had already become one of the mainstays of the Yiddish
school curriculum. Halpern complicated the optimism of Mani
Leib's verse through the introduction of an adult companion whose
foolishness has already marred life's splendor. He was not hailed
quite so readily as a "children's poet," perhaps because those who
defined the category tended to forget how much adult complexity
children are able to tolerate.

Halpern's use of the child as the emblem of joy, goodness, and
pacifism was bound to recall the Christian conception of the child-
ruler who brings peace to men and joy to the world. Ever conscious
of the ubiquity of Christian mythology, Halpern wrote several
poems about Jesus that appear to distinguish his own conception of
goodness from its Christian counterpart. As we might expect, the
distinction turns on the matter of corporeal existence. In "Jesus to
the Children," the resurrected Nazarene, who appears before an
audience of children to tell them of his birth and miraculous rebirth
as the son of God, mourns the bitter irony of his fate. Though God
responded to the desperate loneliness of his mother by granting her
the gift of himself, there can never be an end to his loneliness:

> —Do you know of a blind man hereabouts
> Who could hear a spider in the grass?
> Let him play for me of your loveliness
> That shatters the light of my eyes, like glass.
>
> —Let him hear the broken cry of my name
> That should have remained in a child after me.
> The earth, the sky, everything is mine—
> All the world is mine—except one of you.[21]

Jesus protests that he would have preferred the limits of mortal
existence, which includes the biological possibility of paternity, to
his transcendent and eternal deprivation. Let no one, therefore,
confuse the fantasies of a Yiddish poet with the hankering for divine
redemption. The godliness of a Jesus who can claim that "all the

world is mine" is a cursed abstraction compared to the presence of a real child.

Halpern pressed his case against Christianity hardest when he sensed how close he came to its spirit. A confirmed pacifist—a friend testified that Halpern's only intolerance was for war—he nevertheless wanted to distinguish between his earthy idealism, which took earthly consequences into account, and the religious mythology that seemed never to understand its own irreality and had forever to seek a scapegoat—the Jew—to carry the blame for its failures.[22]

The presence of "Royzele" and "Yingele" (little boy) in Halpern's poetry introduced an element of domestic calm. His son actually became known as "Yingl," as in the poems. But outside the family, Halpern's sense of dislocation grew more profound. Critics in the late 1920s increasingly applied to his work the term "grotesque," which, deriving as it does from a kind of art that interweaves human and animal forms, here retained its full etymological weight. The mixture of animal or insect with human features was one of Halpern's characteristic techniques, and even when no animal features are involved, he notes the identifying characteristics of men and women like a zoologist describing an alien species.

> It is hard to say what this is—
> Here is daybreak, and a man with two feet
> Drags himself up five flights of stairs.
> And here is a door that he opens
> . . . pushing in his beard
> First and then his head.[23]

This odd creature turns out to be the father of five children, deserted many years earlier by their mother. He is bringing home a loaf of bread that he managed to scrounge for them in the jungle below. The movements and grunts of his brood upon receipt of the food are those of a primitive tribe, to which they have been reduced by hunger. The poem's title, "Sunrise in Manhattan," promises an aubade, but Manhattan has worn away all the civilized overlay. Following this human animal to his lair at dawn, we find ourselves back at a stage of civilization when the only organizing principle was the hunt.

Always a master of images, Halpern fragments the human physiognomy with striking results. (He once told a friend that, when stuck in the composition of a poem, he shut his eyes and tried to visualize what followed.) He isolates parts of the body not, as the cubists did, for the sake of visual effect, but almost always to fix a moral judgment:

> The white old maid has an unsweet face;
> Like a rusty lock on an old suitcase
> Were her nose and mouth, it must be said;
> Feet? Hands? With such an old bag, instead
> Of touching her skin, you're better dead.

Taken from a poem about the lynching of an innocent black fifteen-year-old in the South, these lines use the grotesque as a weapon against evil and the social complacency that sustains it. The simile is here a tool of caricature. The encrusted qualities of the valise confirm the repressed sexuality of this unattractive creature, whose sound and smell and texture assure us that her accusation of rape must be false. There is also an irrepressibly comic aspect in the image of her nose as a rusty lock.

The poem in which this image figures is obviously a very harsh indictment of the spinster, the lynch mob that tars and feathers the victim, the preacher who justifies this murder, and even the American flag that is hoisted above the corpse, in honor of which the poem is entitled "Salute." Less predictable, perhaps, is the force of the poem's conclusion, which indicts above all the poet himself:

> It's not the branch, its whining prattle,
> Nor the rope, with its dangling rattle,
> Nor the windblown feather, that had to miss
> Its chance to give the corpse a kiss,
> But you—the whole world's sorrow-stink
> Who stood at a distance there to think—

—Playing pocket-pool, with your fingers curled—
To dream up a poem for yourself and the world.

And he accuses not only himself but the best of art, which is always
ready and willing to turn blood into beauty:

> Now go wake up Chopin, the musician, and let
> Him overflow (if he doesn't forget
> How) with tinkling noises, and you can bet,
> When bloodshed needs background music, that few
> Gentiles can't sing the *Kol Nidre* too.[24]

Among musicians, none more than Chopin used the bloody na-
tional struggle for independence to pump up the fervor of the polo-
naise. He was an entertainer-accomplice, just like the poet of social
protest, who pours out his anguish at the sight of a lynching, and just
like operatic cantors, who had turned the stirring Kol Nidre prayer
into a competitive showpiece. Halpern's eye, trained to recognize
disjunctions, trompes l'oeil, deceptions of every kind, was not
likely to overlook the contradiction between the purported moral
purposes of his poetry and the essential self-absorption of its
creator.

Halpern's tragicomic view of the poet was increasingly reinforced
by the sense of his own superfluity. Independence from the press
gave him absolute freedom to write as he pleased and to say
whatever he wanted in public. But *Freiheit's* withdrawal of spon-
sorship deprived him of the audiences that had once come to hear
him, and of some of the impetus to keep working. "Tuesday evening
was a great success," he reported from a lecture tour in Chicago, the
year after he had severed his official links with the newspaper. "In
addition to the $15 for the rental of the hall, my lecture brought in
another $9.50 clear profit."[25] As an estranged contributor to its
publications, Halpern was under an informal boycott by the mili-
tant Left, so that the people who would have rushed to hear him the
previous year now made a point of staying away.

Halpern's emergence as a political pariah impressed friend and
foe alike. As the Communists intended, some took it as a warning.

A friend wrote to Moishe Nadir, after attending an evening of Hal-
pern's in Detroit, about how sorry he felt for Moishe Leib. A year
earlier, when Halpern had been brought to Detroit under the aus-
pices of the Lenin Branch of the Workmen's Circle, all the other
"progressive" branches of the organization had canceled their
weekly meetings in order to get members out to his lecture. This
year the whole sector of radical youth was missing from his audi-
ence. The correspondent was writing to warn Nadir what would
happen to him if he bolted the movement, as he was threatening to
do.[26] On the tenth anniversary of the Bolshevik revolution, in 1927,
when Trotsky's car was turned back at the official celebrations, Zishe
Weinper made this connection between Moscow and New York:
"Doesn't it remind you of *Freiheit*'s treatment of its poets? When
Halpern didn't speak out against them, he was one of the family.
Every move of his was reported in large type: 'Ours, Ours,
Ours . . .' Now my heart beats for Leivick"—who, Weinper sus-
pected, would be the next boycott victim.[27] But it was Halpern alone
who remained the local "Trotsky," irritant to those who upheld
collective discipline.

The moral strength of the radical Left reached something of a
peak in the spring of 1927 with the execution in Massachusetts of
Nicola Sacco and Bartolemeo Vanzetti. Among immigrant Jews,
Sacco and Vanzetti were almost uniformly regarded as martyrs for
their unpopular beliefs. The Communists, whose popularity had
been damaged in the vicious fight they had waged over control of the
unions, tried to channel some of the spontaneous sympathy for the
accused anarchists into an attack on the capitalist system. They con-
solidated a protest movement that temporarily united most sectors
of Yiddish political life and elicited from every kind of Yiddish
writer an expression of outrage.[28]

Halpern's poem, dated September 4, 1927, two weeks after the
execution, was the product of many painstaking drafts. One would
expect Halpern to react strongly to the execution, as he did to so
many contemporary instances of social injustice. Jacob Glatstein
observed that in Halpern there burned the embers of much unused
social commentary: he once proposed to Glatstein that they publish
a magazine in which he could write poetic editorials even on munici-
pal issues.[29] Yet on this public political occasion, his reaction was

curiously apolitical. The images of the execution take over the mind
of the man who witnesses it and become part of his own struggle
against madness.

You can pull from your head a gray hair
That sometimes comes too early with troubles that are too hard,
But for someone whose troubled head
Feels too hard with its skin and hair,
Too hard to bear any more
On these two wretched bones called—in humans—
Shoulders;
Let him not stand there, mouth and eyes agape,
As in some madhouse:
The stone of the wall is harder than his head,
And to hit himself against it will only yield a lump
No larger than an apple in a tree, that withers
With no one to pick it in due season.
And today, after all, there's an easier way
For anyone who looks for it:
You have only to keep quiet for a while
And submit your head, like a typhus patient, to someone who
    shaves it.
He is, after all, a brother,
And you shouldn't be cross with him
For not scraping up the scalp as well.
He only does what he's told and when he's paid for it.
And the death-smock, as well,
That, too, was sewn up by a hungry brother.
And if a child of the very poorest
Dolled up in good clothes for a holiday
Can allow itself to be led everywhere by the hand,
You, too, may allow yourself to be led to the electric chair
No matter how old you are.
And if the murderous copper gleams on your head
What can still be too hard?
A king—even when the whole kingdom wails around his throne—
Should be silent at his coronation.
And if, elected, his crown is one of fire,

It is a crown of wonder in this desolate world;
And only the wolf, who ranges forever because of his wildness,
And only the thief in the night,
Are afraid of fire.
Infants, speechless, who cannot yet
See anything with open eyes,
Reach out toward fire.
And only the butterfly that longs for the light
In the night's darkness
Welcomes forever with outstretched wings
His fiery death.[30]

The victims are united in a single fused image. By contrast, every-
thing else is extraordinarily fragmented, and the various elements of
the scene summon up such eccentric associations that for long into
the poem the subject remains elusive. Only by degrees does it intro-
duce the prison, the shaven heads, the execution clothing, the elec-
tric chair, the wires, the current, and the final shock. By then, but
only then, do Sacco and Vanzetti emerge triumphant from their
ordeal of fire, not in the flesh, to be sure, but as the powerful and
beautiful symbol of innocence, which death cannot dishonor.

Absent is any political note. The abundant images open up a
gaping social wound, but without isolating the villain or the villainy.
When the poem comments on those who prepare the men for their
death—"He only does what he's told and when he's paid for it"—it
includes the prison brothers in the mad orbit along with the judges
and spectators and executioners. The momentum of the poem
sweeps Sacco and Vanzetti up into the forces of nature: they turn
into a brilliant butterfly, two outspread wings of martyrdom, at-
tracted to destruction as Jesus was to his cross. The person tearing
his hair from his head and banging his head against stone walls in the
opening lines of the poem is not the prisoner on death row, how-
ever, but the lamenting onlooker, wretched and uncomprehending.
His state of mind is expressed through tumbling images of torture,
illness, neglect, and deceit, each of them so vivid that it momentarily
interrupts the grammatical flow. The vertical line of narrative can
hardly withstand the centrifugal pressure of the images that appear
always on the point of snapping it. The speaker's struggle against

what feels like the collapse of reason runs in tandem with the doomed struggle of Sacco and Vanzetti, but in winning posthumous redemption for them, it is not equally certain that he has saved himself.

The Sacco-Vanzetti poem shows how out of joint Halpern was with the political atmosphere. Whether it was his humiliation at the hands of *Freiheit* that turned him inward, or the greater density of his art that precipitated his disengagement from politics, his poetry was losing the aggressive energy that radicalism had originally inspired in him. Injustice, in this later work, is only the sorriest manifestation of man's essential estrangement, a process of severance that begins when he is yanked from the womb, is reinforced when he leaves home and homeland, determines his dealings with his fellow creatures, and is finally revealed as the basic principle of human existence.

In the spring of 1926, Halpern felt he could no longer stay in New York and began listening to friends in various cities who tempted him with offers of support. At first Royzele resisted the move so strenuously that Halpern said "it would be easier to move the ocean than to dislodge her."[31] Their modest home in Seagate, Brooklyn, filled with furniture and artifacts that Moishe Leib had collected and decorated, was a cozy nest, and she was afraid of change. As if to confirm her fear of travel, the family was involved in a car accident on the way home from a visit at Moishe Nadir's farm, and both grown-ups were badly bruised.[32]

Finally matters grew so desperate that the Halperns were forced to vacate their apartment. For a short time they moved in with one of Royzele's brothers in the Bronx. Halpern claimed that the daily *Der tog* offered him $35 a week to become a regular staffer, but as with the offer from *Forverts*, he could not bring himself to accept. "I am destined to wander all my life, and that's that."[33] He moved the family to Detroit, where they stayed for several months at the homes of friends. At a reception in Halpern's honor, $1,000 was pledged for a tractor that would be sent in the poet's name to Jewish colonists in Russia.[34] Though he was genuinely adored by a small circle of admirers, they were too few to maintain him at their expense, and he returned to New York to try working again at *Frei-*

heit. His pride and his poverty were locked once again in battle.

In 1928 the family again set out, this time for California.[35] Yiddish-speaking communities outside New York, less spoiled by the accessibility of Yiddish theaters and cultural organizations, seemed eager to welcome writers into their midst, and the Jews of Los Angeles had already shown their generosity in support of the prose writer Lamed Shapiro. Shapiro, embarked on the most quixotic of his many projects, had set up in Los Angeles a laboratory where he hoped to develop color cinematography for the movie industry. During the course of his solitary work, for which he lacked any formal training, he raised more than $10,000 from local residents, most of whom were still struggling themselves for a toehold in this newer part of the country. After the effort proved futile and Shapiro's heavy drinking began to undermine his health, he continued to receive assistance from a small group of admirers.[36]

The Halperns were warmly welcomed, staying first with wealthy friends and later in a small house on Boulder Street in the center of the city. But the change of place did not bring, as promised by the Jewish expression, a change of fortune. In California as in New York, Halpern was caught between the warring political factions, the anti-Communists complaining that he did not really belong to them and the Left afraid of sponsoring a writer frowned upon by the party newspaper. The welcoming committee was so ideologically torn that even the selection of a chairman for an evening in his honor proved an almost insurmountable problem.[37] Worst of all, he was suffering again from severe abdominal pain. Attributed by a physician to an ulcerated stomach, the attacks continued for weeks until brought under control by a strict diet.[38]

Halpern's physical discomfort may have soured his attitude toward the Jews of Los Angeles, among whom he had hoped to find some peace.

> I wait as though behind a barred window
> For a word of comfort to be passed to me,
> While they, like children with Purim *graggers*,
> Pass their secrets from ear to ear.
>
> The husbands appear to be gaunt with hunger
> Though each has money enough to waste,

And the women—in velvets and silks—are barreled
As if storing sausages around the waist.[39]

To be sure, Halpern received a little support from these scrawny
husbands and bulging wives, but the terms of this "income" were as
compromising as ever. When the Communist magazine *The Waker*,
in order to discredit him further, reported that he was seen at parties
passing around the hat for himself, he protested that he had actually
been collecting for someone else, a writer who was about to be
evicted from his house.[40] It required a certain kind of disinterested
nobility to live off the charity of others, confident that this system of
patronage benefited the culture as a whole. Though apparently rec-
onciled to this arrangement, Halpern showed in flashes of temper
and disgust how much it cost him.

An extended visit to Los Angeles by the Drost family, which
cheered Halpern for the several months that it lasted, left him de-
spondent at their departure. For the first time he thought of taking
out American citizenship papers, ironically, like many immigrants
of his generation, in order to travel overseas. Halpern's reputation
among Yiddish readers in Poland assured him a splendid reception
there, and recent translations of his work into Polish suggested that
he might be accorded welcome by the larger Polish-language literary
community as well. "I dream hard of hopping over to the other
side," he confessed.[41] "The devil won't catch this Los Angeles com-
munity if it costs them a few dollars to rid themselves of a Yiddish
poet," he decided, mocking himself and his benefactors.[42] The com-
munity obliged by collecting the necessary money to send Halpern
and his family back to New York, and perhaps Halpern was right in
believing they would consider themselves well rid of him. He seems
to have given up the plan to apply for American citizenship, and he
never got to Europe.

The one steady accumulation in the Halpern household was the
stack of unpublished manuscripts in the poet's trunk. When a mag-
azine occasionally invited a poem from him, he had plenty of mate-
rial in the trunk to choose from.[43] He was writing but, lacking a
place to publish, he had little incentive to polish the work. Halpern
continued to sympathize with the ideas of the Left, "but its people
are something else again. As for the 'Right,' it was always moving

backwards. *Forverts* was a Zionist organization whose leadership would soon be donning prayershawls and praying in Hebrew, or even in English like the reformers in their temples."[44]

In the summer of 1929 temporary salvation came to Halpern in highly dramatic form. Arab rioting in Palestine, directed by the mufti of Jerusalem, culminated on August 23 in the massacre of sixty-seven yeshiva students and religious Jewish residents of Hebron and in the deaths of many more in Safed. These brutalities, which were not quelled by the local British police, marked a turning point in the history of the *yishuv*, the Jewish settlement in Palestine, which was forced to reconsider its attitudes toward both the Arabs and the British and to refashion its political institutions accordingly. They also brought about changes in American Jewry. The recurrence of the all-too-familiar pogrom, no longer on Russian soil but in the young pioneering settlement that had been established to escape such dangers, shook the Zionist movement and temporarily awakened the sympathies of even non-Zionists to the Jews in the Middle East. As one anti-Zionist radical poet wrote bitterly, "Tens of thousands of Jewish deaths in the Ukraine [in 1918–19] did not create such an upheaval in Jewish organizational life as the 60 slain yeshiva boys in Hebron."[45]

The upheaval in American Jewish organizational life, however, was the result of more than just the violence in Palestine. The reaction of *Freiheit* required of all but the most fervent sympathizers with Communism a reconsideration of their allegiances and political priorities. At first all the Yiddish newspapers had joined in the outcry of anguish, and *Freiheit* too, though it fixed part of the blame on the British and on the Zionist leaders who fomented anti-Arab feeling, condemned the severity of the Arab "response." But after three days, *Freiheit* reversed its position: it joined the Communist front in hailing the mufti as a liberator in the Arab revolution against British imperialism and its Zionist agents. Jewish fellow travelers, who of course remained unaware of party directives, were disgusted by Jewish justifications of anti-Jewish bloodshed. A roster of writers who had been loosely associated with *Freiheit* published a public letter severing their connections with the paper. Six weeks later, they initiated *Vokh* (The Week), an independent Yiddish weekly devoted to literature and politics, which was modeled on the successful *Literarishe bleter* (Literary Pages) of Warsaw.[46]

Having tried to establish his political independence well before the others, Halpern was the ideal contributor to an unaffiliated, left-leaning magazine that considered the October Revolution "the greatest event in the life of recent generations" and yet opposed Jewish assimilation in either the proletarian or the bourgeois cause. Once again, as during the early days of *Freiheit*, Halpern seemed to have found a suitable literary address. Just back from the West coast, he threw himself wholeheartedly into the venture, contributing poems, theater and book reviews, and occasional columns. *Vokh* not only signed up subscribers, but in order to compensate for its lack of institutional backing, it tried to organize associated groups in each of the major Jewish communities that would provide a network of financial support. Halpern was sent out on the road to help in this job. On a trip to Philadelphia he signed up a hundred new subscribers and helped to establish a group of *Vokh* supporters.[47]

In the pages of the weekly, though, Halpern was as much out of step as he had been among the Communists. The paper was distinctly political and, despite its editorial staff of poets and writers, addressed most of its contents to local and international political issues. Having broken away from *Freiheit*, the writers struggled to prove that their differences with *Freiheit* did not diminish their loyalty to the Soviet Union. Their appeal to national unity would not be allowed to obscure the class struggle between the exploiters and the exploited; only the Jewish working class could be the legitimate carrier of the Jewish national ideal.[48]

Of the major contributors, Halpern alone was either apolitical or antipolitical. In fact, one of his columns speculated comically on how a good playwright might represent the twenty-year-long attempt of his literary cohort to reeducate the Jews. He imagines a worker at the center of the stage. Two women on either side of him are tearing the man to pieces. The older woman doing damage to the right side of his face is, like all older women, a dyed blonde. The more violent one on the left, a natural redhead, has the advantage of youth. Though he is losing his breath and blood is streaming from

his eyes, the worker smiles as he falls because he is used to a beating
and enjoys being fought over. The worker finally lies crippled on the
floor. Enter the chorus—the education delegation, like priests with
their hymnals—to recite the last rites. Of all these delegated mourn-
ers, the most pathetic is the representative of *Vokh*, whose screechy
little voice can hardly compete with the robust rhetorical powers of
the others, cultivated over twenty years at Sunday picnics on Coney
Island and under the thundering elevated trains.[49]

Only a few years earlier, Halpern had argued for the distinction
between the useless art of the aesthetes and the compassionate pos-
sibilities of proletarian writing. But by the time he was writing for
Vokh this kind of differentiation also appeared artificial. Take, for
example, the case of a widow with four small children, who is trying
to turn the scrawniest of them into a newsboy so that he can awaken
the pity of his customers. What sort of poem is appropriate to her
situation? One that begins:

> October—father of
> Labor
> For our needs,
> Father of winds, of stones and wheels
> For our mills . . .

The only father she has in mind is the one her children lost. Or
would it be a poem about "our rising strength" and "our cultivated
solidarity"? The woman is enraged by phrases that seem to mock
her predicament.[50] When poets of the Left say that they are writing
for this woman, they seem even more corrupt than the Yunge, who
at least spared the worker and the widow the indignity of pretending
to assist them. The elemental cry for protection Halpern imagined
he heard from his own wife and child could never be answered by
poetry in any form.

A chilling sobriety overtook Halpern in these months of feverish
activity around *Vokh*. Although the full effects of the Wall Street
crash would not be felt among most New York Jews until the end of
1930, when the closing of the Bank of the United States deprived
some 400,000 depositors, most of them Jews, of their life savings,
the economic activity of the community was beginning to slow

down.⁵¹ Marginal as he was to these events, Halpern's economic dependency made him highly susceptible to fluctuations in the general level of prosperity. If he had not been able to sustain his family during the prosperous years, when his friends had extra money and Yiddish publishing ventures were still viable, how would he fare in leaner times?

The well-being of the Yiddish language also seemed to depend on the strength of the economy. One of Halpern's most trenchant contributions to *Vokh* dramatized, in a series of vignettes, the bankruptcy of Yiddish as part of the national atmosphere of decline. During a run on Yarmolovsky's Bank (the column appeared in March 1930), the crowd is so thick it threatens to squash one poor little Jew. A policeman trying to disperse the crowd says to him, "Feter, aheym" (Go home, uncle), in what he knows is their common language. This hint of familiarity is enough to deprive the policeman of authority; the man digs in his heels and the crowd shoves more vigorously than ever.⁵²

Two other brief scenes, of a young man who gets his face slapped when he proposes to his girlfriend in Yiddish and of a female robber who is about to get away with a holdup until she addresses the storekeeper in Yiddish and gets beaten up instead, turn similarly on the ineffectuality of the language and the contempt in which it is held by its speakers. Halpern concludes his column by quoting his "Uncle Henakh Mikhl," who says that if he were a diplomat he would insist that all declarations of war henceforth be issued in Yiddish; this would guarantee peace in the world. It was the fate of most Yiddish writers, from the earliest to the latest, to have to fret over the strength of their language. In contrast to most of his colleagues, however, Halpern had never lamented over Yiddish. That he elected to do so now suggests an unprecedented sense of futility.

Halpern had been among the first to identify with Yiddish radicalism in America and to find in its optimism a new source of creative energy. He vigorously opposed the quietism of Mani Leib and the intellectualism of the younger Introspectivists, whose self-conscious experimentation drew more attention to itself than to the world it promised to refract in its images. He was the first, the most famous if also the most ambiguous, example of the Yiddish prole-

tarian poet, bringing the kind of artistic prestige to the social strug-
gle that ideologues were eager to harness to their cause.

The politicization of Yiddish culture alienated Halpern just when
many of his fellow poets and writers were being drawn into its web.
His early exposure to applied Marxist politics in the increasingly
dogmatic *Freiheit* alerted him to the excesses of the materialist phi-
losophy, just as the spiritualism of the Yunge had once irritated him
with its excess of loftiness. The Marxist belief that art and thought
are the products of material relations denied the primacy of the
imagination and, by raising social analysis to the level of immutable
law, consigned to the poet the role of lackey. In the same way that
religion once seemed dangerous to Halpern because it obscured the
material basis of life, historical determinism, translated into di-
rectives that one write thus and thus and not otherwise, threatened
the mysteries of mind and the spontaneous intelligence.

The other editors and contributors to *Vokh*—H. Leivick, Me-
nahem Boreisho, Ephraim Auerbach—continued to hope that
Freiheit would reverse its stand on the issue of Jewish national
rights. After their own magazine folded, they were lured back into a
common front with Moscow whenever one was proposed. But Hal-
pern had formed an intuitive distrust of Communism. With eyes
wide open—and, indeed, Halpern's late poems are exceptionally
intent on seeing—he dissociated himself from all prophets and
preachers. His struggle against systemetization became part of the
fabric of his later work. Poems often took the form of speeches,
public and private words of counsel, lectures or dramatic ut-
terances. A line of apparent reason maintains the structure of argu-
ment as if the speaker were proceeding along clear lines of cause and
effect. A whole series of conjunctions and adverbial connectives
—but, because, however, then, and, after all, yet, still, and also, but
if—is marshaled to sustain the rational continuity.

Yet the items strung together by this apparently reasoned process
are wildly inappropriate to any coherent statement. They erupt in a
Vesuvius of images, each dragging along a grotesque, compelling
load. Items placed in formal relation to one another are disturbingly
unrelated so that we are pitched into incomprehension through the
very technique that promises enlightenment. The distance between
the ostensible subject of a poem and the succession of pictures and

metaphors that are introduced in its description corresponds to the distance within the speaker between the conscious and unconscious operations of his mind.

The problem of comprehension dogged Halpern, as we have seen. Readers wanted to know by what right a writer of "theirs" so scrambled his message that they could not decipher it. But the disjunctions of Halpern's verse went much further than his editors and readers knew. His poetry challenged not merely *their* understanding (because they were not skilled enough to make out the turns of phrase); it challenged the liberal optimism on which most public communication is based. Public poetry is predicated on the notion that, once man is figured out, he is capable of correction. Halpern's late poetry, in which the impulse of clarity is forever checked by billowing chaos, denies the possibility of social "solutions" or "expressions" of the human problem.

Instead, having traversed a full cycle, Halpern came back to an idea he had expressed many years earlier. Chastened by his experience, Halpern no longer spoke of the moral radiance of the artist but merely of powers that he possessed, through no fault or control of his own. The poet spoke truth and denounced falsehood not because he was morally impelled to do so, but because his genius radiated light even against his will.

> Who am I? Who am I? Who could have guessed right
> That all I imagine would turn into light?
>
> Like a monkey, from head to foot all hairs,
> The prophet's around for thousands of years
> Urging all to acquire his light—free, no cash—
> Like a luminous herring you'd find in the trash.
>
> A herring like that you don't skin: instead,
> You hold it aloft, and eat up from the head,
> And the famished soul who gets to the tail
> At the top, which he also devours, won't fail
> To open his mouth—that crater—so wide
> With his hands outspread
> As if wanting to cram some more inside.[53]

In this poem, called "Likht—mayn vort" (Light—My Word), the poet declares that he does not peddle his message, as the prophet does, leaving those who receive it hungry for more. Instead, the poet's light emanates with a power of its own, shining out from his navel, as unfortunately visible as "a Jew with a *shikse* behind a wall" (the Jew having vainly tried to hide his assignation with a gentile girl). The poet is as powerless to deny his light as the society that tries to avoid him, and society succeeds about as well in escaping him as a train that tries to run from its own smoke:

> What a game that is!
> The faster the train can push smoke out
> The faster the smoke can push it about,
> The faster smoke pushes the train about
> The faster the train will push it out,
> And that's strange. My God!
> But that smoke should push the train ahead
> While the train pushes smoke behind instead,
> Shouldn't be so. My God.

The reader who can hold in his mind simultaneously the cartoon-like interaction between the train with its smoke and the other pair of contestants—the public and its poet—will be rewarded by a comical but not unserious self-image of Halpern and his audience. Benefactor and victim, the dynamic principle that moves things forward and the exhaust that gets left behind, the poet no sooner claims to be one than he is also revealed to be the other.

Both prophet and poet are admittedly engaged in the same activities of spreading the light, but the poet's light is spontaneous and beyond the measure of good and evil. He cannot help himself when he admits wickedness into his work because it imposes itself upon him of its own volition.

> Even Lilith—no sooner thought of, than she,
> Too, turns into light and trails after me
> Like a tarted-up wretch who, you can bet—
> My God—to collect the smallest debt
> Would follow you into the outhouse, yet.

> And if I look, like a goy at an axe
> At a word as lofty as "*Rimzi-Brax*"
> Whose light and whose significance
> Are as alien to me as a shirt and pants
> To a wolf in a cage, that light sticks to me there
> As warmly as cowdung does to a bare
> Foot. My God.

Even the devil's consort wants to collect her due from the true force of poetry. And beauty sticks to him whether or not he is its appropriate vehicle. The many images in the poem of chasing, fleeing, running, stealing, cheating, and hiding show us the degree of anxiety that accompanies the creation of a work of light, which, being outside the poet's control,

> Always flows out of me, come what may,
> Like fire struck from the broken wood
> Of a tree hit by lightning in the night . . .

In fact, by the end of the poem, the speaker lets us catch a glimpse of him as an old Jew, walking around with his head lowered,

> Belatedly leaving the synagogue
> And hurrying toward his grave. My God.

When the light is not bursting through him, the poet is a spent man who lingered a little too long in his service of a spent God. The poet feels no awe, no joy, no triumph in his exploits. To be sure, he resembles Mani Leib's anointed, who has been granted the supreme grace—the ability to create beauty. But this is not, for him, a source of exaltation. He is rather like the comic creature played by the film comedians—Buster Keaton, Charlie Chaplin, or Harold Lloyd— the victim of a beneficence that becomes oppressive in excess. The inspirational light that first appears to the poet as a blessing assumes the quality of a curse when it begins to stream from him unstoppably, inappropriately, with sorry consequences. The very method of the poem with its profusion of elaborate metaphors straining the ostensible line of meaning proves how unsuited is the irradiating presence of the poet to the purposeful tasks of the reformer.

Matters did not improve when *Vokh* folded, less than a year after it had been launched. This left Halpern wholly unemployed once again. The degree of his concern in the spring of 1930 can be determined from his proposal to the Drost brothers in Cleveland that they come to New York to set up a shoe-repair business that could sustain them all.[54] The proposal sounds like a parody of Mani Leib's shoe cooperative that failed six years earlier. Despite their affection for Halpern, the Drosts were practical enough to recognize that the times were not right for a new business venture of this kind. Halpern would not have contributed much to it in any case because he fell sick again, too sick to work. He was told that the ulcerous condition of his stomach had affected his teeth, all of which had now to be extracted. With no money to cover the cost of either the surgery or the dentures, he was forced to appeal to the friends who had helped him so many times before.

In the meantime, younger poets were beginning to make themselves heard. They viewed Halpern as a giant of the golden age of Yiddish in America. Editors of little magazines in Chicago, Los Angeles, and elsewhere invited him to contribute to their pages in the hope that his prestige would attract attention to their own work. As a sign of respect, Zishe Weinper, his literary godson, made Halpern his coeditor of the magazine *Oyfkum* and accepted Halpern's offer to write the introduction for a volume of his collected works. Weinper, who had moved toward the political left as Halpern moved away from it and who tried to stay in the good graces of the Communists without formally commiting himself to them, should have known that he was taking a risk when he agreed to have Halpern bless his book. After World War I, when Weinper had returned to America from serving with the Jewish Legion of the British army, Halpern was chairman of an evening in his honor. The issuance of the Balfour Declaration several years earlier had given the Zionist plan for a Jewish homeland in Palestine its first substantive boost since the death of Theodor Herzl in 1904, and many people believed that the Jewish Legion, fighting in the British ranks, was to be credited for this success. Fully aware of the sympathies of his audience and of the honoree, Halpern used the chairman's prerogative to denounce the Zionist movement for "playing at soldiering" and for stirring up false national pride. Now, ten years later, though Weinper's politics had changed, Halpern had not. The younger poet did worry that his idol would again misappropriate the occasion, but his admiration exceeded his caution.

True to form, Halpern's book introduction berated Weinper for his shift to the left and particularly for his joyous reaction to his recent trip to the Soviet Union. "Great-grandfather on the burning pogrom pyre, grandfather at the Wall where the *Shekhina*, God's Emanation, rests and refuses to linger, and now their grandson, Weinper, purifying himself through the Revolution of the Soviet Union—that's all he needs!" Halpern's prose style was as crabbed as his poetry, but its convolutions and compression distilled the mockery into purer form:

> The truth is, you can catch a snatch of the revolutionary psalms right here among us too, but our alarm clocks only ring when it's time for the buttered rolls with coffee, while [in the Soviet Union] no sooner does the rooster crow than someone must begin worshipping the red divinity, blessed be he, because otherwise no one is allowed to stand around with his hands in the mud, like the Israelites in Egypt.
>
> There is only this difference: there, in Egypt, they kneaded children into the walls, whereas in Sovietland you have only to reshape yourself; you become a new Adam—even without a figleaf.
>
> For the robust goyim this is surely a piece of good luck, but for our kind . . . well, I've heard that they skulk around with their hands over their ——, more afraid nowadays of the puniest little gentile than they ever were before.[55]

No other writer of the time observed with such clarity the humiliation of the Jews at the hands of the Soviet rulers and the self-abuse that some of them were prepared to practice in their adaptation. Halpern saw it because he had been playing the same game off and on for almost a decade.

The introduction did not neglect to praise Weinper for the qualities Halpern had always admired in him, his joy, lack of rancor, and simplicity, qualities he can hardly have been said to enjoy in himself. It also aired his long-standing antipathy to the Zionist Marxists who expressed their ideals of liberty, equality, and fraternity by practicing birth control and promising that when they went together to Eretz-Yisroel to smell tobacco they would sneeze in Hebrew.

Halpern considered Zionism and Communism equally misguided because, while the killing of Jews continued, Zionism for all its idealism was powerless to prevent it and Communism, feigning idealism, was content to exploit it.

Halpern turned the introduction to Weinper's book into a kind of prose poem of his own failed politics, anticipating a hostile response. At the literary evening honoring Weinper's book, he felt that the speakers were organized against him. When Weinper tried to disabuse him of this notion, he accused the honoree of licking the boots of his fellow writers in gratitude for the bit of kindness the literary community had thrown his way. Since this "literary community" consisted of Halpern's erstwhile colleagues of *Vokh*, the writers and poets with whom he should have felt most at home, his impression of them shows the extent of his isolation and distrust.

We know that he too was trying to raise funds for a book. Back in January 1927 a small announcement in *Oyfkum* indicated that $2,000 had been collected for a new collection of Halpern's verse. If true, the money must have been put to more immediate use because four years later he was still planning the project. There was more than enough material for a third collection of poems, and even for a volume of collected prose. Halpern was encouraged to believe that there might even be an audience for it. A questionnaire in Warsaw's *Literarishe bleter* showed him to be the favorite among Yiddish writers, and he thought that if he could get to Europe he might be able to publish his book where the costs were considerably lower.[56]

We have no idea how the poet would have organized this third volume of collected poetry. From the evidence of the earlier books, we know that he would have shaped it carefully, placing the poem cycles and longer works strategically in the text, modulating the whole within a suggestive mythical framework. It would surely have been the most personally revealing of his books, and one of the richest in Yiddish poetry. The dozens of works scattered through newspapers and magazines from 1924 onward, and the scores of unpublished manuscripts that Halpern had on hand, reveal a poet who had passed beyond the "bratty" brilliance of youth to a very wise, though not serene maturity.

Halpern's poem cycle about the *shtotgortn*, Central Park, would certainly have occupied a place of prominence. Here Halpern was

returning to the garden theme that he had placed so rakishly at the
start of his first book:

> What a garden, where the tree is
> Bare, but for its seven leaves,
> And it seems it is amazed:
> "Who has set me in this place?"
> What a garden, what a garden—
> It takes a magnifying glass
> Just to see a little grass.
> Is this garden here our own,
> As it is, in light of dawn?
> Sure, it's our garden. What, not our garden?[57]

Tendentious and raw, the immigrant of this early lyric mocks this
garden of Eden to which he is consigned and mocks those like
himself who should not pretend to be more than they are.

The cycle of poems of the late 1920s about Central Park is, like
the improved location, more generous than its scrawny predeces-
sor. A reflective poet strolls through the city park in winter, pausing
at the statue of Goethe to commune with the noble writer, letting his
mind wander from the passers-by to a conversation with his wife
over dinner to his youth in a distant land. The poet's voice is re-
markably clear and tender. All his poetic life, "Moishe Leib" had
projected his lines like an actor performing before a crowd. Here the
communion is private and unstrained, as if the man were singing for
himself.

> Whose fault is it that your tree can't be seen,
> Garden of snow, my garden of snow?
> Whose fault is it that your tree can't be seen
> When the woman strolling through you displays
> A bosom that rises and falls in the ways
> That a boat on the ocean will toss and careen
> Over troubled waves, with twin pirates, yo-ho,
> Who cry out that they are twin pirates, yo-ho!
> Garden of snow, my garden of snow.

Whose fault is it that there's no stag hereabouts,
Garden of snow, my garden of snow?
Whose fault is it that there's no stag hereabouts
When a priest, who should be as devout as a child
Runs after his hat in the wind so wild—
Hey and ho and hello, he shouts,
And the hat, wildly springing to and fro,
Doesn't hear, wildly springing to and fro,
Garden of snow, my garden of snow.

Whose fault is it that I'm foreign to you
Garden of snow, my garden of snow?
Whose fault is it that I'm foreign to you
When my funny shawl and my cap appear
Like nothing that anyone else wears here,
When I still have a beard that the wind picks through
Like a woman through straw, for the egg below
For her sick child, a chicken's egg below—
Garden of snow, my garden of snow.[58]

ver iz shuldik in dem vos men zet nit dayn boym,
gortn in shney, mayn gortn in shney.
ver iz shuldik in dem vos men zet nit dayn boym,
az se geyt shpatsirn in dir aza froy,
vos ir buzim heybt zikh un varft zikh azoy,
vi iber tseruderte khvalyes un shoym
a shifl in yam, mit yam-royber tsvey,
vos shrayen, az zey zaynen yam-royber tsvey—
gortn in shney, mayn gortn in shney.

ver iz shuldik in dem vos keyn hersh iz nishto,
gortn in shney, mayn gortn in shney.
ver iz shuldik in dem vos keyn hersh iz nishto,
as a galakh vos darf zayn frum vi a kind
loyft nokh dem kapelyush zaynem in vint,
un er shrayt tsu im hey un ho, un ha-lo!
un der kapelyush in zayn vistn gedrey
hert im nit, in zayn vistn gedrey—
gortn in shney, mayn gortn in shney.

ver iz shuldik in dem vos ikh bin dir fremd
gortn in shney, mayn gortn in shney.
ver iz shuldik in dem vos ikh bin dir fremd,
az ikh gey nokh dem shal un dos hitl do,
vos ba keynem in land iz azoyns nishto,
un az kh'hob nokh a bord vos dayn vint tsenemt
vi a yidene shtroy, vu zi zukht an ey
far ir krankn kind, fun der hun an ey—
gortn in shney, mayn gortn in shney.

There is no longer anything rhetorical in the poet's questions, for whose fault is it that the garden and its creatures remain so foreign to one another, that nature, including his own nature, remains so alien to man, who cuts a comical figure in what used to be his domain? The forces of wind and imagination that fracture the peace of the poem and of the garden are not attributable to any specific evil or amenable to any known solution. Summer, the season of Halpern's early poetry, has turned into winter, which softens what it bares, and the combative poet is humbled.

In the absence of a completed third volume of collected poems, one can only guess that the five-poem cycle on the park would have stood at its heart. The odd man strolling along in his "funny shawl and cap" can't stop dreaming about what might have been his fate if, for example, his younger brother who died on the eighth day of his life had survived to join him now, decades later, to relieve his loneliness and poverty. To the walker in the city garden the unrealized possibilities are more actual than his own existence.

The poet of this series is so philosophically reconciled to estrangement that he sees everything and everyone in a comic light, the priest chasing his hat, the woman with bobbing breasts, and himself above all, who has moved from the peripheral immigrant quarter right into the heart of the city without losing his homelessness. He is at once exceptionally solitary and in full possession of the scene, withdrawn into his own past and fantasy but attentive to all that is around him. These, Halpern's most personal poems, capture the mood of the early Depression that set so many ordinary citydwellers afloat, and enter the mainstream of American expression at the very moment of registering their creator's deepest isolation.

In the Magic Valley

Moishe Leib Halpern died on August 31, 1932. His death was such a shock to those who knew him that children remembered many years later where they had been when their parents received the news—on the way to buy new shoes for school or spending a final day in the country.[1] The word went out that he had died of neglect: his close friends had been blind to the severity of his illness, and the Jews indifferent to one of their greatest living writers. One critic was certain that "future Yiddish literary history would consider his death a murder."[2]

He died at an awkward moment on the calendar—the end of summer vacation—and at a low point in Yiddish literary activity. As the news slowly spread among his fellow writers, it seemed oppressively symbolic. Leivick, in the flush of tuberculosis, heard of Halpern's death in the Spivak Sanatorium in Denver. It was hard to believe that Halpern, "the gladiator," was dead while he, Leivick, the perennially sick Yiddish poet, still clung tenaciously to life.

Mani Leib was also ill but tuberculosis had not yet been diagnosed, and he was resting in the Catskills, at a farm in Saugerties, one hundred miles from the city. To his closest friend, David Ignatoff, he confided that the only thing occupying all his waking minutes was rent money for the children. "You are the only witness, these last few years, to my helplessness."[3] Ignatoff and Iceland must have decided to shield him from the news of Halpern's death. They did not summon him back from the mountains, and since he was beyond the reach of the daily Yiddish papers, he learned of it too late to come to the funeral. To Ignatoff he wrote anxiously when he finally heard,

> Moishe Leib Halpern isn't with us—Can't understand it! Halpern dead! Is it all over? Does that mean that it's reached us?—I think of death every day and I'm not afraid of dying . . . It's not death, but our life that is terrible. Halpern's life was so bitter, although I often envied him the easygoing impression it made. But who can judge another's life? Everyone suffers in his own way.
>
> And how come I was not told? [this sentence is mangled]. And I wasn't at his funeral! When I heard the sore news I realized how close he is to us—the same blood flowed through us all.

Agitated and miserable, Mani Leib wanted Ignatoff to write him all the details of Halpern's death.[4]

There was not much to tell. On Sunday afternoon Halpern had severe stomach cramps, but he went out as planned to spend the next day in Far Rockaway with his family. In the evening he took his customary swim in the ocean. This time the effort exhausted him and he collapsed on the beach. By Tuesday he was in such agony that the doctor sent him to a hospital the next morning. It was there on Wednesday that he died.[5] "Memento Mori" he had written many years earlier, describing Death as a familiar that would come to him, color-drenched, among the waves. In league with his ulcerated stomach, it came just as he had invoked it.

If Halpern knew he was in mortal danger, he certainly gave no hint of it to others. His friends saw only the dapper, gray-haired poet with the cane and dismissive arrogance or the doting father and husband. Casting back for omens, Reuben Iceland, who had seen him just two weeks earlier, recalled how "sweetly" Halpern had spoken at a charity evening for unemployed writers that the Peretz Farein had organized at a resort in the mountains.[6] Someone else remembered an unexpected meeting with Halpern, out for a stroll with his wife and child: Halpern had stopped to talk about the "shtetl hypnosis" that still gripped Yiddish literature, of which he claimed only he and David Bergelson were free.[7]

Halpern's death provoked the same anxiety as his verse.[8] Though his friends might try to fix blame for it on themselves and on the callous Jewish community, the dislocation and discontinuity of which Halpern wrote warned that there was no longer any viable "people" or nation to shoulder responsibility for its writers or to identify significantly with their fate. What his poetry affirmed his death seemed to confirm, provoking his fellow writers to recognize that they too might be laid to rest in a charity plot of the Workmen's Circle cemetery and to an equally humble resting place in literature.

At the time of Halpern's death, Mani Leib was beginning to write again after a fairly long period of drought. His "return" to poetry had been heralded by an announcement in the *Vokh* of 1929.[9] Over the next two years he did publish occasional poems and translations, including some long narrative poems, but much of his work had the flavor of self-imitation, as if a very wealthy man had decided to retire and live off his accumulated capital. The terms of this comparison may be cruelly inappropriate, since in every sphere except talent Mani Leib was increasingly burdened by poverty. The delicate balance he had managed to strike between working at poetry and working for a living had been fatally skewed with the onset of the depression.

As long as Mani Leib worked as a craftsman in the shoe industry, he was assured a steady income. He might envy Moishe Leib his "pampered hands," but he knew that he in turn enjoyed the enviable security of dignified labor. When deteriorating health prevented work in the factories, he became only one of the mass of the unemployed. In 1931, the year before his collapse, he worked in the pocketbook trade at $45 a week and also helped his son run a laundry pick-up during his spare hours.[10] This was no easy schedule for a man approaching fifty, and certainly not for a poet. Under the strain he began to lose weight, signaling the onset of serious illness. He was admitted to Deborah Sanitorium in Browns Mills, New Jersey, the last week of November 1932.[11]

A poet's artistic credo is not always manifest in his daily life, but Mani Leib's productive convalescence was like a gloss on his recurring theme of poetry's redemptive powers. Of course the materialist could offer a simpler explanation: by freeing him from his stressful routine, illness temporarily took him away from the city to a country setting and supplied him for the first time in his life with long hours of leisure. Weak and worried, and unable to rid himself of concern for the people who depended on him, he nevertheless profited extraordinarily from the enforced rest. During the year and a half it took him to recuperate, the surrender to hospital rhythm generated a fresh fund of creative energy. He experimented with new verse forms, composed two parts of a poetic autobiography, and wrote a five-act play. He took shy pleasure in the new poems he wrote and sent out for publication.

The letters he now had the opportunity to write to his friends communicated some of this rekindled power and even recreated, in a small way, the sense of a binding literary circle. As he read the literary magazines they sent him, he shared his reactions with his friends, who in turn took up these issues among themselves. Bygone literary conversations of the café tables were reviewed in thoughtful letters they had never before found the time or the need to write to one another. The death of Halpern and the simultaneous confinements of Leivick and Mani Leib forced them to take stock of what was left of their lives.

When Mani Leib was admitted to Deborah Sanatorium, he found that he was not altogether a stranger to the place:

> Do you know that my father died in a sanatorium like this? On a high white bed, among white walls. And now I so resemble my father! With this difference, that I'm not as quiet and compliant as he was, and not as kind-proud-compassionate and pious. I shout. My father spent his last years in sanatoriums and behaved like a man ashamed. He never let fall a word of accusation against us, his sons and daughters, yet we were all so guilty of neglect! I remember how he used to meet us in the sanatorium courtyard; too embarrassed for joy to look at us directly, he would glance at us, somehow, sideways, ashamed. He kept silent . . . but I get excited, and I shout with resentment, not at the children—they are so helpless and they are surely my sacrificial victims—and not at my friends—I have so many blood brothers, and I dare not complain, but I shout. At whom? At our Jewish society? But it doesn't owe anything to me and to those like me. So to whom do I shout?[12]

Though he repudiated his father's silence, he still found no outlet for his anger. The never-ending sounds of coughing reminded him of his kinship with the other patients who were a microcosm of the world. "'We' here are deeply moved when anyone out there in their free homes thinks about us," he wrote after his first week, still surrounding the plural pronoun with quotation marks to under-score the irony of his new collective identification.[13] He became a part of his new "home," took his turn serving table, and indulged his weakness for cards. He had always described himself as a folk-singer, elevated by the accident of his talent to a position of respon-sibility and glory above the others. Here, where as resident celebrity he recited his poems in the evening, organized readings for some of his famous visitors from the outside, and received privileged confi-dences from his fellow patients, the description held true. "I feel in the sanatorium like a man who doesn't like his bride, living it up at his own wedding." He provided the occasion for the pleasure of others, even though it was by no means the one of his choosing.[14]

If it was hard to organize beauty in the outside world, it was harder still in this artificial community united by its fear of death. The neoromantics and symbolists were always flirting with death in their struggle to free themselves from the clutch of ordinary matter. Mani Leib's early poetry regularly and almost eagerly reached for nonbeing as the soothing alternative to life. But now the situation was reversed. Death was the omnipresent reality. The thermometer, the scale, the diet, the bed, the walks at noon, the little gatherings at night, were all strategies for staving off the coughing, blood, and fever.

> The bed on which I lie—as I found out just this week—is where the patient before me died. It doesn't bother me. The night I found it out I slept soundly, like the man who had gone to sleep forever. Yet when I opened my eyes at six in the morning and saw through the window the tree, copper in sunshine, that the dead man used to see with his eyes and will never see again, and that I see, and will see again, and may even write a poem about—I rejoiced.[15]

The presence of death made the ordinary extraordinary. At first this atmosphere engendered in Mani Leib a fear of writing "like the fear that children have of going to sleep," but little by little he did begin to write and sent Ignatoff this first finished effort:

> In poor homes there is so much beauty;
> Hungry lips faith refines.

The hand beaten in aching smallness
Holds all doors open for poorer neighbors.

By the cold fire of feeble coals
Around the table heads rest on elbows
Ears are pricked, and old beards tell
The tale of pain and wisdom and miracles unfathomed.

And overhead—softly, the redeemer
Descends from their words to sit in their midst.
The coals glow with renewed red fire
Reddening all the heads and beards carved of fire.[16]

The scene of this poem was familiar from innumerable earlier Russian poems and Yiddish poems and from Mani Leib's childhood recollections of Jews gathered on Saturday night around the table of his parents' home in Niezhin. The theme, also familiar and simply stated in the opening line, interprets beauty as the refinement of want through faith and loving-kindness, as if to dispel for all time the notion that poor homes are notable merely for their suffering, steadfastness, or sorrow. Words long the staples of Mani Leib's verse—*shtil, sheyn, eydl* (still, lovely, refined)—compose the mood of quietude here too.

But the poor of this poem do not require the poet's mediation for their salvation. The gnarled syntax belies their apparent simplicity and complicates Mani Leib's earlier understanding of beauty and reality. The "hungry lips" that appear to be the subject of the second line are really the object of faith's refinement. Then, when we expect the "hand" of the third line to conform to this pattern, it confounds our expectations by "holding all doors open for a poorer neighbor." We suppose that we know all about poor homes, yet every phrase, cast in novel form, proves us wrong.

This poem complements Mani Leib's famous early lyric that portrayed the Jews as a muted herd, hushed in perpetual anticipation of the Messiah. These men of faith bring the redeemer to life through the energy of their yearning, sparking the dying embers to illumine and warm them anew. The ultimate beneficence is here dependent on ordinary human goodness, the miracle on those who bring it to life. The tremendous flow of movement in this seemingly static picture of a group of bearded Jews, telling stories around a common table, interweaves what is above and what is below—spirit and matter—so densely that it is no longer possible to distinguish which of the two is attendant on the other.

Moved by Thomas Mann's *Magic Mountain*, which someone had given him to read, Mani Leib realized how emblematically a sanatorium could be treated. He noted the essential difference in scale between Mann's monumental work and anything he might attempt:

> On the magic mountain, the whole world of ideas is revealed to Hans Castorp, but in my magic valley, the whole human world comes to life for me in keener miniature . . .
>
> I am not Goethe, nor even Heine. I am a limited Jewish artist with all the shortcomings of a Jew, with his poor cultural inheritance and closeted jargon of a language. With all the flaws of my talent.[17]

This was not an apology but an admission that he lacked the intellectual grandeur of European culture. Taking the measure of his own small achievement against the enormous changes that were disturbing the peace of the world, he saw how sheltered his work had remained and how incapable he would always be of confronting the large events, even those that affected his people directly. Were he a great poet, like Goethe, he would write comedies; a poet of his stature, however, could only corrupt whatever talent he had if he tried to wrestle with enormities. His fall into the "magic valley," where everyone is afraid of the world of the healthy, could not transform him into a writer of greater scope than he was. On the contrary, by coming to know life in death's domain he could better accept his limits.

Mani Leib's attraction to that most strictly controlled poetic form, the sonnet, dates from shortly after this period of imposed confinement and derives from the same impulse that made him write with assurance that "In poor homes there is so much beauty."[18] In the world outside, Marxists, Socialists, Communists, Hitlerites, Fascists, and Technocrats (his list) were busy "organizing life" and pressing language into the service of their large ideas. The poet had to rein himself in even tighter than before if he wished to resist such monstrous powerlust.

Within a few months, the doctors began to find him stronger. But the gradual return to health was a mixed blessing, demanding more frequent contacts with the city and a renewed responsibility for what was happening there. Both his families were in trouble. Rochelle was homeless, without enough money to rent an apartment of her own. The small checks she picked up from *Forverts* and from the few magazines where Mani Leib was publishing his poems were not enough to maintain her. Each helpless partner felt guilty for not being able to assist the other. Mani Leib's wife Chasia was deteriorating, and her social-service agency considered sending her to an institution. His children, unskilled and poorly educated, found it hard to hold on to their sales jobs and to compete in the depression marketplace. The greatest blow to Mani Leib was the arrival as a fellow patient of his youngest daughter Leyke, still a teenager, but already infected by the lung disease that would claim her life a few years later.

From the sanatorium he wrote insistently, trying to borrow money for his family—fifteen dollars so that his son Willy could buy a new motor for his truck, a few dollars to tide Rochelle over a particularly bad stretch, and always what was needed for the family's rent. He pleaded with friends to help when they could, knowing that they were often in great difficulty themselves. The scrawled messages he sent out seem clumsy attempts to salvage as much as possible of the lives he thought he had set adrift. In the end, when he was about to leave the Deborah to return to the city, he had to ask Rochelle for a few dollars to pay up his card debts and to buy the train ticket home.[19]

Nonetheless, the improvement of his health strengthened his writing, or perhaps it was the other way around. He was very pleased with *Justice*, a five-act play that he wrote so effortlessly in the spring of 1933 he thought he might be a "concealed dramatist."[20] The play used a family setting to dramatize the tension in his own life between common duty and artistic freedom. Its pivotal character, whom the author referred to as his hero, is an older musician, a "naive and honest violinist," the father of two talented pianist sons. The younger is a Communist who puts his music at the service of institutional choirs and other applied cultural causes; the elder is a virtuoso with a budding concert career. To support his studies he "borrows" the inheritance of an orphaned cousin who lives as a member of the family. The father sanctioned this financial sacrifice on the part of his niece because he expected that his son would marry her in return, but instead the ambitious concert pianist falls in love with a wealthy widow and refuses to keep his side of the tacit bargain. Thus the father's morally balanced musician's code is split in the next generation into two extremes—the sacrifice of art to the cause of humanity and the sacrifice of the human to the pure ambition of art.[21]

Mani Leib's ability to flesh out this idea in his first effort at playwriting justifies the pride that he took in it. Had he been able to sell the script to Maurice Schwartz, as he hoped to do, he would almost certainly have attempted another drama. He was intrigued by the possibilities of the local Yiddish theater, which had begun to cultivate an experimental branch, and like Halpern a decade earlier he hoped to write a successful play. (He cast certain leading actors in his mind.) But the play was too ideologically neutral to interest the radical ARTEF company, and it lacked the high drama that Schwartz sought in his theater. In the absence of further encouragement Mani Leib returned to the lyric, which it was always possible to place either in *Forverts* or in one of the newer literary magazines.

From the shelter of the sanatorium and the farm where he prolonged his recuperation, the resumption of vigorous literary activity seemed so plausible that by the end of his convalescence Mani Leib considered starting a new Yiddish journal to compete with one that he heard Leivick and Opatoshu were planning. Personal relations between the two poets had improved a little thanks to their common illness (and Mani Leib intended to invite Leivick to contribute to his magazine), but their artistic competition was as fierce as ever and the news of Leivick's plans may have quickened Mani Leib's resolve to draw the old group together again.[22]

He even considered going on the road. There had been some talk of a literary tour to California that could yield Mani Leib a precious few hundred dollars in income, but in addition to the doctors' counsel that he was not yet ready for such exertion, he was discouraged by the figure he cut as a speaker. "They want stump speakers like Leivick," he complained to a friend, "whose talk about our poetry the one time I heard him, made me blush with shame."[23] A magazine of his own would help to counter all this embarrassing rhetoric, but its potential contributors were simply too few and too poor to afford it. Release from the "magic valley" plunged Mani Leib right back into the reality of Yiddish literary life, dominated more than ever by the vying forces of left and right, and quickly dispelled his dreams of an independent literary organ.

The ferocity of debate inside the Yiddish community during the 1930s rose to the boiling point as the pressures upon Jews increased worldwide. In Palestine this same claustrophobic atmosphere exacerbated the quarrel over language between the Hebraists and those who wanted to preserve Yiddish in the Jewish homeland. By 1935 the language struggle had reached such critical proportions that the League for the Rights of Yiddish in Palestine had to be established to maintain, for example, a Yiddish printing establishment in Ramat Gan because many printers were too frightened by the strongarm tactics of the Hebraists to undertake the publication of Yiddish materials. Of course the battle over Yiddish, which was spoken in Palestine by orthodox Jews who opposed Zionism, and promoted as part of their ideological platform by the Communists and some left-wing Labor-Zionists, had an overt political edge, but the American Yiddish writers perceived it as yet another crushing threat to the future of their language. Reports of the "war against Yiddish" did nothing to endear the *yishuv* to those American Yiddish writers who were already anti-Zionist, and even the writers who sympathized with the Zionist cause were offended by the attack on their language. Mani Leib wrote a bitter sonnet addressed to Hebrew poets who laugh as "Queen Yiddish" expires in the drum smoke and dust of hora songs.[24]

The eagerness of the Yiddish writers to believe in the Soviet Utopia was similarly influenced by their dependence on the language, and the promise that there, at least, Yiddish culture would be granted its due. Whenever the Comintern opened a common front with the socialists, it drew back into its orbit a number of poets and writers who believed that Russia offered them their only chance of cultural survival. *Zamlbikher*, the impressive journal that Leivick and Opatoshu managed to launch successfully in 1936, was dedicated to a "positive attitude to man and to his environment"; more accurately, in its first issue this meant a positive attitude to Communism and *its* environment.[25] The editors daydreamed about Russia and tried to justify its policies. "We have forfeited Israel," one wrote in anguish to the other, "let's not lose Birobidhzan." "We are dull and sterile . . . What do we have but dust and dregs (*droyb un shtoyb*) everywhere—here in New York, in Poland, everywhere. Birobidhzan will give us power, will give us a base of support, even here in the Bronx."[26]

Death was the most immediate enemy. Moishe Leib's sudden death was indeed, as Mani Leib feared, the sign that "it had reached them," that their mantle of youth could no longer protect them. Other deaths followed in rapid succession.

Sacha Dilon had never achieved the artistic stature of poets like Landau and Mani Leib, but he was from the start an important member of their circle, an apostle whose wholehearted absorption in poetry and the lives of the poets gave them all a heightened sense of mission. Notorious as a literary gossip, Dilon forgave the poets everything except a bad line of verse. The only one he exempted from criticism was Mani Leib, his poetic ideal, to whom he clung "wordlessly speaking and fluttering" in imitation of his master. Dilon's death in 1934 deprived the Yunge of their most spirited defender, a lonely devotee of the aestheticist ideal whose self-consecration seemed foolishly anachronistic, but a lingering confirmation of how much their art could matter.[27]

Zishe Landau died in 1937. He fell, alone, in the rain in the middle of Broadway. Severe diabetes had limited his activity during the last years of his life and kept him shy of the company of even close friends. The shabby death of this poet, renowned for his fastidiousness, seemed to mock his lifelong ideal of perfection.[28] Landau had played a singular role in the development of American Yiddish poetry, but even before his death it was a role much in dispute. To his defenders he was the purest prophet and practitioner of the art of poetry. When Mani Leib eulogized him as "our rebbe," and the perceptive critic I. Kisin remembered him as "our conscience," they were deferring to his impressive erudition in the field of literature and to the stubborn fight he waged for its appreciation.[29] He would often declaim poetry aloud—the work of others, not his own—swaying back and forth like a Jew at prayer, and so keen was he for exactitude that (perhaps recalling the incanted Torah reading in the synagogue) he wished poetry could develop a system of notation, to capture the poet's full intention. The importance he ascribed to poetry and the intelligence he brought to its analysis kept alive his colleagues' faith in its value at a time when it was suffering its greatest neglect.[30] This same jealous devotion to poetry naturally drew the scorn of the social reformers who made him their favorite target. Even those who admired him as the "poet of pleasure" observed that the aestheticism of the Yunge had the misfortune to be born on the eve of the First World War, forcing the writers into a destructively adversarial relation to their time and place.[31]

Landau's genuine sensitivity made him the best critic of his own verse and of its limited possibilities. In a witty epigram—"Hirsh Lekert shot Von Wahl / And killed my blue nightingale"—he pronounced judgment on his artistic aspirations.[32] In 1902 Hirsh Lekert, the first genuine martyr of the Jewish Workers' Bund, had tried to assassinate the governor of Vilna. Landau's couplet suggests that, despite his failure as a political assassin, Hirsh Lekert, by fueling the radical movement, did succeed in destroying the possibilities of a culture that could tolerate Landau's kind of poetry. All his life Landau was aware of the insistent thumping of history, and his self-mockery derived from just this admission of his own superfluity, of his quixotic excess. (Moishe Nadir, whose artistic indebtedness to Landau was overlooked because he put it to such different polemical use, said he loved the way Landau limped on healthy feet.) His method of understatement and self-deprecation, developed to protect himself against overpowering political reality, eventually undercut the will to sing at all.

> Though I have much to tell you
> I shall hold my tongue.
> You are the doers of deeds,
> I am the man of song.[33]

The death of the man of song broke up the inner circle of the Yunge, and petty squabbles provoked lasting feuds. Mani Leib, in his eagerness to initiate some public form of tribute, took an unfinished poem from Landau's desk to what he considered the best of the current literary magazines: Leivick and Opatoshu's *Zamlbikher*, the very publication he had hoped to rival. His friend, the novelist David Kozanski, never forgave this kind of gesture and considered the published fragment, which the editors framed in black "like an Ex-lax advertisement," an insult to Landau's memory. Kozanski accused Mani Leib of scurrying after the favors of the local literati like a mouse fleeing a burning building. He apparently felt that Landau's death and Mani Leib's fear of loneliness had led him into the arms of the opposition. The quarrel was never quite mended.[34] The intense friendship between Mani Leib and Ignatoff also began to show strain.

At the same time, the deaths of their friends placed the survivors under a clear obligation. All their avowed confidence in the transcendent power of poetry was meaningless unless the poems were accessible. The dignity of the Yiddish word for which Landau had fought so hard could not be expected to emanate from yellowing pages of scattered newspapers and forgotten literary journals. Since the early 1920s none of the small group of the Yunge had managed to bring together his work in a decent volume, and unless the poets' works were now published, their writing was almost certainly doomed to oblivion.

The commemorative activity of the Yiddish writers on one another's behalf is an exceptionally moving testimony to their devotion to Yiddish literature and to their often estranged colleagues. The concern that Mani Leib showed for his fellow writers over the next twenty years contrasts sharply with his neglect of his own work. It angered Rochelle Weprinski to see him mopping the floor with copies of *Forverts* and pretending to be pleased when his own poems and picture appeared underfoot. He did not even keep copies of all his published poems. Except for the original trio of books of 1918 and some volumes of children's verse that were subsidized with an eye to their use in the Jewish schools, Mani Leib never brought together his poems during his lifetime.[35]

This carelessness did not extend to the works of other Yiddish poets. Mani Leib helped to put out the collected poems of Sacha Dilon in 1935 and three volumes of Landau's work beginning in 1937.[36] He coedited a book in honor of David Ignatoff.[37] He tried, unsuccessfully, to assemble a commemorative volume for Moishe

Leib Halpern, but had to give it up when Royzele, "stubborn as a mule," refused to cooperate.[38] Much of Mani Leib's correspondence and effort from this time was consecrated to helping other Yiddish poets. He collected sums of money for writers he knew to be in want and for literary projects that could not otherwise be realized. One friend remarked that Mani Leib was seen in the company of writers much more in his last years than before, as if wanting to make up for the earlier insularity of the Yunge.[39]

Mani Leib was also the object of uncommon tenderness. Unable to return to the shoe factories after he was released from the sanatorium, he found work in the publicity department of the Bakers' Union. At his request, he was also received back on the *Forverts* staff; he defended Abe Cahan as a fine person against charges that he mistreated his writers.[40] He was commissioned by the Workmen's Circle schools to prepare an introductory essay on Mendele Mocher Sforim commemorating the centenary of his birth. He did the work because he needed the money, but found himself unsuited for the task and unequal to interpreting a writer of such biting disposition.[41]

Everyone knew that Mani Leib was without a stable home. During the desperate years following his convalescence, Rochelle moved into a large house in Far Rockaway, one of the many abandoned summer residences that had been taken over by banks and mortgage companies after the stock-market crash; she made ends meet by renting out rooms to boarders. In all their years the couple had never enjoyed anything like a permanent home together, and this boarding-house arrangement was no different.[42] It occurred to his friend Jacob Pat and to some of Mani Leib's other acquaintances that his readers should make him a gift on the occasion of his sixtieth birthday of a home of his own, freeing him from at least one constant source of anxiety. In one of the most unusual gestures in the annals of modern poetry, Mani Leib was given the keys to a small house in Far Rockaway, near the oceanside he loved. The gift, organized in 1943 by *Forverts* and the unions of which Mani Leib had been a member, was presented to the poet by his appreciative readership three years later.

"Come to see how Yiddish poets live in their 'villas,'" he wrote soon after taking possession of the house. "Well, my 'villa' which needs new stucco may not impress you. But when you consider that it is a gift to the Yiddish poet from his battered folk, you will marvel at our people that troubles its bloody head with presents for its poor poets in these days of its own bloody demise."[43] The war was now over. For the Yiddish poet, the destruction of European Jewry was indeed the end of his people because his whole cultural presence derived from its sources and could have no vital existence without them. Mani Leib accepted the gift as a tribute to the generic Yiddish poet in the moment of his people's deepest despair.

Note that the "Yiddish poet" in question is long since done with affirming his separateness from his people, his folk. Mani Leib alongside many of his colleagues had won the battle for individual sensibility only to learn that his individual sensibility was that of a child of Jewish Niezhin, transplanted with the rest of his fellow Jews to New York and part of their collective fate. The Yiddish language was the raw material of the Yiddish poet. His resonance lay within its sources and nowhere else. The greater the poet's ambition, the more it forced him to attend his language, which was not his own creation but the product of a distinct civilization.[44] From the moment they sensed the threat to their language, long before their European counterparts, the American Yiddish poets realized that the distinction they had tried to draw between self and society was untenable. The gift of the "villa"—the grandeur of the gesture and the poverty of the house—expressed their interdependency.

Mani Leib's use of poetry to fuse the torn segments of life into an organic whole gradually erased the distinction between the private and the public voice. Nowhere is this more in evidence than in the sonnet series he began in the mid-1930s. Sometimes through the tension of the octet and sestet of a single sonnet, sometimes in a pair of sonnets that complement one another like two sides of a coin, Mani Leib reconciles the strained contrarieties of doubt and faith, constancy and deceit, guilt and pleasure, hunger and satiety, estrangement and loving accord. Though we do not have his final arrangement of the poems, internal evidence suggests that as the consummation of his work this series intended to create the harmony that life itself does not grant, and granted him least of all.

He did not write very much about what came to be known as the Holocaust. This reticence was not new: even after the First World War, when the apocalyptic vision dominated Yiddish literature, Mani Leib felt unable to adapt his modest style to catastrophe on such a terrifying scale. The only American contributor to a European elegiac ephemeris called *Death-Cycle* (1920), Mani Leib submitted a poem of characteristic obliquity, which said that he "had not heard the screams at night / although the danger was near / only at dawn in the snow on his field / did he find the bloody stain."[45] The poem was as much about his lateness and inadequacy in assimilating the tragedy as about the brutality and its victims. When he addressed the final murder of European Jewry in the 1940s, he was similarly delicate. But the two muted sonnets he did write on the subject are among the most beautiful in the language.

These sonnets are paired: one is metaphysical, the other earthbound; one opens the sore of doubt, the other mourns the ravished landscape. Drawing on the image of messianic expectancy that had become his own affirmation of faith, he calls into question all that he had been prepared to affirm:

> We waited long with prayers for your coming,
> A quiet little flock with pious beards,
> Redeemer, good Redeemer, on your snow-white steed!
> Our wait cut short . . .

The long waiting in the first line, *mir hobn lang gevart mit tfiles oyf dayn kumen*, is altered by the minor change of a prefix in the fourth line, *un nit dervart*, to a wait abruptly terminated. The hushed expectancy of the Jews was finally rewarded by their murder. Remaining is only "a small, small little Jew," the poet, to cast a last shameful question: "To whom, Redeemer, will you come today, to whom?"[46]

As against this diminuitive, plaintive, prayer for the slaughtered innocents, the companion sonnet evokes a muscular Jewry, a resonant and vigorous male chorus:

> There had been multitudes, yea, multitudes, O God—
> So many lively ones, and so many gallant,

So stately and so bearded, and so crowned with talent—
Whose language was astonishing, and nobly odd.

From under every rooftop with its gabled slopes
Such curious songs, and such haughty ones they'd sing,
Of the splendid peacock and Elimelekh the King,
With biblical cymbals, and the appropriate tropes.

But high above their heads, only the sun could see
The raw attack, the cold knife of the murderer
As he descended on them in a violent stir,
And what a lot there was of savage butchery . . .

Now they are melted, they are what violence can remember,
Two or three trees left standing amid the fallen timber.[47]

zey zaynen dort, oy got, geven a sakh, a sakh,
azelkhe lebedike un azelkhe brave,
azelkhe shtaltne, berdike un kutsherave—
un mit a vunderlekher oysterlisher shprakh.

un zingen flegn zey fun unter yedn dakh
azelkhe hoferdike lider un tshikave:
fun meylekh eyli-meylekh un der sheyner pave,
mit mavir-sedre trop un tsimblen fun tanakh.

not iber zeyer kop—di zun hot nor gezen
di roye gvald, dem kaltn meser baym roytseyekh,
vi er iz iber zey arop mit vildn keyekh,
un sara merderay iz dort geven!

itst zenen zey a zeykher nor fun yener gvald:
a tsvey-dray beymer fun an oysgehaktn vald.

The abundance, the stateliness, and the strength of this mass of Jews is actualized only in the final line when the few surviving trees make us see the mighty forest that once stood where the ground is now so barren. Through the multiformity of Yiddish sound and song, the poem confirms the power of the Jews, who are felled by an unfathomable force that strikes them like natural disaster. If, in one sonnet, Mani Leib flings at the conscience of its Shepherd the betrayed innocence of a patient herd, he recalls in the other the virility of the East European Jewish settlement that fatally impoverished the earth that consumed it.

In none of the poems is it easy to distinguish the folk poet from the private man. The strands that he separated so painstakingly when he published his work in three separate volumes in 1918 are here braided into an indivisible unity. One of the most exultant sonnets refers not to the poet, *dem poet*, but to the liturgical poet, *dem paytn*, God's alchemist, who triumphs over mutability and moves quietly to a holiness of word, "to fashion / prayers for the world / to knot the heart / to God: to unbind the heaviness on mute lips."[48] In poems of glory and frustration, whether blessing the Creator for his grace or cursing the Hebrew poets who trample Yiddish underfoot, the poet is inseparable from the civilization whose repository he has become.

The mature *balebos*, or householder, of the sonnets is a man of many moods. Sometimes eroticism breaks through the domestic routine, and another time sexual union estranges man and wife who sit across the supper table in its aftermath, separated like its two edges from one another.[49] In a sonnet that echoes some of Mani Leib's earliest lyrics, a man steals his happiness from the secure home of another, tasting guilt with every drop of his pleasure.[50] In what seems to be its companion piece, a husband offers his wife a taste of the ripe plum he has just plucked from a tree; together they suck the sacramental juice leaving only "skin, / And pit, and flecks of overbrimming foam."[51]

The result of this unending counterpoint of emotions is not a landscape of inner conflict, as one might assume, but discovery of human poise. Without in the least denying his rancor, and the pettier ranges of disappointment that nip away at his lengthening-shortening life, the speaker of these sonnets overcomes his sense of defeat. The approach of death invites a rash of reckonings—for an artistic opportunity that was incomparably promising, but only at the start; for a pair of hands whose dexterity served him perhaps too well; for love that was the more difficult the readier it came; for the destiny of an American immigrant; for the fate of a Jew. The compression of the sonnet, like the bright but limited light of a single day, challenges the poet to complete his reckoning within its bounds.

While only some of the sonnets are cast at the feet of God, they appear to join there like a psalter.

> You're full, sated with wonder as with bread,
> Sated with days—a full river that goes
> Beyond your eye, around the earth, and flows
> With light that God's eternal lamp has shed.
>
> Fed by him from the root up to the face
> With overflowing, as if given suck . . .
> He doomed you to become a pile of muck,
> For death and the blind worm a nesting-place.
>
> His Will your wisdom cannot comprehend:
> You only know you've been vouchsafed to see
> His light, the purple of his drapery.
> Thus when that light leaves your eye at the end,
>
> Throw your head down at his anointed sole:
> Give thanks, till earth has covered your mouth whole.[52]

It is no simple thing for a man to make his peace with God's bounty. The sated mouth that opens in blessing and purses its lips to kiss the purple hem of Glory will also, as in the English expression, bite the dust. To transcend the indignity of his human finitude, the poet must get beyond irony, acknowledging its doubled truth, but without capitulating to its crooked half smile. The poet can only become the *paytn*, a poet of the highest level of sanctity, once his competitive ambition as a creator satisfies itself of God's superior creative power. Mani Leib's sonnets occasionally touch this sphere of holiness.

Since the sonnets authoritatively interweave all the many strands of Mani Leib's experience, their omission of Russia and the Russian landscape cannot escape notice. The only two sonnets to recall the distant past are emanations of a pious Jew; one evokes the odors of the old house of study as sharply as if the poet had spent his youth within its walls, and the other, called "Christmas," captures the annual moment of terror:

> The bronze of bells aroused by the night sky,
> The town has frost, flares, incense on its breath;
> Their God arises joyfully from death
> And the crowds carry, on a pole on high,
> His image. And their tread, heavy and blind
> Bears hate aloft;[53]

The Jews, whose protection must come from their own "compassionate God," are dumb with fear and their blood "clamors in anguish" before the gentile knife. For many years Mani Leib defended his descriptions of harmonious gentile-Jewish relations; he was not to blame, he said, if he came from a peaceful part of the Ukraine and remembered his youth so fondly. Evidently, by the time he wrote the sonnets, contemporary events had either summoned up a different kind of memory or required that he substitute his people's truth for his own.

This does not mean that he ever ceased to mourn the loss of his homeland. But the Molotov-Ribentropp pact of 1939 ended for many Jews whatever illusions they had wanted to nurture about the nature of the Soviet regime and complicated the subject of "Russia" or "the Ukraine" even for such an apolitical poet as Mani Leib. His wish to keep poetry above ideology had always required him to keep a certain distance from the events of the day, but the alliance between the Soviet Union and Nazi Germany would have required him to do much more—to erase the contemporary meaning of Russia, substituting a private aesthetic reality for the revealed political facts. This it seems he could not do. Though the German invasion of Russia in June of 1941 turned the Soviet Union into a common enemy of Hitler for the duration of the war, this temporary alliance did not dull for Mani Leib the revelation of Soviet depravity. He was thus deprived of one of his major sources of imagery and inspiration.

In private, however, Mani Leib continued to dream of his Ukrainian homeland. His sparse archive contains the draft of a long letter (really a fiction in epistolary form) to the Soviet Yiddish poet

Itsik Feffer, who came to New York in 1942. As part of its determination to regain the trust of its democratic allies, Stalin's Central Committee, which always exaggerated the influence of the Jews, decided to send two Jewish emissaries abroad to win sympathy for the common war effort. They selected for the task Solomon Mikhoels, the great actor-director of the Moscow Yiddish State Theater, and Itsik Feffer, the Ukrainian-born Communist, whose poetry radiated enthusiasm. Mikhoels was the best known and Feffer probably, from the Soviet government's point of view, the most trustworthy member of the Jewish Anti-Fascist Committee that allowed Jewish writers in the USSR to work together for the duration of the war. This two-man delegation was intended to impress the Jews, and through them the British and Americans, of the importance of antifascist unity and to dispel the circulating fears of internal Soviet repressions.

We do not know whether Mani Leib was among the estimated 50,000 Jews who welcomed Mikhoels and Feffer at their outdoor appearance at the Polo Grounds, but the letter expresses his wild impatience to meet "his dear and beloved Itsik Feffer," touchstone of his abandoned past:

> I can't contain myself and write this letter many days before your coming to us in America. I am writing you out of the joy that overcame me at the news that you will be our guest. How odd: I have the feeling that with my letter I will be the first to welcome you, and seize the joyous initiative from all admirers, friends, and colleagues and from the poets who rejoice in your visit.
>
> My joy in seeing you is not collectivist, but personal, selfish perhaps, but nurtured from the first day I heard your happy name, Itsik Feffer, because I loved you as my own brother. I loved you, as they say, at first sight.
>
> In the joy of seeing my brother I even forgot that you are coming not to me, not to your lonely brother poets, but to our American Jews on some mission of some Anti-Fascist Committee to unite us with your Soviet Jews in some union to hate the fascists, that may God protect us from such a union.
>
> No: Jews hate the fascists and murderers of our people, and it's wildly alien for someone to demand of the Jews or even call upon Jews to hate their murderers. It's like demanding of people who are alive that they live.

I know that you are a person of the Soviet Government and that yours is a governmental mission and that you are probably the best person your government could choose for this job. In my joy at seeing you, I also forget that you, Itsik Feffer, carry, as I have heard, the rank of colonel. I don't believe it. Why it's comical that this jolly, joyous, and lyrical Yiddish poet, Itsik Feffer, should be a colonel: "Colonel Itsik Feffer!"[54]

Feffer, almost alone among the major Soviet Yiddish poets, was born in Mani Leib's section of the Ukraine, and Mani Leib recognized in his blend of Yiddish and Ukrainian rhythms a more ebullient version of his own kind of lyricism. He was drawn to Feffer like a lover. And like a star-crossed lover he proposed to spirit Feffer away from his Soviet guards for a midnight tryst. Feffer was to make his way down the backstairs of the fine hotel where the "official delegates to the bourgeoisie" are housed and flit across darkened New York to the poor home of a Yiddish poet for a free night of talk. All night the two poets would share the pain of forced separation between two Yiddish sons of the Ukraine who hear the same music in their bones and whose verse exudes the same aroma of Ukrainian roses and acacias.

This remarkable love letter does not stop here. Into Feffer's mouth Mani Leib puts a long, intimate confession of the true condition of the Soviet Yiddish poet, who wakes up in the morning with a Hasidic poem fully formed in his head but must put it aside in the harsh real light of dawn. "Feffer" confesses to his friend how the Soviet poet is forced to adjust at every moment of his life.

The poem does not get written. And before I grasp the calamity that has befallen me, the Soviet reality stands before me with all its horrors and shoves into my hands a ukase: I must write a poem about the Red Army, Stalin, the great progress of the kolkhoz system, the Sovnarkom, the Komsomol, and the devil knows what else; I must write something for the atheists or destroy in verse the world bourgeoisie; I must demolish our literature which serves the imperialists.

And later, during the war, when we fought with blood and limb . . . we Yiddish poets especially, we were free for the duration of the bloody game to sing as we pleased. That was the only time in all these years when we were free to sing of what was in our hearts. Obviously, we were not much inclined to "sing" during such a time, so we yelled, shrieked, sounded the alarm, cursed until we grew hoarse . . . and all that was natural given the danger of death.

Then it was after the war, after we had tasted freedom during the time of battle. The devastation was great in our land and even greater was our Jewish devastation. We, Yiddish poets, were fooled along with everyone else in the country; we thought that the liberty we had known during the war would last after the war as well. And we tried our first experiments, with our customary fear, to be sure, singing songs of our people, of our rebirth—

The conclusion of this letter suggests that it was composed well after the war, perhaps even after Feffer's arrest in 1948, though of this Mani Leib could have had no certain information. It ascribes to Feffer the postwar realization that Stalin's charges of treason against cosmopolitans and nationalists, namely Jews, had only been interrupted and not halted by the war. With tragic prescience Mani Leib charts the thoughts of a doomed man. Feffer, who after his arrest in 1948 was only released from prison once for a staged meeting with Paul Robeson (so that the respected Communist could reassure American Jews that Feffer was hale and free), was shot along with David Bergelson, Peretz Markish, David Hofshteyn, and other major Yiddish writers and artists on August 12, 1952.[55]

The letter reveals that Feffer was not the only one living a secret life. Mani Leib's discomfort with politics and his unwillingness to enter into the arguments raging around him forced him into an inner world of his own. He obviously followed very closely events in his native land and realized how the Soviet system was harming its citizens. But unable to formulate these misgivings artistically, he could only cut the past away from him or indulge in anguished private reflections. In effect, the unsent letter to Feffer was a buried attempt to keep up a contact with his homeland.

Mani Leib's last years were not as serene as his friends had hoped to make them when they gave the poet his house by the ocean. Although his sonnets record his pleasure in evening walks along the shore, Rochelle said that the proximity to the water in a poorly insulated house was not good for his health and gave that as the reason for their temporary move to an apartment in Forest Hills, then to another house in Far Rockaway.[56] Rochelle's influence over

Mani Leib was so suspect among some of his acquaintances that they accused her of seeking out a place in Queens near the cemetery where Mani Leib's daughter lay buried.[57] Because each move of the couple was complicated by unforeseen delays and difficulties, Mani Leib's last years in New York were almost as nomadic as his first.

Although his surviving children came to visit their father, bringing their own children for him to play with, there was no true family reconciliation. Mani Leib tried to make up to his children for the home he had broken, but their resentment of Rochelle could not be assuaged by presents he lavished on his grandchildren or by what they felt to be belated parental concern. Rochelle was also unhappy over the family's distrust and Mani Leib's straying affection. These tensions occasionally made their way into Mani Leib's later poetry.

By contrast, Mani Leib's renewed artistic confidence encouraged him to take a more active and fatherly role of sorts in Yiddish literary circles. In 1945 he assumed for several issues the editorship of the independent literary journal *Epokhe* (Epoch), imposing on it his unmistakable stamp:

> We need a magazine where poetry is not an afterthought . . . but the exclusive or at least the main substance. In our time of *khurbn* [destruction of the Jews], migration, homelessness and reconstruction, *Epokhe* will not be an isolated tower but a small workshop where serious poetic craftsmen can also meet to talk about their work.[58]

Characteristic of Mani Leib is not only the idea of work and craftsmanship but the homely atmosphere in which weighty subjects are to be treated. True, he proceeded as editor to scold David Ignatoff for publishing a memoir of the Yunge that grossly exaggerated his own importance in the formation of the group. This attack ruined the long-standing friendship between Mani Leib and Ignatoff and caused them both much anguish.[59] Nevertheless, Mani Leib's criticism can be read as his desire to rescue the memory of a united and democratic group from one who unfairly distorted the record. For the rest, Mani Leib functioned as a kind of elder statesman, organizing open symposiums in his magazine and mediating quarrels outside it.

One of the questions he raised in a symposium on tradition was the Yunge's old complaint about the missing inheritance of Yiddish poets, their orphancy. The Jews, he said, had written all kinds of poetry during their long history. The borrowings of Jewish poets, including Yiddish poets, from other languages showed their awareness of the poetry and the traditions of poetry in surrounding cultures. But prior to the Yunge there was no appreciation of verbal art as a component of national culture, and even those who wrote poetry did not regard it as the expression of a people's heart and wisdom. As the first mindful poetic group among the Jews, the Yunge were also the first to establish that Yiddish had an indigenous tradition of poetry worthy of cultivated respect. "Thus the poetic tradition begins with us. And our people—woe is us—may yet remember us to the good."[60] Our people—woe is us: a sudden stab of realization that the Jews for whom this tradition was fashioned are fatally altered. The Yunge had pronounced the value of a modern secular literature for Jews everywhere so that no Jewish poet after them need ever doubt his legitimacy. But to whom would it matter?

Happily, this nagging doubt did not silence Mani Leib or dull his enthusiasm for the poetry of others. He extended what hospitality he could to the Yiddish writers who survived the war and came to America as refugees; and if this occasionally involved a bit of intellectual duplicity, he put the person before his art. At a public evening honoring Chaim Grade, who had just arrived in New York (when he was still known exclusively as a poet, having not yet published any of his novels), Mani Leib hailed Grade's place in the tradition of "Rosenfeld, Yehoash, Frug, Peretz, Bialik, Liessin, and Abraham Reisin." An unsent letter in his archive shows what effort this public praise must have cost him.[61] Grade's rhetoric and his inflated attempt to describe the Jewish national sorrow represented for Mani Leib the worst tendencies in modern Yiddish verse—"*fat exaggerated metaphors*," "*forced rhymes*," "*superfluous repetition*"—all introduced to swell the importance of *khurbn*, the subject of the Holocaust. Mani Leib expressed his admiration for Grade's first, prewar book of poems, *Yo* (Yes) but demonstrated what had gone wrong when the poet turned himself into a moralist. Much to his regret, he concludes that he will never be able to share these truths with Grade because "It is hard for me to talk to you as I would like and hard not to talk to you." These unsent communications—there are several among his papers—were an "embarrassed"

attempt to keep the sacred trust of poetry without causing unneces-
sary human damage.

"I envy you the love that thousands of people feel for you," he
was told by Joseph Rolnik, who had always suffered from what he
took to be unfair neglect.[62] Regretful for his own contribution to
that neglect, Mani Leib tried to put out an issue of *Epokhe* devoted
to Rolnik's work. He encouraged the older poet with high praise for
his natural diction and authentic earthiness. His friend of the early
years, the poet I. J. Schwartz, was so impressed by the ripe quality of
Mani Leib's poems that he asked him, "How did you grow so
wise?"[63]

It took all of Mani Leib's diplomatic skill to help arrange the visit
to New York of Itsik Manger in 1951. Manger, who many con-
sidered the outstanding Yiddish poet of his generation, was also its
most difficult personage. His disposition had not improved during
his lonely refugee years in London, where he had managed to escape
in 1940. A hard drinker, he used the facade of drunkenness to do
and say many hurtful things that not everyone was willing to excuse
as an appurtenance of genius. Mani Leib knew he would not be in
for an easy time when he fell in with the critic Abraham Tabachnik's
proposal to bring Manger over to America.[64] Manger's arrival
stirred the whole Yiddish literary community and the thousands of
Jews who came to hear him read his work. Such visits of European
writers to America (or of American Yiddish writers to Europe) had
been common in the 1920s when the Yiddish press was always full
of welcoming speeches and farewell speeches by the travelers and
their hosts. Now Manger came like a ghost from the land of the
dead. Haggard, always with a cigarette at the corner of his mouth
and a performer's talent sharpened by years in the Yiddish theater,
he looked and played the part of the ruined troubador. Through his
brokenness he evoked the Jewish tailor shops of Rumania where he
had worked as a boy and the Jewish cabarets of Poland for which he
had traded them in as an adult, granting audiences a posthumous
glimpse of their liveliness. No one could remain indifferent to
Manger or his poetry.

Manger was closest to Mani Leib of all the New York poets, and
he stayed with him and Rochelle for a while. They were two singers
who delighted in the popular folk sources of song and story. Even

when they knowingly strained at the bonds of their culture, exploring the kind of aberrant urges that tore moderns away from their tradition, their diction and rhythm and imagery recalled a prelapsarian harmony. Manger credited Mani Leib's influence as a popular lyricist, undeniable proof that the "tradition" of modern Yiddish poetry had evolved just as the Yunge had defined it.[65] Mani Leib treated Manger as an irresponsible younger brother. For Manger undeniably had in him more than a little of Moishe Leib Halpern's belligerence. Even before he arrived in New York he was attacking H. Leivick for having his hand in the community dish, that is, profiting from the public he courted. Manger rewarded his acquaintance of the Warsaw years, Melekh Ravitch, who had arranged his visit to Montreal, by denouncing his poetry, his character, and the dishonesty of his friendship. Mani Leib shared many of Manger's dislikes. Faced, however, with exaggerations and distortions of his own prejudices, he came to the defense of Manger's targets and of the local American Yiddish audiences whose bourgeois posture Manger found so offensive.[66]

Thus in addition to the delight that his poetry inspired and the emotional charge that his presence elicited, Manger made Mani Leib feel the weight of his years. Forced to interpret and defend Leivick and the rest of the American Yiddish literary community from Manger's intemperate assaults, he knew how much he had come to value the poets among whom he had lived and the American experience that had given shape to his poetry. Together they had composed their song and it was there, on the stones of East Broadway, that they would have to seek their immortality. Manger felt alien among them; eventually he took his restlessness to Israel, where he was as much at home as he could be anywhere. Each in its way, the visits of Feffer in 1943 and of Manger in 1951, the two poets with whom he had most in common artistically, impressed on him how much he had become a part of America.

It was during Manger's visit that Mani Leib again took sick. Illness was always connected in his mind with the possibility of a tubercular relapse, forcing him to take stock of his life and work. For years his friends had been urging him to do for himself what he was always doing for others: to put out his collected works. Rochelle wanted him to publish his translations as well as his original verse in a separate volume, such as he had put out for Zishe Landau. But all of his work was scattered in newspapers and magazines and would have to be retrieved before it could be used. He had resisted the idea of a new book of verse as long as he was unsure of its quality. Now that he was in the midst of writing his sonnets, with sixty already at hand, he felt ready to do it.[67]

Commenting on the sonnets some time afterward, Jacob Glatstein observed that Mani Leib became a great poet only in the last decade or so of his life. According to Glatstein, Mani Leib had never written poetry of middle years—only a poetry of youth and the sonnets of ripe age.[68] The odd thing about this judgment is that it seems to have been shared by the poet himself. Mani Leib's decision to collect his work in book form once he had written his sonnet series reveals the depth of his self-doubt during the preceding decades, when he did not even save much less republish his work. His popularity would have guaranteed him sponsors because, like the Cleveland-based committee that put out Halpern's *The Golden Peacock*, there were always small groups of Yiddish readers willing to underwrite a worthy project; at least one group in Chicago had made him an official offer of support. His failure to put out a book cannot be attributed to the instability of his life or his finances, but to what he regarded as the insubstantiveness of his work.

Glatstein said of Mani Leib, as it has been said of many other American writers, that his career did not have a second act. Many explanations for his decline were offered, during his lifetime and after:

—Mani Leib's romantic inspiration was essentially a function of youth. When the piercing emotions of love and pain grew blunted, as they do with age, the poetry lost its freshness. Mani Leib's kind of talent does not outlast the first flush of creativity.

—The competitive political atmosphere of the 1920s, which released in his colleague Moishe Leib Halpern a rush of creative energy, damaged the gentler talent of Mani Leib, whether he tried to escape the hostility or to adjust to it by joining *Freiheit*. Wounded by sniping critics, he retreated into translation and self-pity.

—His life grew too complicated to sustain his poetry. His genius was crushed by excessive domestic weight. This was one of the most frequently cited reasons for the falling off not only of Mani Leib but at one time or another of every other major American Yiddish poet.

—The press killed the poet, just as the Yunge initially feared it would. Their movement was born of the realization that the individual writer had to stand free from any commercial or coercive vehicle. As soon as Mani Leib became a regular contributor to *Forverts*, his poetry wilted.

—Mani Leib focused too exclusively on himself. The intelligent English-language journalist and Yiddish poet Judd Teller, who most forcefully advanced this view, complained that the Yunge's "cultivated ignorance of life" resulted in a kind of fetishism of the personal pronoun. Teller felt that the development of poets like Mani Leib had been fatally undermined by the self-centeredness of the Yunge, which unfortunately replaced "Halpern's openness to the world" as the main tradition of American Yiddish poetry. The Yunge were "Hellenistic aesthetes whose spirit ran counter to Jewish tradition" and who deserved to lose their Jewish audience.[69]

Unsatisfactory in themselves, each of these propositions sheds some light on the difficulties Mani Leib faced as a poet after he had established that he was one. To contradict Glatstein, Mani Leib could have gathered a fine—if slender—collection of poems of his middle years from among the works he published. What is more, with the exception of a few years of silence—the exception, not the rule—he continued to experiment and to reach for the larger work to which the Yunge had always aspired. But it did take him a very long time to realize his ambition, and his slow progress, compounded by false starts, temporarily discouraged and embittered him.

Perhaps the question of Mani Leib's progress should be reversed to ask not what weakened his second act but what revived him in the third. Given the difficulties and setbacks of his life and the inimical atmosphere in which he worked, how did Mani Leib recover the artistic confidence he had lost? It is less unusual for a poet to experience a falling off from early exuberance than to produce his strongest work after the age of fifty.

Apparently, when Mani Leib and the Yunge spoke of poetry as faith, it was more than a phrase. Raised in the Jewish faith, they delighted as young men in upending or subverting it by applying its language of sanctity to art and its insistence on moral behavior to an insistence on perfect poems. Landau especially liked to show how far he had traveled in his *commedia dell' arte* treatment of religious personalities like the Baal Shem Tov and Sarah Bas Tuvim, author of Yiddish prayers for women. Mani Leib resisted the irony. The feeling of having been touched by God's grace required that he fulfill his obligation to his talent. He was always miserable after squandering a day or a night in the café or at the card table, guilty over the poem he might have written. He counted on discipline as much as he hoped for inspiration.

Without explaining the creative process, we know that Mani Leib found his voice in the sonnet. In this strict poetic form, he was able to make much out of little, the challenge ideally suited to his talent and his moral view. The sonnet was to him like poverty, like deprivation—small cramped space that only the artist could make resplendent. The sonnet was the very antithesis of those inflated poems on great themes by Leivick and Leyeles and Menahem Boreisho that so annoyed Mani Leib with their "mysticism—mystification—poetic paraphernalia."[70] And yet the sonnets could, when ranged in numbers, assume the weight of a major body of work. They satisfied his contradictory requirements of smallness and greatness, intimate enough for his soft voice yet powerful enough for the summary of a life. He had been looking for something bolder, of epic proportions, like the autobiographical poem he began writing in 1933. He settled for the sonnet without letting it feel like a compromise.

Although he lived so much longer than Halpern, proud of reaching seventy, his poetry was if anything even more scattered and unorganized than Halpern's at the time of his death. Except for the sonnets that he had neatly transcribed in a notebook (though not in order, and with variant phrases still undecided), he had only begun to assemble his manuscript when he was admitted back into Deborah Sanatorium in April 1953. Perhaps having in mind his productive sojourn there twenty years earlier, he brought the manuscript along and worked on it when he felt strong enough.

He fell back into the hospital routine hoping to be sent home quickly "though at my age illnesses come one after another—to help the angel of death escort us to the world beyond."[71] At first Mani Leib saw himself as the hero of a farce. A doctor thought he could treat him for tuberculosis at home, but when the medication proved worse than the disease, he went for a new set of X-rays. The X-rays proved negative, prompting him to exclaim, "What am I without my illness?" To determine who was right, the home doctor or the radiologists, he was admitted once again—this time to a sanatorium in Liberty, New York. The doctors there seemed uncertain whether the spot on his lungs was residual damage or something altogether new. Once again he received visitors and exchanged letters with those on the outside. The notes he wrote to friends this time were hastier than those of 1933–34. They described a strange whistling noise that emerged involuntarily from his lungs, making him sound like a rooster.[72] If the doctors knew that he was dying of lung cancer, they told neither him nor Rochelle, so that both they and their friends expected him to be released shortly.

On Rosh Hashonah for the first time since childhood he attended services.[73] David Ignatoff, with whom he resumed his friendship, had returned to the regular synagogue attendance of his youth, but Mani Leib had never been at ease with any part of the written tradition of Judaism and felt uncomfortable now with the prayers. Through the years he had come to believe that of the two kinds of Jewishness—that of the scholars and that of the folk—certain Yiddish poets owed their inspiration to the one while he and Ignatoff, Landau and I. I. Segal, Rolnik and Iceland, Feffer and Manger, belonged to the other. They belonged to the Hasidic branch of low social status and high spiritual merit. There were times when he cursed his lack of knowledge and the ignorance that narrowed his artistic horizons. But in this, as in so many other things, he felt bound to accept what was granted him.

The sanatorium was a place of reckoning. Leivick, who was also back in a sanatorium and with whom he had reestablished something like a friendship for the first time since the early 1920s, had written to him as if summing up his life. Though the Jews had no monasteries, he said, they had had in Europe *hisboydedus shtiblekh* (little houses of seclusion), whose equivalent he had found in the sanatorium. He admitted to Mani Leib that some of his days of solitary illness were among the happiest he had known.

Why should I deny it? I am very sentimental about you. Though our lives went in very separate and apparently different directions, it only seems that way. Actually we both share the same source of sorrow, and the same light of exaltation—when that light falls on us. It doesn't always. But we are always poised in preparation *for something*, that requires us to gird all our spiritual, all our poetic energies, to be poetic *heroes*. Your poems have even more wings than mine, and their music bears the sadness of that eternity that has no interest in whether we, Yiddish poets, are the last or not. Yes, we are the last. We need not hide it from ourselves. But there is a lastness of which one has to be worthy.

When I recall our *beginning*, I remember that even then we had a premonition that we were the last, and it was just this premonition that strengthened us and revealed to us much beauty. Of the ten heads of beauty you were given the lion's share. So help me, it's true.[74]

Mani Leib, as ever, had a homier style:

A word about the crowing of roosters: As far as I know, roosters crow to wake their wives, I believe three times a night. I have no Kinsey Report on hand, but here at Liberty I hear the crowing of nearby and faraway roosters through the long nights. Their crowing sounds to me full of loneliness, like a call in the desert—whether they are without wives, or so old that their crowing doesn't wake their wives, I don't know—but here one night a rooster's crowing tore my heart and I thought of you: you in your sickbed had thought of me and called out to me, and I didn't immediately answer you . . . Ah, may God help us.[75]

Mani Leib died not long after Rosh Hashonah, on October 6, 1953. Ignatoff locked himself away and cried. A public funeral was held in the hall of *Forverts* on East Broadway, with eulogies among others by Opatoshu, Niger, and Jacob Pat. Both there and at the cemetery his surviving colleagues, now united in grief, read from his works. Representatives of *Forverts*, the Workmen's Circle, the Jewish Teachers' Seminary, the Yiddish Pen Club, and the I. L. Peretz Writers' Union spoke for their organizations.[76] It turned out that, having failed to pay dues, Mani Leib had no more place in the cemetery than Halpern had. He was buried not very far away from his colleague in a Workmens' Circle plot.

Prominent among the works read at the funeral and the cemetery was Mani Leib's "Inscription on My Tombstone," written as if expressly for the occasion.

> Here lies Hersh Itsi's son: on his unseeing
> Eyes are shards; in his shroud, like a good Jew.
> He walked into this world of ours as to
> A yearly fair, from that far town Nonbeing
>
> To peddle wind. On a scale he weighed out
> All that he owned to a wheeler-dealer friend,
> Got back home to light candles, tired at the end
> When the first Sabbath stars had just about
>
> Curtained his town's sky above all the Jews.[77]

The poet had laid himself to rest as a proper Old World Jew, referring to himself, in traditional manner, as his father's son. The burial society had presumably washed and arrayed him properly, with clay on his eyes to speed his return to clay and in the pure white shroud that would keep him until the Redemption. Only the stuff he traded in set him apart from other ordinary Jews. His return to earth came not a moment too soon since rest, an Eternal Sabbath, had already settled over his entire community. Yet as his bereaved friend, Shloime Simon, wrote in one of the dozens of obituaries and tributes that filled the Yiddish press during the ensuing months, what kind of fabrication was this? There in his coffin lay the modern Yiddish poet who had spent the last fifty years of his life in New York. He was dressed in a blue suit and a white shirt, dolled up by the same heavy rouge that American morticians apply to all their clients as a final indignity. What connection could there be between the epitaph and the man in the coffin?[78]

That, of course, was the mystery that went to the grave with the dead man. Mani Leib would have been amused to find himself a posthumous riddle. Of all the Yiddish poets of his generation, he alone had made a supreme virtue of simplicity, cutting against the grain of modernism to poems of elemental freshness:

> The sun is good to all. It shines even to cut
> Across to dead graves through the cemetery fence,

Shining for the grass and for the blindworms thence,
To raise them up from death, from its distended gut.

It must have God's consoling sign of old to give:
That from death, even, there springs forth life that will live.[79]

He did not rail like Halpern against the messianists, but in his own way, without trying to "bend steeples to the ground," he did stay among the wonders of the earth. The sonnets especially had clarity as their ideal, although with their extolling of "life that springs from death," they could not be all that plain and simple. Through his attachment to what he knew, Mani Leib came up against the unknown.

And he leaves no such simple questions: What constitutes identity in a poet who buries himself as the proper Jew he never was? What does the expression of faith mean in poems of charted doubt? How much do the sensations of resolution and harmony in his poems depend on their context of irreparable breakage and loss? Part of the strength of this late poetry derives from its sense of immortality. In the poem "East Broadway" Mani Leib wrote that his brother poets had transmuted a nation's heart on the grime of each stone, which would ever after resound with their song. This raises a question of another kind. Was the new Yiddish psalter imprinted for all time in the stones of East Broadway, or did it sink with the poets into a place as lost as Atlantis?

Acknowledgments

To acknowledge my full indebtedness in the preparation of this book would require an autobiography. My interest in Yiddish poetry began in my parents' home and in the Jewish Peoples School in Montreal. The Yiddish poet Melekh Ravitch, with whom I had studied privately for two years, gave me access to his incomparable archive when I began my research on the Yunge. Abraham Sutzkever encouraged me to pursue Yiddish studies at Columbia University and shared with me his enthusiasm for these poets. An invitation from the Jewish Peretz Schools in the mid-1960s to speak on Mani Leib prompted my first serious interest in his sonnets.

My colleagues at McGill University have been unfailingly helpful through many years of work on this project. I hope that Eugene Orenstein, Gershon Hundert, Lawrence Kaplan, Barry Levy, Leib Tencer, Bracha Muszkatel, as well as my colleagues of years past, know how much I appreciate their friendship. I had the assistance of Esther Frank, Mindy Spiegel, Goldie Morgentaler, and our secretary, Sylvia Gross, and was stimulated by the papers and comments of many fine students in the advanced Yiddish classes.

I never enter the YIVO in New York without feeling gratitude to my teacher Max Weinreich, who had the foresight to establish it as an American "branch" of the YIVO in Vilna. Among its staff I am particularly indebted for help on this book to Dina Abramovitch, Marek Web, Zachary Baker, and Ezekiel Lifshitz. Mordecai Nadav and Yosl Birshteyn made it a pleasure to work in the archive of the National and Hebrew University Library in Jerusalem, and I am thankful to Yaron Sachish for putting the uncatalogued Moishe Nadir papers at my disposal. The Jewish Public Library in Montreal is an invaluable local resource; I appreciate the courtesy of all its staff and the added pleasure of visiting there with my sister, Eva Raby.

The translators of American Yiddish poets—John Hollander, Benjamin Harshav, Barbara Harshav, Kathryn Hellerstein, Nathan Halper, Irving Feldman, Seymour Levitan, Marie Syrkin, Marcia Falk—are acknowledged in the text and notes, but this hardly covers my indebtedness to them for their labors. Without John Hollander's texts in particular, I could not have hoped to present Halpern and Mani Leib as true poets. I appreciate his permission to include two previously unpublished translations and to use the refrain from "Song: Weekend's Over" for the title of the book.

It was very moving to meet and speak with several of the children of the Yiddish writers, including Isaac Halpern, Esther Landau Getzoff, and the late Daniel Ignatoff, who let me catch through their memories the sharpest images I have of their parents. Their love and respect for the poets among whom they were raised softened considerably the published impressions of strife and rancor. I also profited from interviews with Barbara Getzoff, Elka Segal, Rochelle Weprinski, Eliezer Greenberg, Meir Shtiker, Julia Shtiker, Frieda Tabachnik, and the very dear Bessie Drost. When her relatives, the Helprins, kindly took me to visit Moishe Leib Halpern's sister, Frieda, no longer able (or perhaps too clever) to respond to questions, she shouted at me, "You only want to take!" I have a sense that others may have felt the same and am the more thankful to them for having refrained from saying so.

This book benefited greatly from the suggestions of Irving Howe and my brother, David Roskies, who may recognize the depth of their contribution in the finished text. Khone Shmeruk and Gita Rotenberg offered encouraging criticism of early chapters. The wise editorial advice of Neal Kozodoy on my *Commentary* article, "A Yiddish Poet in America," is reflected in the chapters on Halpern.

For her enthusiastic reception of this book I will be forever grateful to Maud Wilcox of Harvard University Press. It was much improved by her suggestions and by the fine editing of Joyce Backman. My thanks to Linda Rozmovits for the index and to Jacob Wisse for his help in proofreading.

My originally proposed study of the Yunge was funded by a grant from the Killam Foundation of the Canada Council; I hope this somewhat scaled-down version vindicates its trust. I was also helped in later stages of the work by a Humanities research grant from McGill.

Dedication of the book to my husband and our children is an attempt to acknowledge a small part of all I owe them. I am inhibited from saying more out of fear of the evil eye on one side of my cultural inheritance and respect for decorum on the other.

Notes

I had originally intended to write a literary history of the Yunge and only later narrowed my sights to two poets. To leave tracks for future scholars, I tried to cite as many useful Yiddish sources on American Yiddish poetry as I could without overloading the text. Except when quoting directly, I did not give a similarly detailed account of my reading in related areas. Among such other secondary sources I would like especially to acknowledge Oleg A. Maslenikov, *The Frenzied Poets: Andrey Biely and the Russian Symbolists* (Berkeley: University of California Press, 1952). Its evocation of a literary circle through the life and work of one major poet suggested to me a similar approach for a study of the Yunge.

Sources. Biographical sources for Mani Leib and Moishe Leib Halpern appear in the notes to Chapters 2 and 4. The main sources of Yiddish literary biography are Zalmen Reyzn, ed., *Leksikon fun der yidisher literatur, prese un filologye* (Lexicon of Yiddish Literature, Press, and Philology), 4 vols. (Vilna, 1926–1929); Shmuel Niger and Jacob Shatsky, eds., *Leksikon fun der nayer yidisher literatur* (Lexicon of Modern Yiddish Literature), 8 vols. (New York: CYCO, 1956–1981).

The following are of special interest on the Yunge:

Iceland, Reuben. *Fun unzer friling* (Of Our Springtime). New York: Inzl, 1954.

Ignatoff, David. *Opgerisene bleter* (Drifted Leaves). Buenos Aires: Idbuj, 1957.

Kozanski, David, ed. *Zishe lande zamlbukh* (Landau Miscellany). New York: Inzl, 1937.

Pat, Jacob. *Shmuesn mit yidishe shrayber* (Conversations with Yiddish Writers). New York: Marstin, 1954.

Steinberg, Noah. *Yung amerike* (Young America), 2nd ed. New York: Lebn, 1930.

Tabachnik, Abraham. *Dikhter un dikhtung* (Poets and Poetry). New York: A. Tabachnik, 1965.

Wisse, Ruth R. "*Di Yunge*: Immigrants or Exiles?," *Prooftexts*, 1 (1981), 43–61.

——— "*Di Yunge* and the Problem of Jewish Aestheticism," *Jewish Social Studies*, 38 (Summer–Fall 1976), 265–276.

Transcription. All Yiddish titles, publications, and quotations, are transcribed according to the standard YIVO system that can be found in the index volume of the *Encyclopedia Judaica*. The single exception is the well-established form for the newspaper *Freiheit*. Since most of the Yiddish writers Americanized their names in various nonstandard forms, I tried to achieve some consistency by following the usage of the *Encyclopedia Judaica*. Here too I made an occasional exception: for instance, I followed the author's choice of Moisei over Moshe Olgin.

Translation. The difficult task of discussing poets in a language not their own was made much easier by the appearance of two new anthologies, *American Yiddish Poetry: A Bilingual Anthology*, ed. Benjamin and Barbara Harshav (Berkeley: University of California Press, 1986); and *The Penguin Book of Modern Yiddish Verse*, ed. Irving Howe, Ruth R. Wisse, and Khone Shmeruk (New York: Viking, 1987). In choosing poems and even artistic issues for discussion, I found myself favoring examples that were already finely rendered in English, a bias that I hope will enhance the reader's appreciation as much as it facilitated my work. Where no adequate translation was available, I provided my own. To give at least some flavor of the original, a few poems are offered in transliterated Yiddish.

Abbreviations. The following abbreviations are used in the notes:

AYP *American Yiddish Poetry*, 1986
JPLM Jewish Public Library, Montreal
JTSA Jewish Theological Seminary Archive, New York
NHUAJ National and Hebrew University Archive, Jerusalem
PBMYV *Penguin Book of Modern Yiddish Verse*, 1987
TYP *A Treasury of Yiddish Poetry*, ed. Irving Howe and Eliezer Greenberg (New York: Holt, Rinehart and Winston, 1969)
YIVO YIVO Institute for Jewish Research, New York

Though I used many archives of Melekh Ravitch while they were still in his possession, and following his death in the possession of Rochel Eisenberg Ravitch in Montreal, I cite their permanent location in the NHUAJ.

1. A Home for Art

1. For maps and statistical information on the Lower East Side before 1914, see Moses Rischin, *The Promised City: New York's Jews, 1870–1914* (Cambridge: Harvard University Press, 1962, 1977). For later years, see *The WPA Guide to New York City* (New York: Pantheon, 1982), and *New York Panorama: A Companion to the WPA Guide to New York City* (New York: Pantheon, 1984). Also of interest is *The Lower East Side: A Guide to Its Jewish Past in 99 New Photographs*, text by Ronald Sanders, photographs by Edmund V. Gillon, Jr. (New York: Dover, 1979). The most comprehensive study of the immigrant Jewish community, likely to remain so for some time, is Irving Howe, *World of Our Fathers* (New York: Harcourt Brace Jovanovich, 1976).

2. Letter from Joseph Bank to Kalman Marmor, September 8, 1906, Marmor Papers, YIVO. Bank writes, "Just as I was about to seal this letter to you Mani Leib walked in. For three months he has been trying unsuccessfully to write your *address* properly. So you can imagine the spirit of our poet, Mani Leib, if he finds it so difficult to write and remember an address. He sent you several poems which were returned because the address was written illegibly." Bank gives Mani Leib's address at the time as "c/o Mr. Borshavsky, 80–82 Beaver, Brooklyn."

3. Isaac Raboy, *Mayn lebn* (My Life), vol. 2 (New York: Book League, Jewish People's Fraternal Order of IWO, 1947), p. 104.

4. Jacob A. Riis, *How the Other Half Lives* (1890), ed. Sam Bass Warner, Jr. (Cambridge: Harvard University Press, 1970), p. 72.

5. Hutchins Hapgood, *The Spirit of the Ghetto* (1902), ed. Moses Rischin (Cambridge: Harvard University Press, 1967).

6. Mordecai Soltes, *The Yiddish Press: An Americanizing Agency*, 2nd ed. (New York: Teachers College, Columbia, 1950), p. 24.

7. Leonard Prager, ed., *Yiddish Literary and Linguistic Periodicals and Miscellanies* (Darby, Pa.: Norwood, 1982). This bibliography provides an excellent guide to twentieth-century periodical literature in Yiddish, indexed also according to place.

8. Howe, *World of Our Fathers*, p. 461. See also Nahma Sandrow, *Vagabond Stars: A World History of Yiddish Theatre* (New York: Harper and Row, 1977); David S. Lifson, *The Yiddish Theatre in America* (New York: T. Yoseloff, 1965).

9. *A Guide to YIVO's Landsmanshaftn Archive*, ed. Rosaline Schwartz and Susan Milamed (New York: YIVO, 1986). The bibliography shows the popularity of these organizations.

10. Shmuel Niger (Charney), "Yung amerike," *Onheyb* (Genesis), 5 (April 1918). An accompanying note indicates that the article first appeared in the Petrograd *Folkstsaytung*.

11. Moishe Leib Halpern, "In der fremd" (On Alien Ground), dated by the poet, New York, 1913; in *Shriftn* (Writings), 2 (1913), 7–20. Each item in the periodical is numbered separately.

12. *Di yungt*, 1–3 (1907–08). The first issue, undated, probably appeared in late fall, 1907; the second issue, dated January 1908, mistakenly identifies itself as the first; the third issue is marked no. 3. Auspices given as "Yugend Publishing Association, 26 Jefferson St., N.Y. Price 5¢. Outside N.Y. 6¢. Overseas 7¢. Annual 50¢." David Ignatoff names Yoel Entin, M. Schmuelzon, M. J. Haimovitch, Yedidye Margolis, and Borukh Senter as those initially responsible for the magazine, with himself and Margolis as editors of the third issue. See David Ignatoff, *Opgerisene bleter*, pp. 68–70.

13. See Prager, *Yiddish Literary and Linguistic Periodicals*, for brief descriptions.

14. Isaac Raboy, "Di royte blum" (The Red Flower), *Di yungt*, 1.

15. Raboy, *Mayn lebn*, pp. 158ff.

16. The question of Yiddish orthography appears to have been raised for the first time at the Czernowitz conference on the status of Yiddish (1908), and among the Yunge by Yude A. Yoffe, "Shraybn oder shrayben?" (Shall *Shraybn* [Writing] Be Spelled with an *e*?), in *Literatur: A zamlbukh* (Literature: A Miscellany), 1 (July 1910), pp. 102–111. Among early contemporary references is one in *Dos naye land*, March 1, 1912, p. 27, by M. Kh. Luner, who draws attention to inconsistent spelling and calls for regularization. After the war, spelling became an issue in the press when *Forverts* resisted reformist pressure and the Communists introduced an ideologically based system of spelling that ignored the Hebrew-Aramaic component of the language.

17. *Di yugnt*, 2. David Ignatoff claimed authorship.

18. Reported in *Dos naye land*, September 22, 1911. Cahan was speaking at a banquet honoring the magazine.

19. Tsivyon (Ben-Zion Hofman), "Di yidishe literatur un ire shrayber" (Yiddish Literature and Its Writers), *Di tsukunft*, May 1908, p. 40.

20. The complaint is cited by Moisei Olgin, "Eygns un fremds in der literatur" (Native and Foreign Elements in Literature), *Forverts*, March 31, 1909, p. 5. He refutes the objection, arguing that writers in different literatures may have the same ideas. Nachman Mayzel gives a detailed account of the reception of the Yunge in "Vegn di amerikaner yidishe 'yunge'" (About the American Yiddish Yunge), *Nayvelt* (New World), July 16, 1954. This article is reprinted in his *Tsurikblikn un perspektivn* (Retrospectives and Perspectives; Tel Aviv: I. L. Peretz, 1962), pp. 303–353.

21. Ronald Sanders, *The Downtown Jews* (New York: Harper and Row, 1969), pp. 359–371. Letters from this column have been collected in English as *A Bintel Brief*, 2 vols., ed. Isaac Metzker (New York: Doubleday, 1971; Viking, 1981).

22. William Dean Howells, review of Rosenfeld's *Songs from the Ghetto*, with prose translation by Leo Weiner (Boston: Copeland and Day, 1898), in *Literature*, February 10, 1899. Kalman Marmor includes Rosenfeld's translation of this review in "Fun moris roznfelds literarishe yerushe" (Morris Rosenfeld's Literary Legacy), *Pinkes*, (Record: A Quarterly of Yiddish Literary History, Linguistics, Folklore, and Bibliography), 1:3 (1928), 200–212.
    On the worker-poets, see Kalman Marmor, *Der onheyb fun der yidisher litera-*

tur in amerike (The Beginning of Yiddish Literature in America; New York: IKUF, 1944); N. B. Minkoff, *Pionern fun der yidisher poezie in amerike* (Pioneers of Yiddish Poetry in America), 3 vols. (New York: N. B. Minkoff, 1956); Elias Schulman, *Geshikhte fun der yidisher literatur in amerike, 1870–1900* (History of Yiddish Literature in America; New York: Biderman, 1943).

23. David Edelshtat, "Tsu der muze" (To the Muse), in his *Gezamlte Verk* (Collected Poems; Moscow, 1935), vol. 2, pp. 284–285.

24. Morris Rosenfeld, "Der trern milioner" (The Teardrop Millionaire) and "Mayn rue plats" (My Camping Ground), *Shriftn*, vol. 1 (New York: Literatur Farlag, 1910), pp. 7, 29. In English, *Moses: Poems and Translations*, trans. Aaron Kramer (New York: O'Hare, 1962), pp. 57, 58.

25. Menakhem (Boreisho), "East Broadway," *East Broadway*, ed. Moishe Leib Halpern and Menakhem (New York: Literarisher Farlag, 1916), p. 11.

26. Reuben Iceland, "Di naye vendung fun der yidisher poezie" (The New Direction of Yiddish Poetry), *Fun mentsh tsu mentsh* (Person to Person), ed. Moishe Leib Halpern (New York: New York Publishers, n.d.), p. 34.

27. David Ignatoff, *Opgerisene bleter*, pp. 69–70. Other sources for this biographical sketch are Reyzn, *Leksikon*; CYCO, *Leksikon*; Pat, *Shmuesn mit yidishe shrayber*, pp. 33–44. Daniel Ignatoff, the writer's son, spoke with me about his father in Montreal (September 17, 1979) and gave me access to papers now deposited in the YIVO.

28. Everyone who wrote about the period produced a slightly different roster of its members. Writers who continued to be identified with the original Yunge are Mani Leib, Zishe Landau, David Ignatoff, and Reuben Iceland. The novelist David Kozanski later became part of their circle, and the somewhat older Joseph Rolnik was aesthetically akin in spirit. The term *Yunge* in the years 1907–1914 applied to a whole movement of younger writers: Moishe Leib Halpern, I. J. Schwartz, Joseph Opatoshu, M. J. Haimovitch, Isaac Raboy, Abraham Moyshe Dilon, Herman Gold (Hillel Gurani), Moishe Nadir (then still writing under his real name, Isaac Rayz), and H. Leivick (Leivick Halper). Mani Leib recalled that the literary club Yidishe Yugnt was already in existence when he and Alexander Zeldin joined it in 1906, several weeks before it disbanded, and that among its members were Moishe Shmuelzon, Menakhem-Mendl Tsipin, Leon Kobrin, Ben Yakir (pseud. Dr. Ephraim Rosenblatt), H. Roisenblatt, Jacob Adler, Yoel Slonim, Shmuel Kotler, and A. Voliner. See "Dovid ignatov shraybt geshikhte" (David Ignatoff Writes History), *Epokhe*, 18 (April 1945), 9–10. Most of these writers later wrote for the humor magazines. M. J. Haimovitch, "A bisl geshikhe" (A Bit of History: Mani Leib and His Friends 25 Years Ago), *Fraye arbayter shtime*, March 20, 1931, p. 4, names Mordecai Dantsis, Khaim Gutman (pseud. Der Lebediker), Borukh Senter, H. Shnayder, A. M. Mandelboym, Joseph Tunkl (pseud. Der Tunkeler), Aaron Baron, A. L. Baron, Shmuel Adler, Mikhl Kaplan, Berl Botwinik, and Shmuel Fox. Selective lists of contributors to the contemporary little magazines are provided in Mayzel, "Vegn di amerikaner yidishe yunge," and Prager, *Yiddish Literary and Linguistic Periodicals*.

29. Iceland, *Fun unzer friling*, pp. 1–2.

30. Yente Serdatski, "Di yunge hobn dos vort" (The Yunge Have Their Say), *Di tsukunft*, June 1908, p. 62.

31. Shtok was reputedly the first to introduce the sonnet form into Yiddish. A book of stories, *Ertseylungen* (New York: Nay-tsayt, 1919), seems to have been both the climax and end of her Yiddish writing career.

32. "No synagogue" is cited from Moisei Olgin, "A. Raboy" (1939), in *Kultur un folk* (Culture and Nation) (New York: IKUF, 1949), p. 228. "No school" is from Joseph Opatoshu, "Vegn der yunger yidisher literatur in amerike" (About the Youthful Yiddish Literature in America), *Bikhervelt*, May–June 1922, p. 246.

33. Aaron Glanz-Leyeles, "Literarishe memoirn" (Literary Memoirs), *Di goldene keyt*, 31 (1958), 126–127. An earlier and probably more authentic account of two such occasions, here collapsed into one, appears in *75 yor yidishe presse in amerike* (75 Years of the Yiddish Press in America), ed. Jacob Glatstein et al., (New York: I. L. Peretz shrayber farein, 1945), p. 88.

34. Slighting reviews by Kh. Alexandrov in *Der yidisher arbeter*, 1908 (not seen; referred to by Mayzel, "Vegn di amerikaner yidishe 'yunge,'" and by Ignatoff, *Opgerisene bleter*, p. 70); Ben Yakir "In der literarisher velt" (In the Literary World), *Di tsukunft*, March 1908, p. 58; Tsivyon, "Di yidishe literatur un ire shrayber." Defenses of the Yunge by Yente Serdatski and Yoel Slonim in *Di tsukunft*, June 1908, p. 62; Shakhne Epstein, *Di tsukunft* (January 1911), p. 41. The first definitive article on the Yunge was Reuben Iceland, "Di yunge," *Shriftn*, 1 (1912).

35. *Der kibitser* (Monthly Illustrated Journal for Humor, Wit, and Kibitsing) became a weekly in August 1911. The history of *Der kibitser* is closely linked with that of its competitor, *Der groyser kundes* (literally, "The Great Prankster" but given the English title of "The Big Stick"). Two of the editors of *Der kibitser*, Joseph Tunkl and Khaim Gutman, also served along with Jacob Adler and Jacob Marinoff as editors of *Kundes*. According to Marinoff, the initial arrangement between the two magazines was that they would appear in alternating weeks. Letter to Solomon Bloomgarten (pseud. Yehoash), June 3, 1909, JTSA. Information on humor magazines may be found in J. Chaikin, *Yidishe bleter* (New York, 1946), pp. 209–214; Khone Grotesfeld, "Di humoristishe zhurnaln—*Der kibitser* un *Der groyser kundes*" (The Humor Magazines—*The Kibitzer* and *The Big Stick*), in *75 yor yidishe presse*, pp. 97–99.

36. *Der kibitser*, April 15, 1908, p. 4.

37. Ibid., May 15, 1908, p. 5.

38. The cartoon appears on July 15, 1908, p. 5.

39. Ignatoff, *Opgerisene bleter*, pp. 75–76.

2. Joseph Among His Brothers

A selective Mani Leib bibliography prepared by Ephim H. Jeshurin appears in Mani Leib, *Lider un baladn* (Songs and Ballads), vol. 2 (New York:

CYCO, 1955). Additional material (after 1954) follows the entry for Mani Leib in CYCO, *Leksikon*, vol. 5, pp. 456–457. See also Reyzn, *Leksikon*, vol. 2, pp. 306–310, and the following major sources:

Mani Leib, "A mayse vegn zikh" (A Story about Myself), *Vunder iber vunder* (Wonder upon Wonder; New York: Workmen's Circle, 1930), pp. 5–12. Reprinted in *Lider un baladn*, vol. 1, pp. 347ff (pages unnumbered).

Iceland, *Fun unzer friling*, pp. 65–108.

Yoel Entin, "Mani Leyb," *Yidisher kemfer*, September 16, 1955, pp. 89–93; September 23, 1955, pp. 16–18; October 14, 1955, p. 13.

Jacob Pat, *Shmuesn mit yidishe shrayber*, pp. 193–210.

Shloime Simon, "Mani leyb in zayn kindheyt" (Mani Leib in His Childhood), *Kinder zhurnal*, March 1931.

Rochelle Weprinski, ed., *Briv, 1918–1953* (Letters; Tel Aviv: I. L. Peretz, 1980); and *Dos kreytsn zikh fun di hent* (The Crossing of Hands; Tel Aviv: I. L. Peretz, 1971). The autobiographical novel should be treated primarily as fiction.

1. Mani Leib, "Oyf nyu yorker shteyner" (On New York Stones), *Lider un baladn*, vol. 1 (1955), pp. 139–143.

2. "Oyf nyu yorker shteyner," part 2, *Lider un baladn* (Tel Aviv: I. L. Peretz, 1977), pp. 121–134.

3. Rochelle Weprinski, "Introduction," *Briv*, pp. 6–7. See also Mani Leib's letter of October 1, 1933, p. 43. This period is discussed more fully in Chapter 8.

4. The biographical sketch here is based largely on Mani Leib, Shloime Simon, and Jacob Pat.

5. Mani Leib, "A mayse vegn zikh."

6. Interview with Rochelle Weprinski, November 2, 1972.

7. Pat, *Shmuesn mit yidishe shrayber*, p. 198.

8. Osip Volitski, "A yunyon man—a poet" (A Union Man—A Poet), *Forverts*, December 22, 1963, and "Mani leyb oyf di gasn in london" ("Mani Leib on the Streets of London," poem), *Nyu yorker vokhnblat*, June 25, 1954, p. 20.

9. Lamed Shapiro, "Der shotn yoysef khaim brener" (The Shadow of Joseph Chaim Brenner), *Der shrayber geyt in kheyder* (The Writer Goes to School; Los Angeles: Aleyn, 1945), pp. 91–103. This sense of Brenner's mood and activities is corroborated in many of his letters to Micha Joseph Berdyczewski (1865–1921), such as one from London, February 21, 1907: "We can no longer believe in the possibility of any achievement in our literature. There is no room among us for literature and there is no need for a literature in the Hebrew language. But from this we cannot conclude that we should stop writing." M. J. Berdyczewski to J. Kh. Brenner: *Exchange of Letters* (in Hebrew; Tel Aviv: Hakibbutz Hameuchad, 1962), p. 16.

10. Kalman Marmor, *Mayn lebns-geshikhte* (My Autobiography), vol. 2 (New York: IKUF, 1959), pp. 707–719, 727–731.

11. Iceland, *Fun unzer friling*, p. 67.

12. Entin, "Mani Leyb," *Yidisher kemfer*, September 16, 1955, p. 90. Rochelle contradicted this account, claiming that Chasia had come on her own.

13. Mani Leib, "Zi shpilt" (She Plays), *Fun mentsh tsu mentsh*. Iceland describes the history of the poem in *Fun unzer friling*, pp. 81–82. Another poem in the cycle, "Lider," *Literatur un lebn*, October 1914, opens with the lines "How could you have left the small child standing there / And walked off slouching alone into the night."

14. Iceland, *Fun unzer friling*, p. 78.

15. Itsik Manger, "Mani leyb der liriker" (Mani Leib the Lyrical Poet), in Mani Leib, *Shirim ubaladot* (Poems and Ballads), bilingual Yiddish and Hebrew edition, trans. Shimshon Meltser (Tel Aviv: I. L. Peretz, 1963), p. 9.

16. *Literatur: A zamlbukh* (Literature: A Miscellany), 1 (July 1910).

17. Yoel Entin, "Tsvishn mizrekh un mayrev" (Between East and West); M. (Moishe) Katz, "Got-zukhenish un zikh-gufe zukhenish" (The Search for God and the Search for Self—a reconsideration of Peretz's *Folkstimlekhe geshikhtn*); and Yoel Slonim, "Oscar Wilde," *Literatur*, 1 (July 1910), 50–78; 79–92; 112–119. The issue also contained an essay on Baudelaire.

18. Mani Leib, "Toybnshtile bloye ovnt-shtundn" (Dovestill Blue Evening-Hours), *Literatur*, 2 (November 1910), 3. The poem is dated 1907. The transliteration here follows Mani Leib's rhyming scheme, not the standard YIVO system.

19. The phrase is from the poet Jacob Glatstein. "Mani Leib's revolution—and he was in his own passive-lyrical way a revolutionary—consisted of vocalizing Yiddish words so as to create a mood even before their meaning was clear . . . No one before him dared to treat Yiddish words so tenderly. A line of Yiddish had always carried weight like a camel. It never issued forth without a load of shrewdness, of allusion, of moral charge." Jacob Glatstein, "Mani Leyb," *In toykh genumen: Esseyen, 1948–1956* (Sum and Substance: Essays; New York: Farband, 1956), p. 113.

20. Ignatoff, *Opgerisene bleter*, pp. 72–79.

21. Itsik Manger, "Adonais iz toyt" (Adonais is dead), *Di tsukunft*, November 1953, p. 459.

22. Moishe Leib Halpern, "East Broadway," *Der kibitser*, March 10, 1911, p. 4.

23. Sologub, *Der kishef fun troyer* (The Magic of Sorrow), trans. Zisha Landau (New York: Di heym, 1919). The word *unexistence* for *nitdoikayt* is adapted from David G. Roskies, *Against the Apocalypse* (Cambridge: Harvard University Press, 1984), p. 101. In a similar vein, Landau also translated Goncharov's *Oblomov* (New York, 1921).

24. Mani Leib, *Lider* (New York: Inzl, 1918). See, for example, "Raise your eyes, see: night will soon enfold / The city of New York" (p. 58—earlier version in *Dos naye land*, September 15, 1911, p. 7); "At midday I drew the curtain on my window" (p. 57).

25. "Ay lyu lyu, nakht un regn," *Lider*, pp. 92–93; trans. "Night and Rain" by Seymour Levitan.

26. "Fun shtoyb hot got mikh ufgeheybn," *Lider*, p. 94.

27. Pat, *Shmuesn mit yidishe shrayber*, p. 202.

28. "Shtiler shtiler," *Shriftn*, 3 (1914); trans. "Hush" by Marie Syrkin in *TYP*, pp. 89–90.

29. Iceland, *Fun unzer friling*, pp. 39–40.

30. Mani Leib, "Ikh hob mayn mames shvartse hor" (I Have My Mother's Black Hair), *Literatur un lebn*, October 1914, p. 3.

31. Joseph Opatoshu, "Vegn der yunger yidisher literatur in amerike" (About the Young Yiddish Literature in America), *Bikhervelt* (Warsaw, May–June 1922), pp. 245–47.

32. Ignatoff, *Opgerisene bleter*, p. 79.

33. Howe, *World of Our Fathers*, p. 432.

34. Iceland, *Fun unzer friling*, pp. 61–63.

35. Isaac Bloom, *In mayn literarisher akhsanye* (In My Literary Hostel; Mexico City: Yiddish Cultural Center, 1964), pp. 30–31.

36. David Ignatoff, "Oyfn ershtn keyver fun di yunge" (At the First Grave of the Yunge), *Yidish*, September 9, 1932, pp. 3–4.

37. I. J. Schwartz, *Kentucky* (New York: Schaulson, 1936).

38. Mani Leib, "Dovid Ignatoff shraybt geshikhte," *Epokhe*, 18 (April 1945), 8.

39. I. J. Schwartz, "In likht fun sof-zumer"; trans. "In the End-of-Summer Light" by Seymour Levitan in *PBMYV*, p. 160.

3. Voices of the Chorus

1. Iceland, *Fun unzer friling*, pp. 18–19, 49–54.

2. Moishe Varshe and Ber Lapin, trans., *Dos lebn fun a mentshn* (The Life of Man) by Leonid Andreyev, in *Gezamlte dramen* (Collected Plays; New York: Maisel, 1911).

3. Moishe Varshe, *Vegn fun a neshome* (Pathways of a Soul), ed. Kolye Teper and Zishe Landau (New York: Pinski-Mazl, n.d.). The quotations are from the unpaginated introduction and from the entry of July 30, 1911, p. 11.

4. Melekh Ravitch, "Kolye Teper," *Mayn leksikon*, vol. 1 (Montreal: Montreal Committee, 1945), pp. 104–106. Additional information on Teper from Reyzn, *Leksikon*, vol. 1, pp. 1183–86; Tsvi Hirshkan, "Borukh Stepner un Kolye Teper," *Di tsukunft*, August 1929, pp. 546ff; Moishe Nadir, "Tint un feder," (Pen and Ink), regular column, *Freiheit*, April 16, 1928.

5. Count D'Abruzzi (pseud. Kolye Teper), *Zigzagn* (New York: Maisel, n.d.), pp. 35–40.

6. Letter from Kolye Teper to Shmuel Niger, undated, in Niger Archive, YIVO; letter from Teper to Moishe Nadir, Leningrad, April 4, 1927, in uncatalogued Nadir Papers, NHUAJ.

7. Aaron Leyeles, "Kolye Teper," *Di tsukunft*, January–February 1958), p. 26.

8. Y. Kisin (Yekutiel Garnitski), "Vegn Zishe Landau" (About Zishe Landau), *Zishe Landau Zamlbukh*, ed. David Kozanski (New York: Inzl, 1938), p. 108.

9. Letter from Zishe Landau to Ezekiel Bronshteyn, December 17, 1934, Bronshteyn Papers, YIVO.

10. On Landau see Kisin, *Zishe Landau Zamlbukh*; Abraham Tabachnik, *Der man fun lid* (The Man of Song; New York: Sklarsky, 1941); Herman Gold, *Zishe Landau* (New York: Aldin, 1945); Iceland, *Fun unzer friling*, pp. 1–31; Ignatoff, *Opgerisene bleter*, pp. 33–51; Shmuel Niger, *Bleter geshikhte fun der yidisher literatur* (History Pages of Yiddish Literature; New York: Sh. Niger Bukh Komitet, 1959), pp. 314–348.

11. *Di literarishe velt*, February 28, 1919, p. 8.

12. Iceland, *Fun unzer friling*, p. 30. The poem "Fun ale teg" (Of the Everyday) appeared in *Shriftn*, 3 (1914).

13. Mani Leib, "Oyf der finfter evenyu" (On Fifth Avenue), *Forverts*, March 1, 1921. Reprinted in Mani Leib, *Lider un baladn*, vol. 1, p. 88. Mani Leib wrote a number of poems about martyrs of the revolutionary movement and poems of social protest. But a characteristic poem, "Revenge," opens with lines like these: "He died young, proudly on the gallows / His lovely (*sheynem*) death was seen only by the hangman and the night."*Di tsukunft*, June 1914, p. 9.

14. Zishe Landau, "Dinstik" (1911–1915), *Lider* (New York: Inzl, 1937), p. 60. In a different version, "Tuesday," trans. Ruth Whitman, *An Anthology of Modern Yiddish Poetry* (New York: October House, 1966), p. 61.

15. Tabachnik, *Der man fun lid*, p. 20: "No matter how much Landau enjoyed clowning (if for no other reason than because it distinguished him from Mani Leib), he liked singing more."

16. Zishe Landau, "Epilog," *Shriftn*, 1 (1912); trans. "Epilogue" by Irving Feldman in *PBMYV*, p. 274.

17. Joseph Opatoshu, "Ciechanow Melody," in *A Day in Regensburg*, trans. Jacob Sloan (Philadelphia: Jewish Publication Society, 1968), pp. 91–98.

18. Interview with Esther Landau Getzoff, October 18, 1979, in East Rockaway, New York.

19. Joseph Opatoshu, "Roman fun a ferd-ganef," *Shriftn*, 1 (1912). "Romance of a Horse Thief," trans. David G. Roskies in *A Shtetl and Other Yiddish Novellas*, ed. Ruth R. Wisse (New York, Behrman, 1973), pp. 146–211.

20. Opatoshu, "Moris un zayn zun filip" (Morris and His Son Philip), *Shriftn*, 2 (1913). The discussion of Opatoshu's "zoological style" by Menakhem Boreisho in "Ideolizirte zoologye" (Idealized Zoology), *Literatur un lebn*, February 1915, pp. 95–104.

21. *Di naye heym* (New York: Literarisher Farlag, 1914), ed. J. Opatovsky (Opatoshu), "1883 Crotona Ave., Bronx." Accounts of the split in the ranks of the Yunge appear in Iceland, *Fun unzer friling*, pp. 32–64; Ignatoff, *Opgerisene bleter*, pp. 80–82; Raboy, *Mayn lebn*, pp. 237–239; Abraham Glanz-Leyeles, "Literarishe memoirn" (Literary Memoirs), *Di goldene keyt*, 31 (1958), 122–132;

Joseph Rolnik, *Zikhroynes* (New York: Ignatoff Literary Fund, 1954), pp. 210ff; Nachman Mayzel, "Vegn di amerikaner yidishe yunge," pp. 315–319; Ruth R. Wisse, *"Di Yunge:* Immigrants or Exiles?," *Prooftexts,* January 1981, p. 44.

22. Borukh Rivkin, cited by Nakhman Mayzel, "Vegn di amerikaner yidishe yunge," *Tsurikblikn un perspectivn,* p. 318.

23. Isaac Raboy, "Her goldenbarg" (Mr. Goldenbarg), *Shriftn,* 3 (1914).

24. Joseph Opatoshu, *Hibru* (Hebrew; New York: Maisel, 1920).

25. Janet Hadda, "Di hashpoe fun amerike oyf der yidisher literatur" (The Influence of America of Yiddish Literature), *YIVO bleter,* 44 (1973), 248–255.

26. The most concentrated source of information about Leivick is in Shmuel Niger, *H. Leivick, 1888–1948* (Toronto: Leivick Jubilee Committee, 1951).

27. H. Leivick, "Ergets vayt," *Hintern shlos* (Behind the Lock; New York: Fornberg, 1918), p. 7; trans. "Somewhere Far Away" by Benjamin and Barbara Harshav in *AYP,* p. 679.

28. Leivick, "Di yunge," *Shriftn,* 4 (Summer 1919), 33.

29. Leivick, "Ikh-mir" (I-We), *Fun tsayt tsu tsayt* (From Time to Time, occasional literary volumes; March 1925), p. 22.

30. Description of Gold in Zishe Weinper, "Herman Gold," *Yidishe shriftshteler* (Yiddish Writers), vol. 2 (New York, 1936), p. 123. Appreciation of schnorrers in Judd Teller, "Yiddish Litterateurs and American Jews," *Commentary,* July 1954, p. 31.

31. Joseph Rolnik, "Hafiz," *Di naye heym,* 1914.

32. Biographical introduction by Sh. Miller, ed. Lamed Shapiro, *Ksovim* (Posthumous Writings; Los Angeles: Shapiro Ksovim Committee, 1949), pp. 7–18. Description of restaurant and clientele in Zishe Weinper, *Moishe Leib Halpern* (New York: Ufkum, 1940), pp. 91–93.

33. Correspondence between David Ignatoff and Jacob Dineson, *Shriftn,* 5 Autumn 1919; "Fun yankev dineson's archiv" (From Dineson's Archive), *Der khodesh* (Warsaw, 1921), supplement ed. Sh. Rosenfeld.

34. Ber Borochov, "Vos ervart dos yidishe folk in Amerike?" (What Awaits the Jewish People in America?), *Literatur un lebn,* January 1915, pp. 71–72.

35. Borochov, "An ofener briv tsu di yunge" (An Open Letter to the Yunge), *Literatur un lebn,* November 1915, pp. 117–123. This and two other articles on the Yunge are reprinted in Ber Borochov, *Shprakh-forshung un literatur geshikhte* (Works on Linguistics and Literary History; Tel Aviv: Peretz, 1966), pp. 298–303, 304–308, 353–354.

36. Reuben Iceland, "Vos iz unz geven I. L. Peretz?" (What Was Peretz to Us?), *Literatur un lebn,* May 1915, p. 101.

37. Zishe Landau, "Far undzer khorev yidish lebn," from the cycle "Du, mayn nitdoik glik" (You My Unpresent Joy) in *Velt ayn, velt oys* (World In, World Out; New York, 1916), p. 54; trans. "For All that Has Been Ours" by Marie Syrkin in *TYP,* p. 97. Cf. Landau, *Lider* (New York: Inzl, 1937), p. 113.

38. David Ignatoff, cited from interview with Jacob Pat, *Shmuesn mit yidishe shrayber*.

39. Isaac Raboy, *Nayn brider* (New York: IKUF, 1936), p. 162; *Nine Brothers*, trans. Max Rosenfeld (New York: IKUF, 1968), p. 110. I have modified the translation slightly.

40. Iceland, *Fun unzer friling*, p. 188; trans. Nathan Halper, "At Goodman and Levine's," *Voices from the Yiddish*, ed. Irving Howe and Eliezer Greenberg (Ann Arbor: University of Michigan Press, 1972), pp. 300–305.

41. Mehakhem (Boreisho), "East Broadway," in *East Broadway*, p. 12.

42. Meir Blinken, *Stories* (Albany: SUNY, 1984), introduction by Ruth R. Wisse, pp. vii–xviii.

43. Iceland, *Fun unzer friling*, pp. 94–95.

44. Interviews with Barbara Getzoff, May 3, 1985; Evelyn Likht, Autumn 1985; Daniel Ignatoff, September 17, 1979.

45. Iceland, "Anna Margolin," in *Fun unzer friling*, pp. 129–172; unpublished paper on Margolin by Adrienne Cooper.

46. Iceland, *Fun mayn zumer* (Of my Summer), poems dedicated to Anna Margolin (New York: Reuben Iceland, 1922).

47. Anna Margolin (Roza Lebensboym), "Ikh bin geven amol a yingling," *Lider* (New York, 1929), p. 5; trans. "Once I Was a Youth" by Marcia Falk in *PBMYV*, p. 218.

48. The rise of this movement is richly documented in *AMP*. See Appendix A: "Documents of Introspectivism," pp. 774–804.

49. Mani Leib, *Lider, Baladn, Yidishe un slavishe motivn* (New York: Inzl, 1918).

50. I. Dobrushin, "Mani Leyb," *Shtrom*, 3 (Moscow, 1922), 50–59.

51. William Wordsworth, "Preface to *Lyrical Ballads*" (1802), in *William Wordsworth*, ed. Stephen Gill (New York: Oxford University Press, 1984), pp. 596–597.

52. Zishe Landau, *Fun der velt poezye* (From the World's Poetry; New York: Ignatoff Literatur Fund, 1947), section on English ballads, p. 54; American and other ballads, pp. 57–70.

53. Mani Leib, "Yingl tsingl khvat" (Young Tongue Scamp) *Shriftn*, 3 (1914).

54. Ignatoff, *Opgerisene bleter*, p. 81.

55. Mani Leib, "Ikh bin der vaynrib der vilder," *Der inzl* (New York, 1918); reprinted in *Lider* (1918), p. 137; trans. "I Am the Creeper" by John Hollander.

56. Manger, "Mani Leyb der lyriker," p. 23.

57. On Mani Leib's classical instincts, see the fine essays by Abraham Tabachnik, "Mani leyb der klasiker" (Mani Leib the Classicist) and "Mani leybs sonetn" (Mani Leib's Sonnets), in his *Dikhter un dikhtung* (Poets and Poetry; New York, 1965), pp. 140–158, 158–168.

58. M. (Moisei) Olgin, review of *Lider*, *Di naye velt*, June 7 and 14, 1918; reprinted

in Olgin, *In der velt fun gezangen* (In the World of Songs; New York: Forverts, 1919), pp. 273–294.

59. Letter from Mani Leib to Rochelle Weprinski, undated, marked by her as Summer 1918, *Briv*, p. 27. Originals in Mani Leib Papers, YIVO; Weprinski's ordering and dating of the letters are inexact.

60. Letter from Mani Leib to Rochelle Weprinski, undated, marked by her as Summer 1918, *Briv*, p. 20.

4. The Street Drummer

A selective bibliography of Moishe Leib Halpern by Ephim H. Jeshurin appears in *In New York* (New York: Matones, 1954), pp. 227–248. See also Reyzn, *Leksikon*, vol. 1, pp. 769–772, and CYCO, *Leksikon*, vol. 3, pp. 31–38. Several other important biographical sources are:

Eliezer Greenberg, *Moyshe leyb halpern in ram fun zayn dor* (Halpern in the Context of His Generation; New York: Halpern Br. 450, Workmen's Circle, 1942).

Z. (Zishe) Weinper, *Moyshe leyb halpern* (New York: Ufkum, 1940).

Jacob Mestel, "Momentn mit moyshe leyb halpern" (Moments with Halpern), *Literarishe bleter* (Warsaw, October 21, 1932), pp. 681–682.

Moishe Nadir (Isaac Reis), "Mit moyshe leyb halpern," *Teg fun mayne teg* (Days of My Days; New York: Morgn-Freiheit, 1935), pp. 169–182.

1. Rochelle Weprinski, *Dos kreytsn zikh fun di hent*, pp. 230–231.

2. For a glimpse by a contemporary of the role of Zlochev, see Gershom Bader, *Mayne zikhroynes* (My Memoirs; Buenos Aires: Tsentral farlag fun poylishe yidn, 1953).

3. Mestel, "Momentn mit moyshe leyb halpern."

4. Hirsh Gutgeshtalt, "Der toyt fun moyshe leyb halpern" (Halpern's Death), *Literarishe bleter*, September 16, 1932, pp. 602–603. See also Meir Khartiner, "Moyshe leyb halpern" (Hebrew), *Hapoel Hatsair* (Tel Aviv), November 23, 1965.

5. Hel-pen (pseud. Halpern), "A briv tsu a khaver" (Letter to a Friend), *Der kibitser*, June 30, 1911. For Yiddish pseudonymns, see Saul Chajes, *Thesaurus Pseudonymorum Quae in Litteratura Hebraica et Judaeo-Germanica Inveniuntur* (Hildesheim: Georg Olms Verlag, 1967).

6. For background on contemporary Viennese Jewry, see Marsha L. Rozenblit, *The Jews of Vienna, 1867–1914* (Albany: SUNY, 1983), particularly her discussion of the limits of assimilation, pp. 144–146.

7. *Di ershte yidishe shprakh-conferents* (The First Conference on the Yiddish Language: Reports and Documents of the Czernowitz Conference of 1908; Vilna: YIVO, 1931). Halpern's name is listed among the delegates on the basis of

memoirs published by Abraham Reisin, p. 61. Confirmation of his attendance is provided by David Klinghofer, "Y. L. Peretz in Lemberg," *Letste nayes,* April 23, 1954.

8. Ibid., excerpts of Peretz's talks, pp. 74–77, 85–86.

9. Moishe Leib Halpern, "Yitskhok leybush perets," in *Y. L. Peretz* (New York: Literarisher Farlag, 1915), pp. 11–12; trans. "Yitskhok Leybush Perets" by John Hollander, *PBMYV*, pp. 176–181.

10. Nadir, "Mit moyshe leyb halpern," p. 176. See also Bloom, *In mayn literarisher akhsanye*, pp. 21–24. In *Der kibitser* of January 13, 1911, there is a mock announcement for a lecture to be given by Halpern at the Farein on "how to sweat and still not make a living."

11. Sh. Margoshes, "Moishe Leib Halpern," News and Views column, *Der tog*, August 31, 1962.

12. Eliezer Sherman, "Bagegenishn mit m. l. halpern," (Meetings with Halpern), *New yorker vokhnblat*, September 4, 1936, p. 54.

13. Nadir, "Moyshe leyb halpern oyf zayn yortsayt" (Halpern on the Anniversary of his Death), *Der tog*, October 5, 1940.

14. *Der kibitser*, February 10, 1911.

15. Mani Leib, unpublished talk on Halpern under heading, "*Di goldene pave* un tsvey bikher nokh zayn toyt" (*The Golden Peacock* and Two Posthumous Books), delivered at an evening marking the twentieth anniversary of Halpern's death (1952). In Mani Leib Papers, YIVO.

16. Alexander Granakh, "Moyshe leyb, der volf" (Moishe Leib, the Wolf), *Literarishe bleter*, October 14, 1932, p. 664.

17. Moishe Leib Halpern, untitled poem from series in *Literatur*, 2 (November 1910), p. 23.

18. Hel-pen, trans. "Daytshland" by Heinrich Heine, *Der groyser kundes*, May 23, 1913–August 29, 1913; "Atta Trol," ibid., November 25, 1913ff.

19. Hel-pen, "Gasn-poyker," *Der kibitser*, September 22, 1911; "Dos lid fun a tremp," *Der groyser kibitser*, November 6, 1914; "La la," *Fun mentsh tsu mentsh*, pp. 64–66.

20. Moishe Leib Halpern, "Der gasnpoyker," *In nyu york* (1919), pp. 33–35; trans. "The Street Drummer" by John Hollander, *PBMYV*, pp. 168–173.

21. Hel-pen, "A friling-tragedye" (A Spring Tragedy), *Der kibitser*, May 19, 1911.

22. "Naye feygl, naye lider" (New Birds, New Songs), *Der kibitser*, June 30, 1911; "In orn-koydesh" (In the Holy Ark), ibid., October 13, 1911.

23. "Oyf tsupikenish" (To Spite), *Der kibitser*, September 29, 1911.

24. Moishe Leib Halpern, "Strike," *Folkstsaytung* (Montreal), June 21, 1912, p. 1. Halpern published additional progressive verse in *Yidisher kemfer*.

25. Hel-pen, "Montrealer notitsn" (Montreal Notes), *Der kibitser*, June 5, 1912.

26. "Der royter hon" (The Red Rooster), *Der groyser kibitser*, November 13, 1914. The poem is dedicated to Meyer London.

27. Greenberg, *Moyshe leyb halpern in der ram fun zayn dor*, p. 19.

28. Morris Rosenfeld, "Berl der piskuter vert a dekadent" (Berl the Piece-Cutter Becomes a Decadent), *Forverts*, November 20, 1910.

29. Halpern, "An ofener briv tsu moris rosenfeld" (An Open Letter to Morris Rosenfeld), *Der kibitser*, December 2, 1910.

30. "Der alter un der nayer moris rosenfeld" (The Old and the New Morris Rosenfeld), *Literatur un lebn*, March 1915, pp. 100–112.

31. Ibid., p. 105.

32. Hel-pen, "Unzere 'yunge'" (Our Yunge), *Der groyser kibitser*, September 4, 1914.

33. Moishe Leib Halpern, "In der fremd," *Shriftn*, 2 (1913). Sections 1, 3, 5, 7, 8, and 10, trans. "In a Foreign World" by Kathryn Hellerstein, with facing originals, in Moyshe-Leyb Halpern, *In New York: A Selection* (Philadelphia: Jewish Publication Society, 1982), pp. 45–59.

34. Yoel Slonim, "Ven moyshe leyb hot geshribn 'In der fremd'" (When Moishe Leib Wrote "On Alien Ground"), *Yidishe kultur*, November–December 1940, pp. 44–45.

35. Nadir, "Mit moyshe leyb halpern," pp. 169–182; Halpern, "Mit moyshe nadir," *Freiheit*, February 7, 1925.

36. David G. Roskies, *Against the Apocalypse: Responses to Catastrophe in Modern Jewish Culture* (Cambridge: Harvard University Press, 1984), p. 95.

37. A version of the mentshele appears earlier in a poem, "Azoy iz es" (That's How It Is), *Der kibitser*, December 15, 1911. A man tells his beloved that, by giving in to his desire, she ruined his dream of love. In part two of the poem the man tells the mentshl in the mirror that he has grown old and that his heart is dead. His beloved is invited to accompany the dead heart to burial. The figure of the mentshele first appeared in one of the pioneering works of modern Yiddish fiction, *Dos kleyne mentshele* by Mendele Moykher Sforim (Sholem Yankev Abramovitch). In the first version of this novel of 1864, the boy protagonist, trying to find the "little man" his mother is always talking about, thinks he sees him when he looks into his mother's eyes. By the end of the book, the phrase is understood to mean a man of little moral worth, a parasite.

38. Halpern, "A nakht," *East Broadway*, ed. Moishe Leib Halpern and Menakhem (Boreisho) (New York: Literatur Farlag, 1916), pp. 20–60. Revised version in *In Nyu York* (1919), pp. 237–304. Excerpts trans. by Kathryn Hellerstein, with facing originals, in Halpern, *In New York*, pp. 126–155. The translations here are my own from *In nyu york* (1919), pp. 266, 291, 304.

39. Zishe Weinper, *Moyshe leyb halpern*, p. 56.

40. Ibid., pp. 63–64.

41. David Ignatoff, *Opgerisene bleter*, p. 92.

42. Aaron Leib Baron, *Libe un benkshaft* (Love and Longing), poems (New York, 1910).

43. Halpern, "De la hester," *Der kibitser*, August 18, November 24, December 1, and December 22, 1911; January 1, 1912.

44. "Unzer gortn," *In nyu york* (1919), p. 7; trans. "Our Garden" by Benjamin and Barbara Harshav and Kathryn Hellerstein in *AYP*, p. 395.

45. Seth L. Wolitz, "Structuring the World View in Halpern's *In New York*," CMJS Annual (joint issue of *Yiddish*, 3.1, and *Studies in American Jewish Literature*, 3.2 (Winter 1977–78), 56–67.

46. Halpern, "Gey fartrayb zey," *In nyu york* (1919), p. 121; trans. John Hollander.

47. "Memento Mori," *In nyu york* (1919), pp. 141–142; trans. John Hollander in *PBMYV*, p. 174.

48. Letter from Halpern to Shmuel Niger, August 15, 1921, Niger Archive, YIVO. The return address on the envelope is "2773 West 37th Street, Coney Island."

5. The King of Freiheit

1. Letter from Mani Leib to Melekh Ravitch (Zecharye Bergner), September 11, 1919; return address "c/o *Forverts*, 175 East Broadway." Ravitch Archive, NHUAJ.

2. Zishe Landau, ed., *Antologye: Di yidishe dikhtung in amerike biz 1919* (New York: Farlag Yiddish, 1919), pp. i–viii.

3. Mani Leib, "Nyu york in ferzn" (New York in Verse), *Der inzl* (New York: Inzl, 1918), 29 pages.

4. Y. Kisin, "Nyu york," *Der inzl* (1918).

5. See e.g. Isaac Raboy, *Nay england* (New England) (New York: I. Raboy, 1918); *Dos vilde land* (The Wild Country), *Shriftn*, 5 (1919). David Ignatoff, *In keslgrub* (In the Melting Pot; New York: Amerike, 1919); *Tsvishn tsvey zunen* (Between Two Suns; New York: Amerike, 1919).

6. "Don't even think of coming to America, Ravitch!" wrote Mani Leib. "First— what do you need this for? All of us here, the people like you, have a very hard, one might say gray, existence. It only looks attractive from afar, as I for example am drawn—powerfully!—to Russia." Mani Leib's changing mood was affected, among other things, by serious illness in the winter of 1919–20. Letter from Mani Leib to Melekh Ravitch, March 1, 1920, Ravitch Archive, NHUAJ.

7. Letter from Joseph Opatoshu to Melekh Ravitch, July 8, 1921, Ravitch Archive, NHUAJ. This view differs from the one Opatoshu expressed publicly in Warsaw a year later, when he declared that the prospects for Yiddish in America were wonderful, that America had become the world center of Yiddish literary creativity. "Vegn der yunger yidisher literatur in amerike," *Bikhervelt* (Warsaw), May–June 1922, pp. 245–247.

8. H. Leivick, "Presse un bukh," *Tealit* (Theater Literature), November 1923, p. 40.

9. Menakhem (Boreisho), "East Broadway," *East Broadway*, pp. 12–13.

10. Moishe Leib Halpern, "Mit moyshe nadir" (With Nadir), *Freiheit*, February 7, 1925.

11. Moishe Nadir and Moishe Leib Halpern, *Unter der last fun tseylem* (Under the Burden of the Cross), 139-page unpublished typescript, not consecutively numbered, with handwritten corrections by both authors. Uncatalogued Nadir Papers, NHUAJ.

12. Inserted by Halpern opposite p. 30 of Act 1.

13. Inserted by Halpern opposite p. 28 of Act 2.

14. Lamed Shapiro, "Der tseylem," *Dos naye land*, 1 (May 1909), 15–30; trans. "The Cross" by Curt Leviant, in Lamed Shapiro, *The Jewish Government and Other Stories* (New York: Twayne, 1971), pp. 114–130. Analysis of this story in Esther Frank, "An Analysis of Four Short Stories by Lamed Shapiro," *Working Papers in Yiddish and East European Jewish Studies*, 28 (November 1978); Roskies, *Against the Apocalypse*, chap. 6.

15. For general information on this period, I have relied on Melekh Epstein, *The Jew and Communism, 1919–1941* (New York: Trade Union Sponsoring Committee, 1959); Melekh Epstein, *Jewish Labor in the USA* (New York: Trade Union Sponsoring Committee, 1953); Zosa Szaykowski, *Jews, Wars, and Communism*, vol. 1 (New York: KTAV, 1972); Irving Howe, *World of Our Fathers*; Theodore Draper, *American Communism and Soviet Russia: The Formative Years* (New York: Viking, 1960); and in particular on the knowledge of my colleague Eugene Orenstein of McGill University.

16. Epstein, *The Jew and Communism*, p. 104.

17. Halpern, "Yid, mayn bruder" (Jew, My Brother), *Freiheit*, April 2, 1922.

18. David Bergelson, ed., *In shpan* (In Harness), 1–2 (Vilna), April and May 1926. Parts of his novel *Midas hadin* (The Letter of the Law) appeared in this journal.

19. Susan Slotnick, "The Novel Form in the Works of David Bergelson," dissertation, Columbia University, 1978.

20. Halpern, "Arum a vogn" (Around a Wagon), *Freiheit*, March 3, 1922; included in *Di goldene pave* under the title "Keynmol shoyn vel ikh nisht zogn," p. 65; trans. "I Shall Never Go On Bragging" by Benjamin and Barbara Harshav in *AYP*, pp. 417–419. For a different English version, see Sarah Zweig Betsky, *Onions and Cucumbers and Plums* (Detroit: Wayne State University Press, 1969), poem 10.

21. "Zlochev, mayn heym," *Freiheit*, May 5, 1923; in *Di goldene pave*, pp. 16–18; trans. "My Home, Zlochev" by Nathan Halper in *TYP*, pp. 109–110.

22. Unpublished manuscript in Halpern Archive, YIVO, nos. 181–186. This was apparently the talk Halpern delivered about himself as a poet during his 1925 speaking tour: see below.

23. "Dembes" (Oaks), review of the play by F. Bimko, *Freiheit*, April 21, 1922. "In the first place you insulted all the living oaks . . . because the characters you present are not oaks but bulls."

24. Letter from Halpern to Yosl Drost, undated, marked by recipient 1923, Halpern Papers, YIVO. "A miracle: Maurice Schwartz heard that I needed money so he forced me (actually forced me) to borrow $100. He promised to give me

work later." Schwartz later hired Halpern to translate *The Chalk Garden* and Ernst Toller's *The Machine Breakers*.

25. Sandrow, *Vagabond Stars*, p. 262. The passage is from Schwartz's manifesto "Can a Better Yiddish Theater Survive in New York?" that appeared in *Forverts* in 1918.

26. The play is *Shabtai Tsvi* by Y. Zhulovsky, trans. Israel Joshua Singer (Warsaw: Di tsayt, 1923).

27. Halpern, "Tsu der oyfirung fun 'shabtai tsvi' " (On the Production of "Shabtai Tsvi"), written in the form of a letter to Moisei Olgin, *Otem*, 1 (October–November 1923), 9–12.

28. "Vos viln unzere estetiker?" (What Do Our Aesthetes Want?), ibid., p. 1.

29. Letter from Halpern to Yosl Drost, July 16, 1923, Halpern Papers, YIVO. These letters provide a running commentary on Halpern's speaking tours between 1923 and 1927.

30. Some of Halpern's advertised topics of 1924 and 1925 were "The Old and the New Literature," "Proletarian Culture," "The Artist and the Revolutionary," "Can There be a Proletarian Literature?" and "Moishe Leib Halpern about Himself."

31. P. (Pinchas) Novick, "Tsvishn yidishe shrayber" (Among Yiddish Writers), *Freiheit*, February 24, 1923. This was the beginning of an open forum that continued through March 4, 15, and 18. The issue was referred to as the debate over *grobe reyd* (vulgar speech).

32. Halpern, "A grus fun yener zayt" (Regards from the Other Side), *Freiheit*, January 18, 1923. Included in *Di goldene pave* as "Der foygl," pp. 11–13; trans. "The Bird" by John Hollander, *PBMYV*, pp. 180–184.

33. Novick, "Tsvishn yidishe shrayber," ascribes this argument to Halpern.

34. *Freiheit*, March 18, 1923; in *Di goldene pave*, pp. 125–128.

35. Over two dozen letters are quoted and summarized under the heading "Grobe verter un sheyne literatur" (Vulgar Speech and Belles-Letters, *Freiheit*, March 4, 1923, and "Tsi darf di naye tsayt a naye shprakh?" (Does the New Age Require a New Language?), March 15, 1923.

36. Jacob Glatstein, A. Leyeles, and N. B. Minkoff, "Introspectivism," manifesto-introduction to *Inzikh* (In the Self: A Collection of Introspectivist Poems; New York: Max Maisel, 1920; trans. by Anita Norich in *AYP*, pp. 774–784. This book contains a large selection of the poetry of Leyeles and Glatstein and selected documents tracing the development of the movement.

37. Halpern, "Der poet yankev glatshteyn," *Freiheit*, January 6, 1923, review of Glatstein's first book of poems, *Yankev Glatshteyn* (New York: Farlag Kultur, 1921).

38. Moyshe Taytsh, "Ikh bet a vort" (I Ask for the Floor), "A Letter from our Moscow Correspondent," *Freiheit*, April 29, 1923. The article is datelined Moscow, April 7.

39. Halpern, "Di mayse mit der velt," *Di goldene pave*, pp. 114–115; trans. "The Tale of the World" by John Hollander, ATYP, pp. 102–103.

40. "Broyt un fayer," *Di goldene pave*, pp. 47–48.

41. Letter from Halpern to Yosl Drost, undated, numbered by Drost as no. 6 of 1923, mistakenly according to internal references; probably written just after the evening in his honor on November 21, 1923. Halpern Papers, YIVO. As part of the advance publicity for the evening, Zishe Weinper published a preview-report: "And he with his gray stiff hair . . . will sit the whole time on the stage, sullen and restless, with the feeling of a baited wolf behind iron bars, and when the time comes for his *aliye* [being called to the Torah] he will get up in confusion, not knowing what to do first—whether to curse the communists or mock the aesthetes or read his own poems. Once he will have survived the ordeal, with God's help, he will return to his Coney Island cave; the ocean, as yesterday and a thousand years ago, will sing its stormy song, which will remind Halpern of his own song, and he will find it strange to be reminded that both the ocean and his heart were already storming even before the Bolshevik revolution in Russia." (Such sarcasm at the expense of the revolution was still possible in the *Freiheit* of 1923.) Zishe Weinper, "Vegn m. l. halpern" (About Halpern), *Freiheit*, November 11, 1923.

42. Meir Shtiker, "Di tragedye moyshe leyb," *Morgn zhurnal*, February 14, 1950. Shtiker also described him to me in these words in an interview, August 16, 1979.

43. Halpern, "Onheyb vinter ovnt" (At the Beginning of a Winter Evening), *Freiheit*, January 14, 1923. Included under the title "Di letste" in *Di goldene pave*, p. 136; trans. "The Last" by Nathan Halper in TYP, p. 108.

44. "Der mentsh der af," *Freiheit*, August 18, 1923; in *Di goldene pave*, pp. 109–110; trans. "Man, That Ape" by John Hollander in TYP, pp. 103–104.

45. "Dos lid funem yidishn koval" (Song of the Jewish Blacksmith), p. 50.

46. "Baym shayn fun lempl" (By Lamplight), *Di goldene pave*, p. 60.

47. Halpern writes to Drost about the project. See also Khone Shmeruk, "Umbakante shafungen fun moyshe-leyb halpern" (Unknown Works of Halpern: The Zarkhi-Myrtle Romance and Its Prose Versions), *Di goldene keyt*, 75 (1972), 212–29.

48. Halpern, "Zarkhi zogt toyre" (Zarkhi Teaches), *Di goldene pave*, pp. 246–249; trans. "From Zarkhi's Teachings" by Benjamin and Barbara Harshav in *AYP*, pp. 425–427.

49. Khone Shmeruk, "Umbakante shafungen," suggests that the source of the name was Herman Gold's story "Khaveyrim" (Pals), *Literatur*, 2 (November 1910), 56–70. The romantic triangle in the story resembles that of the Zarkhi-Myrtle characters. Moishe Nadir writes that Halpern took the name from the truck of a local tradesman, Zarakh, in Coney Island: "Halpern," *Der tog*, October 5, 1940.

50. "I won't be able to go from Toronto to Cleveland because my wife will be

weaning the boy around March 14–15 and I have to be at home then." Letter from Halpern to Drost, undated but marked by recipient as no. 1, 1924, Halpern Papers, YIVO.

51. Letter from Halpern to Drost, marked by him as no. 12 of 1925, Halpern Papers, YIVO.

52. Interview with Eliezer Greenberg. See also Zishe Weinper's descriptions of Halpern's home life in *Halpern*.

53. Halpern, "Fun a briv maynem," *Freiheit*, July 15, 1923, in *Di goldene pave*, pp. 69–70; trans. "From One of My Letters" by John Hollander in *PBMYV*, p. 188.

54. Halpern, untitled, section 38 of "Zarkhi bam breg yam" (Zarkhi at the Seashore), in *Di goldene pave*, pp. 300–301; trans. "The End of the Book" by Benjamin and Barbara Harshav in *AYP*, p. 429.

6. Allure of the Red-Haired Bride

1. Melekh Ravitch, *Dos mayse bukh fun mayn lebn* (The Storybook of My Life), vol. 3 (Tel Aviv: Peretz, 1975). A useful guide to Jewish life in Poland between the wars is Ezra Mendelsohn, "Poland," in *The Jews of East Central Europe Between the World Wars* (Bloomington: Indiana University Press, 1983), pp. 11–83.

2. Letter dated from Moscow, November 29, 1924, in *Briv fun yidishe sovetishe shraybers* (Letters of Soviet Yiddish Writers), ed. Ezekiel Lifshitz and Mordecai Altschuler (Jerusalem: Hebrew University, 1979), p. 17. Leivick's criticism of Einhorn had appeared in "Yidishism in dovid einhorn," *Der inzl* (1918).

3. Interview with Bobby Getzoff, May 3, 1985, based on her conversations with Rochelle Weprinski and others.

4. Rochelle Weprinski, "Fun mayne shlanke glider" (From My Slender Limbs), in her book *Ruf fun fligl* (Call of Wings; New York, 1926), p. 42.

5. Weprinski, *Dos kreytsn zikh fun di hent*, pp. 241ff.

6. Letters from Mani Leib and Zishe Landau to Melekh Ravitch, autumn–winter 1919–20, report on the progress of his illness; Ravitch Archive, NHUAJ. Mani Leib writes (November 5, 1919) that unlike Landau, who also complains that he is ill, he is *really* ill.

7. Told to me by Elke Segal, widow of I. I. Segal, in Montreal, 1985. Mrs. Segal spent the early 1920s in New York with her husband, who worked in Mani Leib's shoe cooperative.

8. Anna Margolin (Rosa Lebensboym), *Dos yidishe lid in amerike*, 1923 (New York, 1923).

9. Weprinski presents a lively portrait of Margolin as Ada in her novel *Dos kreytsn zikh fun di hent*. Since this book was written in reaction to Iceland's memoirs of the period, her portrait may have been influenced by his. Letters from Weprinski to Iceland in Iceland Papers, YIVO.

10. Letter from Mani Leib to Melekh Ravitch, September 11, 1919, Ravitch Papers, NHUAJ.

11. Mani Leib, "Der hirsh" (The Deer), 1920–1930, *Lider un baladn* (1955), vol. 1, p. 130. A variant manuscript is in Mani Leib Papers, YIVO.

12. Aaron Rapoport, "Mit mani leyb in shop" (With Mani Leib in the Shop), *Di tsukunft*, April, 1957, pp. 167–69.

13. Kalman Marmor Papers, YIVO.

14. Mani Leib, "Ikh bin," *Di tsukunft*, October 1932, p. 568. A variant manuscript in Mani Leib Archive, YIVO; trans. "I Am" by John Hollander in *TYP*, pp. 87–88.

15. Gordon McVay, *Isadora and Esenin* (Ann Arbor: Ardis, 1980).

16. McVay, trans. "The Song About a Dog," ibid., pp. 69–70. Mani Leib's translation appeared in *Forverts*, October 22, 1922.

17. Several contemporary reports of the event appeared in the Yiddish press. Later accounts by Leib Feinberg, "Skandaln fun groysnrusishn poet in moskve, berlin, un nyu york" (Scandals of the Great Russian Poet), *Tog-morgn zhurnal*, October 8, 1961, and Rochelle Weprinski, "Iz der poet yesenin geven an antisemit?" (Was the Poet Esenin an Anti-Semite?), *Forverts*, June 2, 1963.

18. Letter from Esenin to Mani Leib (in Russian), Mani Leib Papers, YIVO.

19. "When I was in New York Mani Leib grabbed hold of me and asked me to take part in a concert that he wanted to make for Esenin. I should come in from the mountains [where Leivick was recuperating from tuberculosis] to read something. For what purpose? Because Esenin has to return to Russia and doesn't have the money and is quarreling with Duncan, etc. From the way he spoke and from a few others too I felt that our crowd is very pleased that a poet like Esenin—Duncan's husband, a Bolshevik in boots, the true Muscovite—has a good opinion of Yiddish poets and wants to drink whisky with them . . . And here, suddenly, 'kikes' and 'Trotsky' [Esenin's curses] . . . What a blow it must be for Mani Leib." Letter from H. Leivick to Shmuel Niger (Charney), February 2, 1923. "Selection of the Leivick-Niger Correspondence," ed. E. Lifshitz in *Pinkes far der forshung fin der yidisher literatur un presse* (Register for the Study of Yiddish Literature and Press), vol. 2 (New York: CYCO, 1982), p. 419.

20. Mani Leib, trans., *Ertseylungen* (Stories) by Alexander Kuprin (New York: Nay-tsayt, 1920), 248 pp. Contains two works, "Olesya" and "Molokh."

21. These translations appeared not only in *Forverts* but also in *Tsukunft, Epokhe*, and other Yiddish journals.

22. Mani Leib, "A yidish yingl" (A Jewish Boy), *Lider un baladn*, vol. 1 (1955), p. 151.

23. See *Forverts*, October 1922. The first volume of Vera Figner's memoirs, *When the Clock of Life Stopped*, appeared in Russian in 1921, in English in 1927.

24. Interview with Rochelle Weprinski, November 2, 1972.

25. The question of yearning for Russia is treated more fully in my article, "Di Yunge: Immigrants or Exiles?"

26. Letter from Moishe Nadir to Melekh Ravitch, dated Kovno, October 12, 1926, Ravitch Archive, NHUAJ.

27. Zishe Landau, "Notitsn" Notes, in *Der inzl*, 8 (October 1925), 40.

28. H. Leivick, "Ikh-mir" (I-We), *Fun tsayt tsu tsayt*, pp. 22–32.

29. Zishe Landau, "Farn koved fun vort" (For the Dignity of the Word), *Der inzl*, 1 (March, 1925), 3–8.

30. *Der inzl*, literary monthly issued by Inzl Publishing Co., 12 Jefferson St. This publication should not be confused with the miscellany of the same name, 1918.

31. Mani Leib, "Kum, pashtes," *Der inzl*, 3 (April 1925), 3; trans. "Ode to Simplicity" by Marie Syrkin, *TYP*, p. 89.

32. Reuben Iceland, "In yaddo park," ibid., 8 (October 1925), 14.

33. "Fun reyner kunst tsu natsishn meshikhizm" (From Pure Art to Nazi Messianism), *Studio*, 2 (October–December 1934), 144–156. Iceland's earlier discussion of poet and prophet is in "Kunst un profanatsye" (Art and Profanation), *Der inzl*, 1 (March 1925), 13–16.

34. Letter from Joseph Opatoshu to Melekh Ravitch, February 2, 1923, Ravitch Archive, NHUAJ.

35. Yoel Entin, "Mani Leib," *Di tsukunft*, September 16, 1955, pp. 92–93.

36. Mani Leib, "A mayse vi azoy eliyohu hanovi hot geratevet vilne fun shney" (A Story About How the Prophet Elijah Rescued Vilna from Snow), *Zamlbikher*, 5 (1943), 151–160. An accompanying note says the rhymed story was written in 1939 for the grade-five class of the Vilna Real-Gymnazye, taught by Mira Bernshteyn, whose students had sent him descriptions of Vilna so that, having never seen the city himself, he could tell the story he had heard from his grandmother.

37. Shloime Simon, "Mani leyb in zayn kindheyt" (Mani Leib in His Childhood), *Kinder zhurnal*, March 1931, p. 3.

38. See e.g. "Baym taykh" (By the River), comp. Solomon Golub (New York: Metro, 1924); "Dos lid fun broyt" (The Song of Bread), comp. N. L. Saslavsky (New York: Joseph P. Katz, 1922); "Shneyele" (Snowfall), comp. M. Gelbart (New York: Joseph P. Katz, 1922); "Der soykherl fun perl" (The Pearl Merchant), comp. Samuel Bugatch (New York: Metro, 1931), and note on Pinchos Jassinovsky in chap. 3. The Mel and Shifra Gold Yiddish Music Project of the National Yiddish Book Exchange, Amherst, Mass., has a computer listing of hundreds of American Yiddish songs.

39. Letter from Joseph Opatoshu to Melekh Ravitch, September 9, 1923 (eve of Rosh Hashonah), Ravitch Archive, NHUAJ.

40. Mani Leib, "An entfer h. leyvikn" (A Reply to H. Leivick), in the form of a poem, *Der inzl*, 3 (May 1925), 29–30. This was in response to Leivick's earlier attack on the Yunge (see note 28 above).

41. B. I. Bialystotsky, "Vig lider un andere lider" (Lullabies and Other Songs), *Oyfkum*, September 1926, p. 16.

42. Zishe Weinper, "Mani leyb," *Oyfkum*, January 1928, pp. 30–31.

43. *Oyfkum*, February–March, 1931, special issue in honor of Mani Leib's twenty-fifth year as a poet. "Passed into history," A. Nissenson; "socially deaf," Kusman; "never changes," H. Leivick.

44. Howe, *World of Our Fathers*, pp. 332–333.

45. This headline is from *Freiheit*, July 22, 1927, box at the bottom of p. 1.

46. These changes of affiliation were treated as victories or defeats. From Kiev the literary scholar and critic Nokhum Oyslender wrote to Leivick: "Today I read Mani Leib's first poems in *Freiheit*. So, you see, the ice has broken after all. He still writes a little icily and that isn't his tone. But apparently he feels that a dignified tone, even if it isn't his own, is necessary in the present situation. Now you are both my cousins in New York. I've always dreamed of this. I seem to be gushing like a woman but it makes me happy, frightfully happy, that Mani Leib has left *Inzl* . . . Become what you both are if you aren't it already. It can't be otherwise." Letter from Oyslender to Leivick, dated Kiev, December 6 [1926], in *Briv fun yidishe sovetishe shraybers*, p. 28.

47. Mani Leib, "A lid" (A Poem), *Freiheit*, March 20, 1927.

48. Shifra Vays, "Mani leybn" (To Mani Leib), *Freiheit*, March 3, 1927. In the issue of January 16 there had appeared Mani Leib's "O, mayn torbe" (O, My Wanderer's Pack) in which he portrays himself as a passerby on his way to the land of the holy fool. Vays's reply turns the wanderer's sack and cane into a baton of freedom that will be passed on proudly from land to land.

49. Paul Johnson, *Modern Times* (New York: Harper and Row, 1983), p. 226.

50. H. Leivick, "Yidishe poetn," *Freiheit*, March 6, 1927; trans. "Yiddish Poets" by Benjamin and Barbara Harshav in *AYP*, p. 741.

51. Borukh Glazman, *In goldenem zump* (In the Golden Swamp), a novella in two parts, vol. 9 of *Geklibene verk* (Works; New York: Yidishe bukh-gezelshaft, 1940), p. 82.

52. Interviews with Meir Shtiker, August 16, 1979, and with Esther Getzoff, October 18, 1979.

53. Letter from Mani Leib to Yosl and Basia Drost (undated, probably 1926), Mani Leib Papers, YIVO.

7. Radiant Exile

1. Mani Leib, "Evenyu B," *Di tsukunft*, September 1913, p. 25; reprinted in *Baladn* (1918), pp. 97–103.

2. Moishe Leib Halpern, "Dos lid fun sof-zuntik" (1924), *Moyshe leyb halpern*, vol. 1, pp. 42–44; trans. "Song: Weekend's Over" by John Hollander, *TYP*, pp. 106–107.

3. Portrait of Halpern in YIVO.

4. Nos. 78–81A in Halpern Papers, YIVO, is a story about a flatulation contest between Mechele and Tsipele, won by Tsipele. The story concludes with the peacemaker, Khatskele the tailor, pronouncing the moral: "One plays the flute and another the trumpet/ The bird twitters and the lion roars/ But all praise God, blessed be He, in their own way./ Mechele in hers and Tsipele in hers." I don't know whether this was ever published.

5. Letter from Halpern to Drost, undated, marked by recipient as no. 5 of 1923, Halpern Papers, YIVO. All letters from Halpern to Drost are from this file.

6. Letter from Halpern to Drost, December 3, 1923. "There's been a whole upheaval because of me. Our editor to date [Shakhna] Epstein resigned and there's no one for the time being except [Benjamin] Gitlov, the boss."

7. Letter from Halpern to Drost, marked January 1924 as no. 4 of the year (probably mistakenly according to internal evidence).

8. Letter from Halpern to Drost, marked no. 16 of 1924. By this time *Freiheit* had wooed Halpern back with the promise of $30 a week. Halpern had taken a slightly larger flat in Seagate for which he was paying $35 a month.

9. Ibid. Drost apparently scolded Halpern for returning to *Freiheit* and Halpern defends himself heatedly: "You can understand that I'm not yet rich enough to live off my investment income."

10. There are many accounts of Halpern's break with *Freiheit*, all of them evasive or uninformed. See Weinper, *Moyshe leyb halpern*, p. 10; Greenberg, *Moyshe leyb halpern in der ram fun zayn dor*, pp. 54–55.

11. "I am now in Chicago. The Left [*di linke*] here canceled all the lectures that they were supposed to sponsor for me because in the first lecture I defended Nadir." Letter from Halpern to Meir Shtiker, undated, on stationery of L. Miller Embroidery Company, Chicago. This letter is in my possession.

12. Meir Shtiker, "Di tragedye moyshe leyb" (The Tragedy of Moishe Leib), *Morgn zhurnal*, February 14, 1950. Corroborated by letter from Halpern to Shtiker (see note 11): "My lip has healed on the outside. Somewhere in the soul the wound is still there. The tooth will have to be removed."

13. Letter from Halpern to Drost, marked no. 1 of 1925.

14. Letters from Halpern to Drost, marked 1925. They describe a visit to him in the hospital by Shakhne Epstein, who tried vainly to persuade Halpern to return to *Freiheit*.

15. Letter from Halpern to Moishe Nadir, July 19, 1925, in uncatalogued Nadir Papers, NHUAJ.

16. Letter from Halpern to Drost, March 24, 1924, describes the offer from Detroit. In Chicago Halpern helped to raise money for the periodical *Kultur* and was invited to become a steady contributor. It lasted from October 2, 1925, to February 26, 1926.

17. B. I. Bialystotski, "Tsvishn bikher un kolegn" (Among Books and Colleagues), *Oyfkum*, August 1926, pp. 19–22.

18. Halpern, "Fun mayn royzele's togbukh" (1924), in *Moyshe leyb halpern*, vol. 1, pp. 62–65; trans. "From My Royzele's Diary" by Benjamin and Barbara Harshav and Kathryn Hellerstein in *AYP*, 441–445.

19. "Mayn zunele ven er vet zayn a meylekh" (My Son When He Becomes a King), *Freiheit*, April 2, 1927; reprinted in *Moyshe leyb halpern*, pp. 59–61.

20. Morris Rosenfeld, "Mayn yingele," *Shriftn* (1910), vol. 1, p. 16; trans. "My Little Son" by Aaron Kramer in *TYP*, p. 79.

21. Halpern, "Yezus tsu di kinder" (Jesus to the Children), *Freiheit*, January 23, 1927; reprinted in *Moyshe leyb halpern*, pp. 92–94.

22. Zishe Weinper, "Moyshe leyb halpern," *Oyfkum*, September–October 1932, p. 42.

23. Halpern, "Zun oyfgang in manhatn" (Sunrise in Manhattan, 1924), in *Moyshe leyb halpern*, pp. 51–53.

24. "Salut," *Vokh*, January 24, 1930; trans. "Salute" by John Hollander in *PBMYV*, pp. 210–212.

25. Letter from Halpern to Drost, marked no. 4 of 1926.

26. Letter from S. Starosvetsky to Moishe Nadir, dated Detroit, April 8, 1926, uncatalogued Nadir Papers, NHUAJ.

27. Zishe Weinper, "Ale khoydesh" (Every Month), column in *Oyfkum*, November 1927, p. 43.

28. See e.g. Lamed Shapiro, "Der shtul" (The Chair) in *Studio*, 1 (July–September, 1934), 1–23; H. Leivick, "Sako un vanzetis mitvokh" (Sacco and Vanzetti's Wednesday), *Lider* (New York: H. Leivick Jubilee Committee, 1940), pp. 280–284.

29. Jacob Glatstein, "Tsu moyshe leyb halpern's yortsayt" (On the Anniversary of Halpern's Death, 1945), *In toykh genumen* (Sum and Substance; New York: Matones, 1947), p. 131. Glatstein also discusses the plans for a magazine in "Moyshe leyb halpern," *Tog morgn-zhurnal*, September 8, 1963.

30. Halpern, "Sacco-Vanzetti," *Freiheit*, September 4, 1927; trans. by John Hollander in *PBMYV*, pp. 212–214. Variants of the poem can be found in Halpern Papers, YIVO, items 63–65.

31. Letter from Halpern to Drost, April 17, 1926.

32. Letter from Halpern to Drost, marked 1927: "Driving back from the mountains [the previous letter was sent from Nadir's farm in Loch Sheldrake, New York] we had an accident. The car turned over. We should have been killed, but survived—Royzele and I with bruised foreheads and each of us with a black eye. Nothing happened to the boy."

33. Letter from Halpern to Drost, marked no. 2 of 1927.

34. Notice in *Oyfkum*, January 1927, pp. 46–47: M. L. Halpern spent several months in Detroit as a guest of S. L. Cohen, where a fund of $2,000 was collected for a new book of poetry and $1,000 for a tractor to be sent to Russia in his name.

35. They lived first at 2811 Boulder Street "in a separate house of 4 rooms for $25 a month." Letter from Halpern to Drost, marked 1927. On the train trip to California, Isaac drew a landscape that Halpern later copied in oils.

36. Sh. Miller, "Biographical Notes" in Lamed Shapiro, *Ksovim* (Posthumous Writings; Los Angeles: L. Shapiro Ksovim Committee, 1949), pp. 13–14. Ezekiel Bronshteyn, "L. shapiro," *Fun eygn hoyz* (From Our Own House; Tel Aviv: Hamenorah, 1963), pp. 189–190.

37. Yekhezkel Bronshteyn, "M. l. halpern," *Fun eygn hoyz*, pp. 206–207.

38. Letter from Halpern to Drost, marked 1928.

39. Halpern, "Los angeles," *Vokh*, October 11, 1929; reprinted in *Moyshe leyb halpern*, pp. 231–234.

40. Letter from Halpern to Drost, undated, marked no. 6 of 1928.

41. Letter from Halpern to Drost, undated, marked no. 4 of 1928. Zishe Weinper was in Warsaw in 1929 lecturing about Halpern as part of an optimistic appraisal of American Yiddish literature. He discovered a good deal of interest in Halpern and stimulated more. See report by B. Karlinius in *Moment* (Warsaw), October 4, 1929.

42. Letter from Halpern to Drost, marked no. 5 of 1928.

43. Bronshteyn, "M. l. halpern," p. 212.

44. Weinper, *Moyshe leyb halpern*, p. 105.

45. Ephraim Auerbach, "A khurbn far a khurbn" (One Destruction for Another), *Vokh*, November 15, 1929, pp. 4–5.

46. *Vokh*, ed. M. Boreisho, H. Leivick, and L. Shapiro; appeared from October 4, 1929, to May 16, 1930.

47. Notice in *Vokh*, November 22, 1929, reports Halpern setting out for Philadelphia; report of December 6 says he is being enthusiastically received, signed 50 subscribers, will try to establish chapter; report of March 21, 1930, says Halpern is in Boston for *Vokh*. Halpern's published reports of these missions mock his own enterprise and that of the magazine.

48. *Vokh*, October 4, 1929, editorial.

49. Halpern, "Inem likhtflek" (In the Limelight), *Vokh*, December 13, 1929, p. 15.

50. "A yingele, a mame, un etlekhe lider" (A Little Boy, a Mother, and a Few Poems), *Vokh*, November 15, 1929, pp. 13–14.

51. Judd L. Teller, *Strangers and Natives: The Evolution of the American Jew from 1921 to the Present* (New York: Delacorte, 1968). Himself a Yiddish poet, Teller provides useful social background for the study of Yiddish literature in America between the wars.

52. Halpern, "Anti-yidishism," *Vokh*, March 21, 1930.

53. "Likht—mayn vort," *Freiheit*, March 13, 1927; trans. "Light—My Word" by John Hollander in *PBMYV*, pp. 196–202.

54. Letter from Halpern to Drost, undated, marked 1930: "New York is a big city and there's certainly room for one more shoe-repair shop." See also Weinper, *Moyshe leyb halpern*, pp. 36–37.

55. Halpern, "Introduction" to Zishe Weinper, *Geklibene verk* (Collected Works; New York: Oyfkum, 1932), pp. i–xiv.

56. Letter from Halpern to Drost, marked no. 2 of 1930.

57. Halpern, "Unzer gortn," *In nyu york*, p. 7; trans. "Our Garden" by Kathryn Hellerstein in *AYP*, p. 395.

58. "In sentral park" (In Central Park), *Vokh*, February 14, 1930, p. 6; trans. John Hollander in *PBMYV*, pp. 206–208. Khone Shmeruk first pointed out to me, on the basis of his earlier examination of Halpern's manuscripts and publications, that this poem is part of a series that also includes the poems "Monument Goethe," "Gey Ikh Azoy" (I Walk Along), "Shmuel, My Brother," and "Der gezetshiter" (The Law Abider).

8. In the Magic Valley

1. Interviews with Elaine Friedman, daughter of Yosl and Bessie Drost, Cleveland; and with Daniel Ignatoff.

2. Borukh Rivkin, "Halb veg tsu geoynes" (Halfway to Genius), *Brikn* (Bridges), 2 (Chicago, February 1934), 110. He also quotes Leivick at the funeral: "One of our greatest poets has been murdered!" The eulogy was published in *Literarishe bleter*, September 23, 1932, p. 615.

3. Letter from Mani Leib to Ignatoff, stamped (by recipient?) September 1, 1932; return address "c/o Sacks, Saugerties, N.Y." All Ignatoff letters are among his papers, YIVO.

4. Letter from Mani Leib to Ignatoff, undated.

5. Notice in *Forverts* of September 2 gives his last address as "1724 Weeks Avenue, Bronx." Weinper, *Moyshe leyb halpern*, gives it as "1275 Weeks Avenue, near 74th." Details of his last days reported there.

6. Iceland, *Fun unzer friling*, pp. 109–114.

7. Eliezer Sherman, "Bagegenishn mit moyshe leyb halpern" (Meetings with M. L. Halpern), *Nyu yorker vokhnblat*, September 4, 1936, p. 5.

8. The critic Shmuel Niger, a moderate admirer of Halpern's, wrote to Leivick: "Halpern's odd death (as odd as his life) took everyone by surprise, but—it seems to me—there was no real grief, no human and comradely grief. At the funeral there was only family—I mean literary family—so there might have been an intimate, human atmosphere, but there wasn't. I'm afraid that Halpern's character—his tendency to kick up rows—is responsible for this, though I feel that somewhere deep within him there was a deeply religious person and he was, as you characterized him, tragic in the real sense, in the sense of an innermost rupture, of a permanent battle between God and demon . . . What interests me now, when I read him again, is the primitiveness of his rhyme and rhythm. Was this deliberate—or could he do no better? Or maybe had had a simple, not a complicated, nature; even the struggle within him was only between two sides, without any forces in the middle, without nuances, without complications. One of his close friends should write a purely

personal description of him. Couldn't you do this? . . . I often think that we live in a kind of madhouse where everyone thinks he is sane and the others mad. The worst thing is that in moments of clarity I begin to fear that I too am among those who think that others are drunk when they can barely stand on their feet or talk. That's why I think it's better not to look too deep into the hold of our little ship which has been sinking for so long that sinking becomes known as swimming. Better not to think about it. Why, just today a highly respected poet, someone I hold in esteem, tried to convince me over the phone that M. L. Halpern can be summed up in the single word, *contemptible* . . . well, isn't it better not to think, not to speak, not to hear?" Letter from Niger to Leivick, dated Brooklyn, September 11, 1932. In "Selection from the Leivick-Niger Correspondence," ed. E. Lifshitz, pp. 484–485.

9. Notice in *Vokh*, October 11, 1929. Mani Leib began to publish fairly regularly in *Tsukunft*.

10. Letter from Mani Leib to Abraham Liessin, dated Deborah Sanatorium, Browns Mills, N.J., November 27, 1932, Liessin Papers, YIVO.

11. Rochelle Weprinski writes in the introduction to *Briv* that Mani Leib fell sick and entered the sanatorium in 1933. She may have based this on the first of the letters she includes in the book, dated January 10, 1933. But letters sent the previous autumn to Ignatoff, Iceland, Liessin, and others indicate that he was at a farm in Saugerties from at least late August, then entered the sanatorium around the third week of November.

12. Letter from Mani Leib to Ignatoff, stamped (by recipient?) November 27 [1932].

13. Letter from Mani Leib to Ignatoff, stamped December 2, 1932.

14. Letter from Mani Leib to Shloime Simon, undated, Simon Papers, YIVO.

15. Letter from Mani Leib to Ignatoff, December 31, 1932.

16. "In hayzer oreme" (In Poor Homes) appeared in *Di tsukunft*, January 1933; mistakenly included among poems of 1920–1930 in *Lider un baladn*, vol. 1 (1955), p. 127.

17. Letter of Mani Leib to Meir Shtiker, January 5, 1933; published in *Tsuzamen* (Tel Aviv, 1974), pp. 493–497.

18. Yekhiel Bronshteyn, "Mani Leib," *Keneder odler* (Canadian Eagle, Montreal), November 27, 1961; reprinted in Bronshteyn, *Fun eygn hoyz*, pp. 222–225. Bronshteyn says that Mani Leib was writing sonnets when he met him in 1935.

19. Letter from Mani Leib to Rochelle Weprinski, February 27, 1933, *Briv*, p. 54. Details of this period are from postcards and letters to Reuben Iceland, David Ignatoff, and Rochelle Weprinski, their papers, YIVO.

20. Letter from Mani Leib to Reuben Iceland, undated, Iceland Papers, YIVO.

21. "Yoysher" (Justice), a play in five acts, in Mani Leib Papers, YIVO. It is mistakenly described by Dr. E. Shulman as having been written in the late 1930s, when Mani Leib was living at 603 West 140th Street, the address that appears on the manuscript (*Forverts*, December 25, 1977). Letters of 1933 to Iceland et al. explicitly date the play's completion then.

22. Letter from Mani Leib to Iceland, undated, asking him to keep the project secret for the time being. In another letter to Iceland he gives a lengthy assessment of Leivick's poetry, objecting to the crude criticism of it by Borukh Rivkin and distinguishing between Leivick's fine lyrics and his failed bombast.

23. Letter from Mani Leib to I. J. Segal, undated, Segal Papers, JPLM.

24. Mani Leib, "Zey lakhn" (They Laugh), In *Lider un baladn*, vol. 1 (1955), p. 286 (Lines 2 and 3 are reversed). See also Mani Leib, *Sonetn* (1962), p. 17. Because of its greater accuracy I will cite sonnets according to this volume.

25. Eight *Zamlbikher* (Miscellanies) were published between May 1936 and 1952. The last volume, dedicated to the "silenced or murdered" Soviet Yiddish writers, reflects the changed attitude toward Soviet Russia.

26. Letter from Joseph Opatoshu to H. Leivick, December 23, 1934. See the correspondence between these writers through 1942 in Leivick and Opatoshu Papers, YIVO.

27. A. (Abraham) M. (Moishe) Dilon (Zhukhovitski), *Di lider* (New York: Committee of Friends, 1935), biographical note, pp. 120–124. The book contains the poem "To Mani Leib" from which the quoted phrase is taken. Dilon's sonnet cycle very likely influenced Mani Leib, one of the book's editors, to begin his sonnet series.

28. A. (Eliyohu) Almi, "Der estet in shturem" (The Aesthete in the Storm), *Kritik un polemik* (Warsaw), 1939, pp. 123–126.

29. Mani Leib, "Ot azoy, azoy, azoy" (Just so, so, so), *Zishe landau zamlbukh*, ed. David Kozanski (New York: Inzl, 1938), pp. 7–18; I. Kisin, "Zishe landau's oyftu in der yidisher poezye" (Landau's Accomplishment in Yiddish Poetry, 1938), *Lid un esey* (New York, 1953), p. 224.

30. Tabachnik, *Der man fun lid*, p. 57.

31. Sh. D. Singer, "Zishe landau" (1937), *Dikhter un prozaiker* (Poets and Prose Writers; New York: Education Department, Workmen's Circle), p. 46.

32. Abraham Tabachnik quotes Landau as having said this before his death. Landau's verse comedies, "Der bloyer nakhtigal" (The Blue Nightingale), "Der royter nakhtigal" (The Red Nightingale), "Shipe zibele" (Seven Months' Child), and "Jimmy fun Scotland Yard" were published posthumously by a committee of friends under the title, *Es iz gornisht nit geshen* (Nothing Happened; New York, 1937).

33. Zishe Landau, "Ikh bin der man fun lid" (1925–1937), *Lider* (New York: Inzl, 1937), p. 215. Tabachnik used the last line for the title of his book on Landau.

34. Kozanski, "Oyf morgn" (The Next Day), *Zishe landau zamlbukh*, p. 166.

35. Letters from Mani Leib to Kh. Pomerantz in Chicago, probably from the late 1930s (YIVO Correspondence File), show that a local committee proposed to put out a book of 300 pages, but Mani Leib lacked the time and energy to submit the manuscript. Weprinski's sharpest comments during my interview with her concerned Mani Leib's failure to publish his work in book form.

36. Dilon, *Di lider*; Landau, *Lider*; *Es iz gornisht nit geshen*; *Fun der velt poezye* (Of the

World's Poetry, translations; New York: Ignatoff Literature Fund, 1947). The same group put out the commemorative *Zishe landau zamlbukh.*

37. Mani Leib, coeditor with Sh. Rosenfeld, *Dovid ignatoff: 25 yor literarisher shafn* (volume of tribute to Ignatoff's years of literary creativity; Chicago: Coshinski, 1935).

38. Letters from Mani Leib to H. Leivick, undated but probably from 1952, Leivick Papers, YIVO. The book was to commemorate the twentieth anniversary of Halpern's death. Mani Leib complains that Royzele, having collected $1,000 for a new volume of Halpern's poetry, was reluctant to turn it over to the committee and worried lest someone write disrespectfully about her husband.

39. Sh. D. Singer, "Mani leyb's geshtalt" (The Figure of Mani Leib), *Der fraynd* (The Friend, journal of the Workmen's Circle), November–December, 1953, p. 12.

40. Bronshteyn, "Mani leyb," *Fun unzer hoyz,* p. 223.

41. Mani Leib, *Mendele mokher sforim* (New York: Mendele Jubilee Project for the Workmen's Circle Schools, 1936), 32 pp.

42. Rochelle Weprinski, *Briv,* pp. 6–8.

43. Letter from Mani Leib to Yosl Drost, June 11–12, 1948, return address "3010 Dwight Avenue, Far Rockaway," Mani Leib Papers, YIVO.

44. This point is eloquently made by Abraham Tabachnik, "Tradition and Revolt in Yiddish Poetry," trans. Cynthia Ozick in *Voices from the Yiddish,* pp. 289–299.

45. Mani Leib, "Ikh hob nisht farnumen bay nakht keyn geshrey" (I heard no scream at night), *Toyt tsiklus* (Death Cycle), ed. Melekh Ravitch (Vienna, Warsaw, Lvov: Der Kval, 1922), p. 1.

46. Mani Leib, "Tsu vemen?," *Sonetn,* p. 15. Variants of this, as of many sonnets, are among Mani Leib's papers, YIVO.

47. "Zey," *Sonetn,* p. 14; trans. "They" by John Hollander in *PBMYV,* p. 132. A different translation by David G. Roskies and Hillel Schwartz in *Voices within the Ark: The Modern Yiddish Poets,* ed. Howard Schwartz and Anthony Rudolph (New York: Avon, 1980), p. 298.

48. "Der paytn," *Sonetn,* p. 13; trans. "The Bard" by Nathan Halper in *TYP,* pp. 94–95.

49. "Fremde," *Sonetn,* p. 26; trans. "Strangers" by John Hollander in *PBMYV,* p. 136.

50. "Baym shvel fun glik," *Sonetn,* p. 25; trans. "By the Threshold" by Nathan Halper in *TYP,* p. 94 (slight inaccuracy in concluding lines).

51. "A floym," *Sonetn,* p. 27; trans. "A Plum" by John Hollander in *PBMYV,* p. 134.

52. "Du veyst nor," *Sonetn,* p. 55; trans. "You Only Know" by John Hollander in *PBMYV,* pp. 132–134.

53. "Nitl," *Sonetn,* p. 16; trans. "Christmas" by John Hollander in *PBMYV,* p. 140.

54. Unsent letter by Mani Leib to Itsik Feffer, Mani Leib Papers, YIVO; published in *Di goldene keyt*, 88 (1975), 174–78.

55. For an overview of Yiddish literature in the Soviet Union, see Khone Shmeruk, "Yiddish Literature in the USSR," in *The Jews in Soviet Russia since 1917*, ed. Lionel Kochan (New York: Oxford University Press, 1970), pp. 232–268.

56. Interview with Rochelle Weprinski. See also her introduction to *Briv*.

57. Interview with Barbara Getzoff, May 3, 1985.

58. Mani Leib, "Derklerung fun der nayer redaktsye" (Comment of the New Editors), *Epokhe*, 2 (April 1945), 2.

59. "Dovid ignatof shraybt geshikhte" (David Ignatoff Writes History), ibid., pp. 5–13.

60. "On traditsyes" (Without Traditions), *Epokhe*, 2 (December 1945), 86–88.

61. Notes of talk on Grade and unsent letter both in Mani Leib Papers, YIVO.

62. Letter from Joseph Rolnick to Mani Leib, May 8, 1949, Mani Leib Papers, YIVO.

63. Letter from I. J. Schwartz to Mani Leib, dated Havana, Cuba, March 2, 1950. Schwartz was in Cuba on a speaking tour for the local Jewish community.

64. See letters from Manger to Mani Leib, esp. July 2, 1949, from "2 The Arcade, Swiss Cottage Station, London." This letter occasioned an unsent letter that remained among Mani Leib's papers, chiding Manger for extravagent comments.

65. Itsik Manger, "Adonais iz toyt," *Di tsukunft*, November 1953, pp. 458–460; Manger, "Mani leyb der liriker" (Mani Leib the Lyricist), introduction to Mani Leib, *Shirim ubaladot* (Poems and Ballads, bilingual edition; Tel Aviv: I. L. Peretz, 1963), pp. 8–29. Before arriving in New York, Manger wrote from Montreal: "I feel physically closer to you now. Aesthetically I always felt close to you." Dated Montreal, April 3, 1951, Mani Leib Papers, YIVO. For Mani Leib's reciprocal warmth see his letters to Manger, Manger Archive, 401357, NHUAJ.

66. As chairman of the Manger Committee, Mani Leib had a hard time raising funds from people that Manger antagonized. Letter from Manger to Mani Leib, September 4, 1951, Mani Leib Papers, YIVO; letter from Mani Leib to I. J. Segal, July 4, 1952, Segal Papers, JPLM.

67. Jacob Pat, *Shmuesn mit yidishe shrayber*, says that by 1951 Mani Leib had written 60 sonnets and was still composing more.

68. Jacob Glatstein, "Mani leybs sonetn," *Tog morgn-zhurnal*, November 11, 1962; reprinted in *In toykh genumen*.

69. Judd L. Teller, "Yiddish Literateurs and American Jews," *Commentary*, July 1954, pp. 31–40.

70. Letter from Mani Leib to Reuben Iceland, undated, Iceland Papers, YIVO.

71. Letter from Mani Leib to David and Minnie Ignatoff, September 1953, Ignatoff Papers, YIVO.

72. Letter from Mani Leib to H. Leivick, dated Liberty Sanatorium, August 23, 1953, Leivick Papers, YIVO. Mani Leib attributes the whistling sound in his lungs to emphysema "or bronchial ecstasy."

73. Letter from Mani Leib to Rochelle Weprinski, September 10, 1953, in *Briv*.

74. Letters from Leivick to Mani Leib, April 15 and April 24, 1953, Mani Leib Papers, YIVO.

75. Letter from Mani Leib to Leivick, August 23, 1953, Leivick Papers, YIVO.

76. Obituary reports in *Forverts*, week of October 6, 1953.

77. Mani Leib, "Oyfshrift oyf mayn matseyve," *Sonetn*, p. 20, published with manuscript facsimile in *Lider un baladn*, vol. 1 (1955), pp. 340–341; trans. "Inscribed on a Tombstone" by John Hollander in *PBMYV*, p. 142.

78. Shloime Simon, "Dray bagegenishn mitn dikhter mani leyb" (Three Meetings with the Poet Mani Leib), *Di presse* (Buenos Aires), November 14, 1953.

79. Mani Leib, "Di zun iz gut," *Sonetn*, p. 68; trans. "The Sun Is Good" by John Hollander in *PBMYV*, pp. 140–142.

Index

Index

Rivkin, Borukh, 52
Robeson, Paul, 226
Rolnik, Joseph, 2, 14, 56, 229, 234
romanticism. *See* neoromanticism
Rosenfeld, Morris, 10–11, 43–44, 91–92, 179, 228; Morris Rosenfeld Reading Circle, 33
Russian poetry, 35, 65, 150, 152, 154
Russian revolution: (1905) 12, 14, 37; (1917) 47, 107, 114–116, 199

Sacco and Vanzetti, 184–186
Sanger, Margaret, 46
Sardatski, Yente, 15
Schnitzler, Arthur, 61
schnorrers, 55
schools, Yiddish and Hebrew, 53, 68, 161, 179
Schwartz, I. J., 14, 43, 44, 52, 53, 54, 229
Schwartz, Maurice, 24, 122, 123, 154, 212
Segal, I. I., 147, 234
Senter, Borukh, 7
Shapiro, Lamed, 28–29, 56, 112, 188
Shmuelzon, Moishe, 7
Sholem's Café, 16, 60
Sholom Aleichem (Rabinovitch), 8, 9, 10, 24, 27, 58, 59
Shomer (N. M. Shaikevitch), 25
Shriftn, 40–41, 48, 51–57, 67, 69, 93, 99, 160
Shtiker, Meir, 134, 166
Shtok, Fradl, 16
Shtolzenberg, Aba, 166
Simon, Shloime, 236
Singer, I. J., 143
Slonim, Yoel, 31, 94
socialism, 23, 79, 89. *See also* political ideology
Sologub, Fyodor, 36, 152; Sologubism, 163
sonnet, 218–223, 233
Soviet Union, Jews in, 143, 155, 223–224
Spivak Sanatorium, 204
Stavski, Moishe, 63
sweatshop poets, 10–11, 38, 106. *See also* individual poets
symbolism, Russian, 8–9, 35, 38, 55
symbolism, Yiddish, 7, 31–41
Syrkin, Nahum, 39

Tabachnik, Abraham, 229
Tageblatt (New York), 87
Tageblatt (Lemberg), 77

Taytsh, Moishe, 130
Teller, Judd, 232
Teper, Kolye (Count D'Abruzzi), 45–50, 98, 121
theater, Yiddish, in America, 3, 109–110, 113, 121–123, 212
Tolstoy, Alexei, 152
traditionalism, Jewish, 4, 87–88, 236
traditionalism, Yiddish literary, 58–59, 230
Treistman, Rabbi Eliezer Leib, 46
Trotsky, Leon, 184

Varshe, Moishe, 45–48
Velt ayn velt oys, 65
Verlaine, Paul, 43, 67, 157
Vokh, 190–194, 198, 200, 206

Waker, 189
Weininger, Otto, 45
Weinper, Zishe, 99, 163, 166, 175, 184, 198–200
Weprinski, Rochelle, 63, 65, 71, 72, 74, 75, 144–146, 216, 226, 227, 230
Whitman, Walt, 54, 56
Wilde, Oscar, 31, 32, 45, 50
Winchevsky, Morris, 10, 92, 98
women writers, Yiddish, 15–16, 63, 146. *See also* individual writers
Wordsworth, William, 67
Workers' Party of America, 114
Workmen's Circle, 173, 179, 184, 206, 217, 235
World War I, 41, 46, 57, 59, 95, 97–98, 107, 117, 143, 198
World War II, 219, 223, 228

Yanofsky, Shaul-Joseph, 30
Yehoash (Solomon Bloomgarten), 43–44
Yiddish, as a literary language, 28–29, 33, 79, 107–109, 193, 213–218
Yiddish Pen Club, 235
Yunge, 6–20, 29, 31, 36, 39–44, 46–67, 91–93, 103, 106, 108, 117, 123, 142, 155–163, 192, 214–216, 228, 232. *See also* *Di yugnt*

Zamlbikher, 213, 216
Zhitlowsky, Chaim, 6, 39, 80
Zionism, 4–5, 46, 76, 79, 95, 107, 122, 155, 190, 199, 200, 213
Zunzer, Eliokhum, 43, 92